Implementing EU environmental policy

MANCHESTER
UNIVERSITY PRESS

Issues in Environmental Politics

Series editors Mikael Skou Andersen *and* Duncan Liefferink

As the millennium begins, the environment has come to stay as a central concern of global politics. This series takes key problems for environmental policy and examines the politics behind their cause and possible resolution. Accessible and eloquent, the books make available for a non-specialist readership some of the best research and most provocative thinking on humanity's relationship with the planet.

already published in the series

Implementing EU environmental policy

New directions and old problems

edited by
Christoph Knill and Andrea Lenschow

Manchester University Press
Manchester and New York

distributed exclusively in the USA by St. Martin's Press

Copyright © Manchester University Press 2000

While copyright in the volume as a whole is vested in Manchester University Press, copyright in individual chapters belongs to their respective authors, and no chapter may be reproduced wholly or in part without the express permission in writing of both author and publisher.

Published by Manchester University Press
Oxford Road, Manchester M13 9NR, UK
and Room 400, 175 Fifth Avenue, New York, NY 10010, USA
http://www.man.ac.uk/mup

Distributed exclusively in the USA by
St. Martin's Press, Inc., 175 Fifth Avenue, New York, NY 10010, USA

Distributed exclusively in Canada by
UBC Press, University of British Columbia, 2029 West Mall,
Vancouver, BC, Canada V6T 1Z2

British Library Cataloguing-in-Publication Data
A catalogue record for this book is available from the British Library.

Library of Congress Cataloging-in-Publication Data applied for

ISBN 0 7190 5928 3 *hardback*

First published 2000

07 06 05 04 03 02 01 00   10 9 8 7 6 5 4 3 2 1

Typeset in Sabon
by Northern Phototypesetting Co. Ltd, Bolton
Printed in Great Britain
by Bookcraft (Bath) Ltd, Midsomer Norton

Contents

Part three The impact of new instruments

Figures and tables

Figure

Tables

Contributors

Tanja A. Börzel is a Research Associate at the Robert Schuman Centre of the European University Institute, Florence, and a Research Fellow at the Max-Planck Project Group, 'Common Goods: Law, Politics, and Economics', Bonn. She is currently conducting a research project on state compliance with international norms. Her Ph.D., which she completed at the European University Institute, analysed the impact of Europeanisation on the political institutions of Spain and Germany.

Jan Jaap Bouma is a Senior Researcher at the Erasmus Centre for Environmental Studies at the Erasmus University, Netherlands. He is a business economist and holds a Ph.D. in environmental management. His current research focuses on environmental management accounting and the relationships between environmental management and financial institutions.

Joanne Caddy earned a BA in Natural Sciences at Cambridge University (UK), an MA in Political Science at the Johns Hopkins University (USA) and completed her doctoral dissertation in Political Science at the European University Institute (Italy). She currently holds the post of Administrator at SIGMA, a programme which provides support to public administration reform in Central and Eastern European countries, based at the Organisation for Economic Cooperation and Development (OECD) and financed mainly by EU-Phare. Research interests include: public administration reform in transition countries, public participation and environmental policy.

Rasmus Dilling is a Ph.D. Researcher at the European University Institute, Florence, in international and European law and has a background as attorney-at-law in commercial and European law. The contribution in this book is part of his research on the European Environment Agency and transnational environmental regulation.

Marieva Favoino took her BA in Political Sciences at the Public University of Milan. She was Parliamentary Assistant at the European Parliament (1990–93) and a Consultant at the Italian Second Chamber for parliamentary activities in the Commissions Environment, Health, Public Transports and Infrastructures (1994–95). She is presently a Ph.D. candidate at the European University Institute and a Public Relations Officer of the City of Desio.

Clíona Kimber is a Lecturer in Law at the University of Aberdeen and Director of the Centre for Environmental Law and Policy. She has written and published widely in the field of environmental law and in particular European environmental law and access to environmental information.

Christoph Knill is a Research Fellow at the Max-Planck Project Group, 'Common Goods: Law, Politics, and Economics', at Bonn. He has been Research Associate at the European University Institute (1995–98) and received his post-doctoral degree (*Habilitation*) from Hagen University in 1999. His research interests include governance in multi-level systems, European integration, comparative politics and public administration, environmental policy making and implementation.

Andrea Lenschow is a Lecturer at the Political Science Department at Salzburg University. She received her Ph.D. at New York University in 1996 and has been Research Fellow at the Erasmus University in Rotterdam (1996) and Jean Monnet Fellow at the European University Institute (1997). Her research interests include European integration and policy making, environmental policy making and implementation and comparative politics in Western Europe.

Konstantinos Tsekouras studied Law at the University of Thessaloniki, and at the University of Hannover, Germany. Since 1995 he has been a Researcher at the European University Institute in Florence, where he is writing a Ph.D. thesis on causation problems in environmental liability law in a comparative perspective.

Robert Wright is Senior Associate and Head of the EU Environment Policy Practice at the Association of Public Safety Communications Officials (APCO) Europe, in Brussels. Before joining APCO, he worked for DG XI of the European Commission where he was responsible for coordinating the EU Ecolabel consultation process. He was a Doctoral Researcher in the Department of Social and Political Sciences at the European University Institute in Florence and holds a Master of Science Degree in Government from the London School of Economics and Political Science.

Preface

This book had its origin in the 1997 spring workshop on *The Implementation of EU Environmental Policy* held by the Robert Schuman Centre of the European University Institute in Florence, Italy. The workshop was organised by the Working Group on Environmental Studies which provides an interdisciplinary forum that encourages discussion on environment-related research within the framework of the Robert Schuman Centre. It was the aim of the workshop to discuss the potential of new concepts and approaches for overcoming the implementation deficit in EU environmental policy.

Neither the organisation of the workshop nor the production of this book would have been possible without the support of Yves Mény, the director of the Robert Schuman Centre. We are particularly indebted to Yves not only for providing us with logistical and financial support through the Robert Schuman Centre, but also for his scientific commitment and continuous advice. We also want to express our gratitude to Monique Cavallari and Annette Merlan for their administrative assistance.

In addition to the scholars represented in this book, a number of others participated in the workshop and contributed to the ideas presented here through their formal papers and commentaries, informal discussions and camaraderie. We are thankful to Patricia Bailey, Lucien Chabasson, Ute Collier, Renaud Dehousse, Kenneth Hanf, Adrienne Héritier, Rudolfo Lewanski, Francesc Morata, Eckard Rehbinder, Helmut Weidner, Julia Werner as well as the members of the Working Group on Environmental Studies. In preparing the publication of this book, we received many valuable comments in order to improve and streamline its argument and structure. In this context, we want to express our particular gratitude to Duncan

Liefferink for his invaluable suggestions and Nicola Viinikka for her assistance.

Moreover, the book and workshop project benefited from generous financial support from DG XI in the European Commission. We are particularly grateful to Georges Kremlis for his cooperation and his valuable scientific contributions to the spring workshop.

Christoph Knill and Andrea Lenschow
Bonn and Salzburg

Abbreviations

AI	Access to Information
BAI	Best Available Information
BAT	Best Available Technology
BATNEEC	Best Available Technology Not Entailing Excessive Costs
BEUC	European Consumers Organisation
CAP	Common Agricultural Policy
CE	Central European
CEC	Commission of the European Communities; Central European Country
CEE	Central and Eastern Europe
CEN	Committee for European Normalisation
CEPI	Confederation of European Paper Industries
COM	Commission
CORINE	Coordinating and Ensuring the Consistency of Information on the State of the Environment in Europe
CSCE	Conference on Security and Cooperation in Europe
DG	Directorate General
EAP	Environmental Action Programme
EBRD	European Bank for Reconstruction and Development
EC	European Community
ECJ	European Court of Justice
ECSC	European Coal and Steel Community
EEA	European Environment Agency
EEB	European Environmental Bureau
EEC	European Economic Community
EEO	European Ecolabel Organisation

EIA	Environmental Impact Assessment
EIONET	European Environment Information and Observation Network
EIS	Environmental Impact Statement
EMAS	Environmental Management and Auditing System
EMS	Environmental Management System
EPRG	Environmental Policy Review Group
ERDF	European Regional Development Fund
EU	European Union
EWWE	Environment Watch: Western Europe
GATT	General Agreement on Tariffs and Trade
GCFE	General Consultative Forum on the Environment
GDP	Gross Domestic Product
IMPEL	Implementation and Enforcement of EU Environment Policy
IPP	Integrated Product Policy
IPPC	Integrated Pollution Prevention and Control
JRC	Joint Research Centre
LCA	Life Cycle Assessment
LCP	Large Combustion Plant
NGO	Non-governmental Organisation
NIMBY	Not In My Back Yard
NPI	New Policy Instrument
OECD	Organisation for Economic Cooperation and Development
OJ	Official Journal
PCA	Parliamentary Commissioner for Administration
PPM	Production Process Method
PUMA	OECD's Public Management Service
REC	Regional Environment Center
SIGMA	Support for Improvement in Government and Management in Central and Eastern Europe
TEC	Treaty on the European Communities
TEU	Treaty on European Union
UNEP	United Nations Environment Programme
UNICE	European Union of Employers Confederation
WHO	World Health Organisation
WWF	World Wide Fund for Nature

Part one

The implementation of EU environmental policy: deficiencies in theory and practice

1 *Christoph Knill and Andrea Lenschow*

Introduction: new approaches to reach effective implementation – political rhetoric or sound concepts?

The 'winds of change' in EU environmental policy

The context and priorities underlying environmental policy making in Europe have undergone fundamental changes since the early 1990s. The most important development was the growing relevance of effective implementation of European policies at the national level. The implementation deficit associated with many EU regulatory policies has gained in importance and political salience throughout Europe (CEC 1996, EP 1996; see Collins and Earnshaw 1992). Formerly, the effective implementation of European policy, i.e. the realisation of European policy objectives at the national level beyond their pure formal transposition, played a more peripheral role in both political and scientific discussions. The main emphasis lay on policy formulation. With EU environmental policy makers now focusing increasingly on implementation, the topic has equally been 'brought back in' to political science, where it had been a flourishing industry in the late 1970s.

Closely related to this reorientation in political attention to the implementation phase, we observe the emergence of new institutions and new policies which differ significantly from traditional approaches in EU environmental policy. The latter rely on technocratic and interventionist forms of top–down policy making where uniform and detailed requirements apply to all national administrations involved in practical implementation and enforcement, as well as to private actors, such as industrial operators, who are addressed by the European policy in question. At the heart of the 'new approach', which is reflected in the 1993 fifth Environmental Action Programme of the EU (CEC 1993), is a reorientation in the mode of governance towards network-style and bottom–up forms of policy formulation and implementation (Lenschow, 1999).

Increasing importance is placed on procedural regulation, self-regulation, public participation and voluntary agreements as well as horizontally rather than hierarchically structured processes of policy development and enforcement. Thus, the ideal-type of a 'new instrument' works bottom–up towards the creation of environmental responsibility and awareness on the part of the polluting actors (economic and communicative instruments) as well as towards the integration of the typically rather diffuse environmental interests in the policy formulation, implementation and evaluation processes (a new emphasis on public participation and availability and dissemination of information). Its link to the policy addressees (businesses, consumers, general public) is often indirect, providing incentives or establishing new communication and participation channels; the obligations for the immediate implementing actors (local public authorities) are supposed to be flexible, permitting the instrument's integration in the local political, socio-economic and institutional context.

What are the factors that have induced these 'winds of change' in EU environmental policy making? Here we need to distinguish two dimensions, namely the realisation of policy failures *per se* and second, the related political implications jeopardising the legitimacy of EU-level policy making in general. With regard to policy failure, the Commission's own statistics on the implementation of EU environmental legislation reveal serious deficits: In 1995 Member States notified their implementation for only 91 per cent of the Community's environmental directives, some Member States leaving more than 20 per cent not transposed (CEC 1996). In the same year, the Commission registered a total of 265 suspected breaches of Community law, whereby the environmental field accounts for 20 per cent of all infringements registered by the Commission during that year. In October 1996 over 600 environmental complaints and infringement cases were outstanding against Member States, with 85 cases awaiting determination by the European Court of Justice (ECJ) (CEC 1996, 2).

Politically even more explosive is the link between policy outputs, outcomes and the legitimacy of EU policy making in general. Thus, there is a growing awareness that implementation deficits might call into question the legitimacy and credibility of the integration process (CEC 1996, 6). EU legitimacy is intimately tied to the effectiveness of its 'outputs'; in other words, it rests with the problem solving capacity of the European multi-level system. The theoretical discussion on the EU's problem solving capacity (see Scharpf 1997, 207) has been primarily concerned with the European capacity to *formulate* and develop regulatory policies. In this volume we turn attention to the *implementation* phase which is an equal aspect of the capacity of a multi-level system to solve regulatory problems. Indeed, it is in response to experiences with ineffective implementation, that EU critics call to drive back the EU regulatory output. In this context it is often difficult to distinguish the analytic from the ideological – undoubtedly EU sceptics have exploited the 'news' of implementation deficits to push a deeper, systemic anti-EU agenda (see EP 1993; Golub 1993). Hence, policy implementation is more than a technical issue and of high political significance.

It is in the context of these fundamental implementation deficits and their political implications that we have to understand the emergence of new approaches in EU environmental policy. The 'new approach', in many instances, is praised as a panacea to overcome problems of ineffective implementation. The advantage of new instruments *vis-à-vis* traditional regulatory measures is considered twofold. First, new instruments are argued to leave Member States more leeway to comply with EU requirements by taking account of domestic context conditions. In contrast to the detailed and rigid forms of top–down instruments that are to be uniformly implemented regardless of the physical, economic or political context, new instruments focus on establishing basic procedures for improving environmental awareness and behaviour while no concrete environmental targets are set. Second, new instruments also target the policy context directly and aim to change context factors in order to facilitate the formal and practical implementation of environmental policy in general. By enlarging the channels for societal mobilisation through more transparent processes and participatory opportunities and in providing economic incentives for industrial self-regulation, new instruments are explicitly directed at increasing the environmental awareness and responsibility of societal actors. Hence, by raising the level of acceptance with environmental objectives, it is hoped that new instruments may not only be effectively implemented themselves, but that they also provide a positive framework for the implementation of other measures. For instance, new information requirements may trigger greater public control of potentially polluting actors who may otherwise fail to comply with obligations imposed by other policies. Furthermore, these institutional and procedural innovations are equally directed at policy makers and implementers. By creating a more deliberative context for policy making they raise awareness of possible implementation problems among the policy makers; equally, participatory procedures induce a higher level of acceptance with EU policy on the part of policy implementers.

The analytical and empirical focus of the book

Against this backdrop, it is the objective of this book to assess the contribution of those reforms in EU environmental policy intended to improve implementation effectiveness. How successful is the implementation of new concepts? To what extent do they achieve their objectives? Does the flexibility and context orientation associated with new concepts really lead to better implementation results than traditional top–down regulation? Or do new concepts also face new problems that provide additional obstacles to an effective implementation performance? To put it more generally, to what extent and under which conditions do new regulatory concepts actually lead to better implementation results?

To address these questions, the selection of empirical cases presented in this book includes the major activities that were so far enacted or are currently discussed in the context of the new approach of EU environmental policy. With respect to institutional changes, this includes the organisational reforms in the European Commission which are intended to improve policy integration by establishing horizontal links between various Directorates General and to establish a dialogue between varying public and private actors involved in the policy making process. Moreover, a particular focus is placed on the role and potential of the recently established European Environment Agency (EEA) in improving the overall implementation performance of EU environmental policy.

Turning to policy changes, the book provides a complete implementation assessment of new instruments currently applied in EU environmental policy, including both participatory and communicative instruments (such as the Directives on Environmental Impact Assessment and Freedom of Access to Environmental Information) and economic instruments (such as the Eco-Audit Regulation and the Eco-Label Award Scheme). The analysis, however, is not restricted to policies already enacted, but also includes new instruments currently on the political agenda. In this context, the impact of varying design options on the implementation effectiveness of environmental liability funds is explored.

Moreover, as the book intends to assess the impact of new instruments from a comparative perspective, the presentation of empirical findings is not restricted to the implementation of new instruments, but includes the corresponding performance of traditional concepts characterised by an interventionist top–down philosophy. The 'classics' investigated in this respect refer to the Directives on Large Combustion Plants and Drinking Water Quality, which are both characterised by rather detailed and rigid regulatory requirements for domestic compliance.

The analyses of the different activities undertaken in the context of the new approach to EU environmental policy reveal that there exists a significant gap between the political rhetoric praising the benefits of the new concepts and the actual implementation results. New concepts suffer from considerable implementation deficits, and – when compared with old approaches – hardly any improvements in policy performance can be observed, yet. We argue that there exists no simple causal relationship between policy approach and implementation effectiveness.

The structure of the book

To illustrate this basic argument and to elaborate on the analytical questions posed above, the book is divided into three parts. In this first part, we intend to provide an overall synthesis of the empirical and theoretical findings presented in the individual chapters. Starting from the empirical evidence of persisting implementation failures, it is the basic intention of the following chapter (2) to come up with a theoretical explanation for this puzzling result and to develop more promising analytical criteria for the linkage between policy design and implementation performance. In emphasising both empirical and theoretical deficits characterising the current political and scientific debate on policy implementation, it is not only conceived as an introductory survey of the chapters to follow, but as a concluding theoretical interpretation of the empirical and analytical evidence presented in this entire book.

The following parts can therefore be read as an illustration of the general theoretical considerations developed in this introductory part. In part two, the focus is on institutional changes associated with the new approach to EU environmental policy and their impact on implementation effectiveness. The case studies contained in part three, by contrast, explore this relationship for the varying policy instruments enacted and currently discussed in the context of the new approach, including the assessment of varying policy designs for the implementation of EU environmental policy in future Member States.

References

Commission of the European Communities (CEC) (1993). *Towards Sustainability: A European Community Programme of Policy and Action in Relation to the Environment and Sustainable Development.* Luxembourg: Office for Official Publications of the European Communities.
CEC (1996). *Thirteenth Annual Report on Monitoring the Application of Community Law (1995).* Luxembourg: Office for Official Publications of the EC.
Collins, Ken and David Earnshaw (1992). 'The Implementation and Enforcement of European Community Environment Legislation'. *Environmental Politics*, 1 (4), 213–49.
European Parliament (EP) (1993). 'Application of Principle of Subsidiarity to Environment and Consumer Policy'. *Europe Environment*, 402 (January).
Golub, Jonathan (1993). 'Recasting EU Environmental Policy: Subsidiarity and National Sovereignty'. In Ute Collier, Jon Golub and Alexander Kreher (eds), *Subsidiarity and Shared Responsibility New Challenges for EU Environmental Policy*. Baden-Baden: Nomos.
Lenschow, Andrea (1999). 'Transformation in European Environmental Governance'. In Beate Kohler-Koch and Rainer Eising (eds), *The Transformation of European Governance*. London: Routledge, 39–60.
Scharpf, Fritz W. (1997). *Games Real Actors Play: Actor-Centred Institutionalism in Policy Research*. New York: Westview.

On deficient implementation and deficient theories: the need for an institutional perspective in implementation research

Introduction

As pointed out in chapter 1, the ever widening implementation gap in the environmental policy area (CEC 1996) as well as the serious concerns with the problem solving capacity of the European multi-level system led to the introduction of several institutional as well as policy changes generally associated with the so-called new approach in EU environmental policy. As implementation problems are widely associated with classical forms of regulation and intervention, namely technocratic, interventionist policy making from the top (EU) down (national/local implementation), the new approach places particular emphasis on flexibility for domestic implementation and context orientation, i.e. the mobilisation and stimulation of domestic support in favour of effective implementation. To achieve these objectives, attention is turned to procedural regulation, self-regulation, public participation and voluntary agreements rather than the prescription of detailed and rigid regulatory requirements 'from above'.

Indeed, there is a lot to be said for this shift in environmental regulation. It seems quite reasonable to expect that the implementation of policy measures, which allow for compliance in the light of the specific institutional, political and socio-economic conditions at the domestic level, are less likely to suffer from the resistance of subordinate administrative actors dealing with practical enforcement, or of societal actors addressed by the policy in question. In a similar way, it seems to make considerable sense that the explicit orientation to stimulate and motivate domestic support might further improve implementation performance.

Besides these plausibility arguments, advocates of the new approach can rely on theoretical support, as the new approach responds to the insights gained in implementation research. The various schools in this field have converged in acknowledging the need to secure the support of the implementing actors and the relevant interests in the policy planning process. Likewise, there is some agreement that the socio-economic context needs to be considered during the design phase (Sabatier 1986). In this context the new regulatory approach is praised for its holistic view of the policy process, rejecting the perspective that policy formulation and implementation processes are clearly distinct.

In view of this 'advance praise' rendered on behalf of the new approach, it is the objective of this book to assess the actual contributions of these regulatory and institutional (governance) reforms to improve environmental policy effectiveness. In this chapter we take the broad range of empirical material analysed to investigate the merits as well as the limitations of the new approach to regulatory policy making from a theoretical and practical perspective.

In our endeavour to assess whether these measures fulfil their promises we ask several questions. First, how successfully are these new measures implemented themselves? From a comparative perspective, are new policy instruments implemented better than top–down, interventionist regulations? Second, are network institutions and new policy instruments indeed capable of raising awareness, acceptance and initiative on the level of implementation? More generally, to what extent are they successful tools to increase the problem solving capacity of the European multi-level system?

The analyses of the different activities undertaken in the context of the new approach to environmental regulation suggest two responses to these questions. First, both institutional and instrumental policy innovations suffer from significant implementation deficits questioning their overall effectiveness. Second, when comparing old and new policies in terms of implementation effectiveness, no significant differences emerge. Instead, successes and failures vary across policies and countries, without indicating a direct causal linkage between policy type and implementation effectiveness.

The fact that the new approach has achieved only limited success so far may have two possible explanations. Either the theory remains deficient, or its practical application. We will argue in this chapter that some truth lies in both. From this conclusion another question emerges: are there solutions to these theoretical and practical deficits with respect to the implementation of EU environmental policy? Which concrete steps, if any, can be taken to improve the implementation effectiveness of European policies, and hence the problem solving capacity of the Community?

We argue that at least some of the above problems can be addressed by adopting an institutional perspective in evaluating the promises of either top–down or bottom–up instruments. Such an institutional perspective, which so far plays only a minor role in implementation theory, takes account of institutional adaptation requirements implied by European institutional and policy changes. We suggest that the institutional implications of European policies rather than the choice of the policy type are primarily responsible for implementation performance. An institutional perspective will not only provide a synthesis in the sometimes polarised debate between old and new approaches and address some of the resulting theoretical confusions, but it may also provide a more promising departure for practical policy design.

To elaborate on our argument, we proceed in five steps. In section two, we explain the conception of effective implementation under-lying the chapters in this book. Based on this definition, section three summarises the content of the various activities associated with the new approach in EU environmental policy and evaluates successes and failures in their implementation. We proceed in sec-tion four to present different explanations for the rather modest suc-cess of different institutional and policy reforms. Finally, in section five we develop an institutionalist explanatory framework and pre-sent potential solutions to overcome both theoretical and practical deficits.

The concept of effective implementation

Before moving to the empirical and theoretical discussion of effec-tive implementation, we need to clarify what we mean by this term. This is no easy task as the literature offers a variety of definitions and, notably, the proponents of top–down and bottom–up approaches to implementation differ in their conception of effec-tiveness. For reasons further specified below, we define effective implementation as the degree to which the formal transposition and the practical application of institutional and instrumental changes correspond to the objectives defined in European legisla-tion. Hence, it is the compliance with these objectives rather than an evaluation of environmental quality improvements that concerns us here.

This definition, comparing compliance on the ground with what was decided from above, is more narrow than that usually applied by advocates of the top–down policy approach who equate successful implementation with the achievement of the desired policy outcomes. Implicit in this latter definition is an assumption of a mechanistic causal relationship between policy objectives, instruments and policy outcomes. According to this definition, implementation implies a match between objectives and outcomes. If the objective of European legislation is, for instance, to achieve a certain level of drinking water quality throughout the Community, effective implementation is achieved as soon as the prescribed level is reached. This concept is analytically problematic as it obscures the *actual* link between policy instruments and outcomes. Whether policy objectives are achieved or not depends on contingencies of the political, economic, and social policy context besides the deliberate choice of policy instruments. Hence this perspective passes over important questions such as: 'How do we know whether drinking water quality has improved as a result of European legislation rather than as the consequence of other factors completely independent from European developments, such as different weather conditions, privatisation or economic decline?' It ignores that the success of policy implementation in terms of policy outcomes is not predictable given the scientific uncertainties and socio-economic complexities underlying a given problem constellation (Baier *et al.* 1990; Lane 1995, 110).

The bottom–up approach, by contrast, tries to address these problems by applying an even broader perspective on implementation. Here, policy objectives are no longer defined as benchmarks to be reached, instead it is expected that they may undergo modifications during the process of policy implementation. Implementers should have the flexibility and autonomy to adjust the policy in the light of particular local requirements, changes in the perception or constellation of policy problems, as well as new scientific evidence on causal relationships between means and ends. From this perspective, successful implementation is judged by the extent to which the perceived outcomes correspond with the preferences of the actors involved in the implementation process (Ingram and Schneider 1990). Effective implementation is analysed from a process-related rather than output- or outcome-based perspective. The crucial question for evaluating implementation success is to what extent did a certain policy allow for processes of learning, capacity building and support building in order to address policy problems in a decentralised way consistent with the interests of the actors involved? Implicit in this, however, is the absence of a baseline for evaluating implementation results. First, it fails to offer a measuring rod for learning, capacity or support. When do these processes actually occur and work successfully? Second, and maybe even more significantly from the perspective of evaluating the impact of new policy instruments, this definition ignores the nature of the link between the (EU) policy and the local process of learning and problem solving. After all, local processes could have entirely different origins. In order to assess whether the EU policy has had some impact on these local processes, we need to observe whether its – however open – 'instructions' have been complied with.

Our definition of effective implementation avoids the conceptual problems of both top–down and bottom–up approaches. Rather than analysing the accomplishment of policy objectives in terms of outcomes, we restrict our investigation to the compliance with the legal-administrative tasks (i.e., output factors) specified in the legislation. These also act as the baseline for evaluating the impact of new instruments and institutions. Hence, we start from the assumption that changes in outcome (be it environmental quality or local learning and capacity) depend on – more or less demanding – legal and procedural adaptation to EU policies. EU policies may require the reallocation of administrative competencies, the creation of new administrative structures or the adaptation of existing procedures and rules. We ask, whether both the formal transposition and the practical application of the activities associated with the new approach in EU environmental policy took place in a way that is consistent with the concrete output requirements of these measures. Have existing legal and institutional arrangements been modified in a way that corresponds to the objectives underlying European legislation?

This in some ways narrow conception of implementation effectiveness offers several advantages for the purpose of this book. Not only do we escape conceptual problems implicit in other definitions discussed above. Even more important in our context, the investigative path from EU policy – via compliance with output objectives –

to the substantive impact of the new approach allows us to develop a tight linkage between implementation effectiveness and the problem solving capacity of the multi-layered system of the EU. Effective implementation, in terms of the Member States' general preparedness to accept and comply with European policies, is a basic factor indicating the level of the EU's problem solving capacity. Changes in policy outcomes follow from this, even though the causal path becomes more blurred at this stage and hence more difficult to follow empirically; in cases of ineffective implementation the link between EU policy making and the achievements of the desired outcomes would in any case be interrupted mid-way.

Besides these substantive reasons for investigating (first) the level of compliance with output objectives, this definition of implementation effectiveness has an analytical advantage. Such a formal definition provides the opportunity to compare the implementation results even of widely different policy measures. By contrast, it would be problematic to measure and hence compare the contributions of different policies (e.g. the Directive for Free Access to Environmental Information and the Large Combustion Plant Directive) to the achievement of a policy objective (such as air quality). In other words, our definition of implementation effectiveness allows us to compare and draw conclusions between the individual contributions to this book.

Let us now turn to the question of whether the EU problem solving capacity may improve due to a turn towards the new regulatory approach. The following review of empirical results sheds a rather critical light.

Empirical evidence: the limits of the 'new approach'

This book consists of a number of contributions that reflect in a rather comprehensive way on the Community's recent efforts to improve environmental implementation, and begin to evaluate these attempts. The following chapters cover both institutional innovations, intended to improve the framework for policy making in light of the challenge of implementation lying ahead, as well as concrete policy instruments, thought to either ease the context for the execution of other policies or to represent a lesser challenge for implementers on the ground. In this brief preview of the empirical results we highlight the rather mixed picture that emerges with respect to the merits of the so-called new approach before we turn in the remainder of this chapter to the theoretical and practical implications following from the contributions to this book.

The integration of bottom–up elements in the process of policy making is reflected in a number of institutional innovations that shall provide the institutional foundation for a more deliberative interaction between policy designers and implementers, the public and the private sector, and across policy fields and even countries. Marieva Favoino, Christoph Knill and Andrea Lenschow (chapter 3) examine the effectiveness of changes in the governance structure on the level of the European Commission, which built horizontal links between Directorates General to improve policy integration and which established a series of dialogue groups bringing together public and private actors involved in the various stages of policy making. Rasmus Dilling (chapter 4) investigates the role of the new European Environment Agency (EEA) in improving the level of information for more effective policy making as well as for the control and monitoring of implementation. These efforts at institution building share the assumption that an exchange of information and experiences will improve the mutual awareness regarding the intentions of environmental policy, on the one hand, and the potential problems and conflicting interests of actors on the ground, on the other. It is expected that mutual awareness, increased quality of policy designs, as well as a higher level of acceptance among affected actors will go hand in hand.

Not much positive can be said yet, however about the contribution of these institutional reforms to greater implementation effectiveness. Dilling attributes the not quite satisfactory results to a lack of resources or imperfect institutional design. Though hinting at the political conflicts that were responsible for the present structures, he remains optimistic with respect to the ultimate potential of institution building in support of a better implementation record. Favoino, Knill and Lenschow appear more fundamentally sceptical. They argue that the success of any institutional reform depends on its level of congruence with already existing structures and practices. Some degree of congruence is needed to moblise effectively the support of strong actor coalitions in favour of effective institutional adjustment. On the basis of this assumption they are able to explain the successful implementation of the new dialogue groups and the varying implementation success of the horizontal institutional structures created in the Commission linking the environmental Directorate with other policy fields. While the dialogue groups and horizontal integration in the sector of regional policy implied less challenging adaptations, horizontal integration requirements were in fundamental contradiction with the dominant principles and traditions in the agricultural sector, hence implying negative implementation results in the latter case. Taken together, these chapters suggest that the building of institutional structures that would be capable of facilitating a better compliance with EU environmental law in the future depends not only on the results of the complex EU decision making process (see Dilling) but also on the level of fit between new and old structures (Favoino, Knill and Lenschow).

Applying these conclusions to the general discussion of problem solving capacity in the EU we can identify two positions. Implicit in the chapter by Dilling is the dominant perspective that problem solving capacity depends on the policy formulation and decision making phase. The author departs from the dominant scepticism (see Scharpf 1985) however, by anticipating a technocratic learning process rather than focusing on (inevitable) traps. Favoino, Knill and Lenschow shift the analysis to the merits of the already decided institutional designs and the implementation phase. Their framework could be used to extend the investigation by Dilling, asking whether a 'perfectly designed' EEA would operate effectively and hence contribute to the Community's problem solving capacity. This, they suggest, depends on the 'goodness of fit' with existing structures.

The question of the 'goodness of fit' is also raised in the last two chapters of this book. Christoph Knill and Andrea Lenschow as well as Tanja Börzel have included traditional and so-called new policy instruments in their survey of implementation effectiveness. Börzel (chapter 10) looks at the case of Spain, and the region of Catalunya, in particular. She concludes that not the type of instrument but the institutional and socio-political context are decisive with regard to successful implementation. Börzel shows clear limits to the implementation of new instruments, and hence questions whether the hope raised by the shift to new instruments is justified. In particular, she points to the limits of EU legislation to effectively mobilise domestic support for implementation. The sceptical perspective regarding the potential of new instruments is shared, and due to a cross-country comparative analysis, strengthened in chapter 11 by Knill and Lenschow. Comparing implementation processes in

Britain, France and Germany in the first part of their piece, they emphasise the critical role of the institutional context in which new (and old) instruments are placed. The institutional 'goodness of fit', not the policy type, are decisive for the level of compliance with EU law. This, for instance, explains why the 'new' EU Directive on Access to Environmental Information is implemented rather poorly in Germany. The institutional fit factor also needs to be kept in mind for the planned accession of East-Central European countries to the EU, they argue.

With this institutional perspective we have introduced the bridging element in the evaluation of implementation performance of new and old instruments, as the factor of institutional fit can be applied to both. Even within such an institutional perspective, advocates of the new approach may be justified in supporting the increased use of new instruments, as their objective is to permit flexible handling on the ground and hence the policy's adaptation to institutional conditions (rather than forcing institutional adaptation to the policy requirements). The remaining chapters of this book ask whether new instruments actually meet this goal. Looking in some detail at the compliance and performance of the handful of new instruments that are presently discussed or were recently adopted as part of the EU's attempt to improve implementation, some doubts emerge about whether new instruments are what they claim to be. Several chapters also approach the more fundamental question of whether new instruments – even in an institutionally favourable context – are capable of achieving their promises, namely, of raising environmental awareness and of 'greening' the behaviour of industry and private actors. Before turning to the more systematic, theoretical discussion elaborating on these questions and observations, let us briefly summarise the conclusions of the chapters dealing with the performance of single new instruments.

Clíona Kimber (chapter 8) investigates in a comparative country study the level of compliance with the 1990 EU Directive on the Freedom of Access to Environmental Information. She focuses on the policy design in explaining the, at best, mixed results. At the most general level, she argues that the instrument lacks enforceability and hence top–down pressure that can be applied to ensure compliance. Dealing with the concrete legislation at hand, the design of the instrument is too ambiguous and incapable of sending clear signals to both implementing actors and the potential users of the new legal right. In contrast to advocates of flexible policy designs in the EU context, Kimber argues that different national traditions further increase the need for clear signals. She identifies in her analysis the real possibility of escaping policy obligations as a weakness of new instruments, especially if their design implies additional ambiguities.

Robert Wright (chapter 5) equally focuses on the nature of the policy in his analysis of the ecolabel scheme. On the general level he makes the insightful observation that the ecolabel scheme combines attributes of old and new policy instruments; i.e., it is characterised by a complex regulatory framework on the one hand, but permits voluntary application on the other. A similar mixing of characteristics is also implicit in the EU Directive on Environmental Impact Assessment, namely a tightly regulated procedural framework with flexible substantive implications (see Caddy, chapter 9). The hybrid instrument type, Wright argues, goes hand in hand in the case of the ecolabel scheme with complexities in design that result in ambiguities and inconsistencies. Wright shows that the problematic design of the ecolabel scheme is not primarily the result of poor planning and analysis but rather a consequence of the complex process of policy making. Conflicts of interest – rooted in the multinational decision making context as well as multiple target groups of the policy – have prevented a more coherent policy design. It follows from this that the problem solving capacity of EU legislation, to the extent that it depends on the multi-level decision making processes, may not be *principally* different for new or old instruments even though new instruments are often presented as less controversial and hence less subject to complex compromises.

The issue that multiple design options for new instruments exist and that competing political coalitions may form in support of one design or another is also implicit in Kostas Tsekouras' chapter (7) on environmental liability as a new EU policy instrument. His systematic analysis of the advantages and disadvantages of the many variants of such legislation currently discussed brings home the point that policy performance is a multi-dimensional affair and hence has the potential for various disagreements. Achieving policy success is linked to focusing on environmental objectives in a 'technically' appropriate way as much as to being responsive to the national institutional, administrative and political conditions. With respect to new instruments, this complexity is by no means reduced. The administrative and political feasibility of implementation may be eased somewhat by the greater flexibility and discretion implied in some new designs; nevertheless, most communicative and economic instruments require considerable procedural adaptation and often institution building. On the level of targeting the policy problem, new instruments face even more obstacles as they work only indirectly, leaving room for obstruction.

Jan Jaap Bouma in chapter 6 focuses on the Environmental Management and Auditing System (EMAS) Regulation and precisely on this latter aspect of indirect targeting. The EMAS scheme is intended to raise the awareness of business actors with regard to the environmental costs that they may produce for society. Even more significant for the anticipated learning process, this instrument helps in pointing to the economic benefits to be gained by industry if it moves toward more environment friendly production practices. Bouma suggests that awareness raising may not be sufficient for actual behavioural changes. Besides the resource problems which affect particularly smaller businesses, which may not be able to afford the required short-term investments for longer-term benefits, the true range of economically and environmentally beneficial measures remains limited as long as the overall regulatory framework imposes no limits (i.e. costs) on environmentally harmful behaviour. In other words, new instruments and top–down regulations may complement each other as polluting actors are more likely to comply with regulatory baselines if legal pressure is met by a newly realised self-interest (e.g., due to a different incentive structure produced by new instruments such as the EMAS scheme).

Joanne Caddy in her chapter (9) on the evolution of the legislative framework for environmental impact assessments in East and Central Europe, deals with the problems of administrative, political and societal feasibility more closely. The Directive on Environmental Impact Assessment falls under the new approach as it targets environmental awareness as the path to increase environment friendly behaviour. Her chapter shows that this new instrument is by no means easier to implement than old instruments. While other authors point to the institutional challenges new instruments impose despite all talk about flexible implementation (Knill and Lenschow), Caddy highlights the challenges for administration as well as the societies to be mobilised (see also Börzel, chapter 10; Knill and Lenschow, chapter 11). Similar to Kimber, Caddy suggests that acquiring capacity on the ground should be developed with the assistance of clear signals from above (and institution building) rather than open-ended instructions. The empirical analysis by Knill and Lenschow, however, points to an issue that may complicate matters further as those 'clear signals' may or may not fit in the overall administrative tradition. Only in the case of 'fit' can we expect that clear instructions have a mobilising effect, in cases of poor fit we may just as well experience the complete negligence of EU legislation, hence the persistence of the implementation and capacity gap.

Considering this preview of the empirical contributions to this volume we have now arrived at a rather sceptical view with respect to the promise of new environmental instruments and institutional innovations. A variety of explanatory factors are mentioned in these chapters. Let us now attempt to deal with them systematically on a more general level.

Explaining persisting implementation failure: deficient theory or deficient application?

The above overview reveals that new approaches directed towards horizontal governance, regulatory transparency, procedural regulation or self-regulation do not automatically imply effective implementation. In order to explain these implementation failures, that seem puzzling considering the theoretical and political rhetoric surrounding their application, one could either question the validity of implementation theory or the correct application of the theory. In this section we advance three arguments explaining some gaps in the performance of the new approach. First, the theoretical literature on implementation and on the use of bottom–up policy instruments, in particular, suffers from inconsistencies and ambiguities in its argumentation and hence, its implications for actual policy making. Second, political practice rarely reflects the 'pure' application of theoretical insights; i.e. in many instances new policy instruments are actually hybrids containing elements of both old and new approaches. Third, it is often overlooked in theory and practice that the new approach even in its pure form suffers from its own distinctive weaknesses which might lead to additional implementation problems. In particular, the factor usually viewed as the basic advantage of new concepts, namely their context orientation, remains a theoretically diffuse and practically complex category.

Theoretical ambiguity

The fact that the emergence of new strategies to improve the implementation effectiveness of EU environmental policy are well in line with recommendations drawn from implementation theory does not automatically imply that the relevant theoretical body reflects a dominant and undisputed paradigm. To be sure, there are numerous studies emphasising the advantages of bottom–up concepts, indicating the need to consider the specific context constellation in which a certain policy is implemented (such as interests, capabilities, motivations of implementers and target groups) (Lipsky 1980; Berman 1980). The top–down approach, by contrast, focuses on policy content, design and the presence of enforcement mechanisms as the basic factors affecting implementation performance (Krämer 1992; Lübbe-Wolff 1996). Yet other analyses suggest a mix of top–down and bottom–up elements as the perfect solution (see Sabatier 1986, 23–5) or advocate a contingent approach to the choice of policy instruments (Ingram and Schneider 1990; Peters 1993). In short, implementation theory is characterised by no single and consistent conclusion which allows for general policy recommendations in order to improve implementation effectiveness.

The empirical richness of the implementation case studies of the 1980s, in particular, had the consequence that scholars increasingly shied away from seeking a universal model (Mayntz 1983; Windhoff-Héritier 1987). Instead, the focus was on mid-level conclusions (e.g. on the appropriateness of certain policy instruments in light of distinctive policy problems and context characteristics), in the best case amounting to general contingency models (Hanf and Scharpf 1978; Linder and Peters 1989; Ingram and Schneider 1990; Peters 1993). But even these mid-level or contingency models, identifying different problem/context constellations in which either top–down or bottom–up measures are expected to be more successful, ended up contradicting one another. For instance, Ingram and Schneider (1990) argue that in constellations of low support for a policy, bottom–up instruments that emphasise learning and support building will lead to better implementation performance than detailed top–down intervention. This view contrasts with an argument advanced by Cerych and Sabatier (1986), stating that clear and specific objectives might enhance learning by lower level agents because it produces obvious performance indicators. Equally contentious is Ingram and Schneider's (1990) recommendation to apply bottom–up concepts in constellations characterised by high uncertainty and complexity in order to allow for sufficient flexibility to react to new developments in the light of specific context conditions and the generation of ideas useful for the further evolution of a policy. There are good arguments to justify detailed top–down regulation in such constellations instead. First, too much discretion for subordinate agents might imply that nothing happens at all (Lane 1995, 112; Lübbe-Wolff 1996). Second, even a top–down policy that takes little account of the problem complexity, might succeed in stimulating learning processes by trial and error.

Such a litany of contradictory advice that can be derived from implementation research could be continued. It illustrates the general ambiguity of implementation theory. Even attempts to classify contingencies, identifying particular problem or context constellations, fail to establish convincing causal linkages between policy choice and implementation effectiveness. This insight is not entirely new, but it seems that it has been forgotten in the EU context, considering the sometimes euphoric reception of new approaches by many of the political and societal actors involved.

To be sure, this euphoric response should not only be read as the result of Commission bureaucrats and Member State politicians misreading implementation theory. It must be traced to a number of political factors as well. Besides processes of simple trial and error learning (abandoning deficient top–down concepts in favour of new approaches) or mimetic learning (the imitation of successful domestic concepts), political and ideological aspects have had an impact on recent institutional and policy changes at the supranational level. The empowerment of sub-central levels of governance as well as the increasing reliance on market forces and industrial self-regulation resonate well with the current subsidiarity debate and the neo-liberal call to 'slim' the regulatory state. But even though political factors may have contributed to ignoring the theoretical ambiguities with respect to the merits of the new approach, the political reality of its increasing adoption justifies some further investigation of its inherent limits or problems.

Is 'new' really new?
Implicit in the controversial discussion of the potential of the new approach is the assumption that such an approach is clearly delineated and that new policy instruments as well as the appropriate

institutional innovations are distinct from traditional, top–down instruments and structures. The empirical evidence presented in this book suggests that this distinctiveness is a myth, at least on the level of actual application. Most new instruments or institutions are hybrids, combining deliberative and discretionary with hierarchical and inflexible characteristics. As a consequence, they share many problems with traditional tools, both during the decision making process as well as at the implementation stage.

To elaborate, it is often argued that new instruments are preferable as they render greater political acceptability in the decision making as well as implementation process. Their flexibility and responsiveness to local framework conditions suggests that new policy designs are less prone to inviting political conflict. Consequently, decision making is expected to be relatively smooth. Equally, given the context orientation and discretionary structure, new instruments imply a lesser imposition on implementing actors than classical regulation, hence favouring acceptance and compliance also on the ground. Political acceptance is expected to increase even more if deliberative institutional structures are developed in addition. The reality, however, looks less rosy.

Several studies of environmental policy making show that political conflict does not stop, or even diminish, at the issue of new instruments. The work by Héritier *et al.* (1996) for instance investigates in some detail the conflicts around the adoption of the EMAS Regulation and the Information and Environmental Impact Assessment Directives. Moreover, institutional innovations are far from unproblematic, considering, for instance, the protracted battle prior to the establishment of the EEA (Jimenez-Beltran 1996). These experiences show that the measures in this new approach are rarely free from competency conflicts, nor do they 'fit' every regulatory system. On the contrary, because new instruments typically focus on the procedural level – e.g., establishing channels for awareness raising and learning – they may impose quite significant reform pressures for national and local administrations. Hence, we may ask whether new instruments are really 'new' with respect to the implied reduced adaptation challenge for the decision makers and implementing actors.

Take for example the Impact Assessment Directive. In administrative terms the Directive assumes horizontally integrated structures that enable a comprehensive assessment of any public or private project across environmental media, such as water or air as well as across geographical areas (regardless of political or administrative boundaries). Both administrative requisites violate against the federal and hierarchical structures in Germany, which therefore fought the Directive in the decision making process and now stands out with a minimalistic approach to implementation (Héritier *et al.* 1996; Knill and Lenschow 1998). It seems doubtful that the substantive objectives of the Directive will be reached this way. Similarly, Robert Wright (chapter 5) elaborates on the political fights affecting the decision of the ecolabel scheme as well as on the procedural challenges implied in the application of this – after all voluntary – instrument. On a hypothetical level, Tsekouras (chapter 7) equally draws on the administrative and political challenges implicit in different designs for an EU environmental liability framework. Hence, the hybrid character of many new instruments may imply ineffective implementation as a result of the nevertheless quite demanding procedural requirements, which may be in conflict with already existing structures and trigger administrative opposition or simply exceed administrative capacities. In addition, implementation of new instruments may suffer from the consequences of the conflictual decision making process. A typical result of political conflict, if it can be resolved, is the adoption of a compromise solution catering for a multitude of often incompatible interests, thereby losing clarity and cohesion. These weaknesses were mentioned as the cause for implementation problems on the ground in a number of the chapters. Kimber (chapter 8), for instance, mentions the ambiguities in the Information Directive as a primary reason why some Member States either misunderstood or wilfully escaped their obligations under the Directive.

Political conflict and administrative resistance during the implementation of new instruments follow not only from their 'lack of purity' and the presence of regulatory elements that contradict national structures despite the assumed flexibility of the policy tool. Conflict and resistance may have even deeper reasons, touching on key questions of regulatory philosophy. It must be realised that new and old regulatory approaches are rooted in a more general belief system (or causal theory; see Sabatier 1986) and certain assumptions with regard to human behaviour in the policy process. In brief, advocates of the new approach trust in citizens' self-initiative (particularly if the institutional framework and knowledge base facilitates initiative) while classical regulation assumes more passive but typically law-abiding citizens (especially if the threat of sanctions adds pressure to comply). In most Member States such either society- or state-centred thinking has become institutionalised in the form of regulatory philosophy or administrative traditions and will influence the decision making process. Hence, not all policy types will resonate equally well with the national administrative tradition. Even though the concrete challenges for adaptation may be lower for new instruments (which is already a questionable assumption, as indicated above), on the level of regulatory philosophy the political, and in the end also administrative, challenge for adaptation may be substantial (Knill and Lenschow 1998). There exists no principal difference between old and new instruments, even in their 'pure' form.

Are new instruments and structures really new; that is, do they escape some of the problems usually attributed to traditional regulatory measures? The answer seems to be a rather unambiguous no. Most new instruments are in fact hybrid solutions, implying, usually on the procedural dimension, considerable adaptation pressure for at least some EU Member States. From this follows political conflict in the policy formulation and decision making stages, deficits in the resulting compromise solutions and the rather doubtful acceptance on the part of the policy implementers as their discretion to mould the instrument according to local needs and facilities is in fact more limited than expected. Even if new instruments and institutions are pure in their novelty with respect to the substantive requirements, we must realise that they *cannot* be new on the 'philosophical' level. Here they will imply quite inflexible challenges to the regulatory traditions of at least some Member States.

Is 'new' really better?
The previous discussion was not supposed to imply that so-called new instruments are in fact no different at all from traditional approaches. The intention was to show that the contrast is less encompassing than often thought and that both approaches share some characteristics, and hence problems. The main difference between old and new policies remains the more procedural emphasis of the latter, going hand in hand with more flexible and open-ended implications on the substantive side. This openness to context factors of the new approach may carry its own set of problems, however, as several chapters in this book indicate.

A somewhat idealistic and ad hoc notion of 'context orientation' among advocates of the new approach has resulted in wide-spread unawareness of inherent problems. The first question that arises is whether the open-ended nature of new instruments, as opposed to clearly specified obligations, really provides sufficient incentives for motivating and mobilising sufficient administrative and societal support in favour of effective implementation. As part of its open and flexible design, the new approach assumes the presence of motivated and capable implementers who are willing and able to work with the policy instrument in the local context and toward the intended goal. Several chapters in this book suggest that there is reason to question this assumption of principally motivated actors. Kimber (chapter 8) shows that ambiguities in the legal text may help local administrators to escape their legal obligations to make environmental information accessible rather than induce them to fit the legislation into existing structures. The chapters by Börzel (10), Bouma (6), Caddy (9) and Knill and Lenschow (11) point out that many new instruments are too passive in their design to mobilise either the administration or the general public. These actors either lack the clear incentive, general inclination or skills and resources to actually respond to new (communicative) instruments. Furthermore, Bouma presents a rather sceptical view on the extent to which the indirect strategy of many new instruments, trying to achieve environmental goals via awareness raising and attitude change, is sufficient to promote effective implementation of environmental policy in general. More concretely, he suggests that new instruments require a substantive counterbalance that provides concrete incentives to change behaviour; he shows that the EMAS Regulation suffers from the missing coercion of financial instruments imposing costs on environmentally harmful behaviour.

Second, notwithstanding their flexible and open-ended nature, new instruments may trigger not only positive responses but also resistance or active opposition. Experiences with the adoption of the ecolabel scheme indicate that the political and economic context for economic instruments in particular may be highly conflictual due to the market effects of such instruments, hindering their effective implementation (Wright, chapter 5). Several other chapters point to instances of administrative resistance or sabotage (see Kimber; Knill and Lenschow, in this book); rather than responding to new channels for learning, national administrations maintain old practices and routines. Advocates of new instruments seem to overestimate the (positive) malleability of the local context. To push the theoretical framework further in this respect, we need to develop general indicators concerning this malleability. We argue in the next part that an institutional perspective contributes to distinguishing more or less malleable and/or favourable framework conditions.

In summary, aside from sharing some characteristics and problems with the classical regulatory approach, new instruments have a number of inherent weaknesses. Flexible design and open institutional and procedural structures may create confusion rather than incentives to act. Furthermore, the frequently indirect signals sent by new instruments presuppose favourable context factors. Hence, the context orientation of the new approach works only for a limited set of *already favourable* context constellations (e.g., low initial opposition, sufficient capacity and resources, some initial motivation, complementarity with regulatory and institutional structures, etc.). Ambiguous theory has helped to mystify the latter aspect particularly.

Addressing the deficits: towards an institutional perspective in implementation research

In previous sections we have considered some empirical evidence that new institutional designs and new instruments have not contributed to reduce the implementation deficits that were widely attributed to the predominant use of hierarchical, command-control structures and instruments. Our analysis has pointed to an overstated distinction between old and new as well as several particular weaknesses of new institutions and instruments in order to explain this disappointment. We now show that these explanations have an institutional perspective in common.

Implementation and institutions: the argument
Notwithstanding the overall revival of neo-institutional approaches, implementation research has remained surprisingly unaffected by these theoretical developments. This may be due to the fact that implementation research was already an 'industry in decline', when institutions came 'back in' to the work of political scientists from the mid-1980s onwards (Evans *et al.* 1985). Only recently, and especially in the context of research on the implementation of EU policy in the Member States, scholars began to analyse the impact of

institutions on implementation effectiveness in an explicit and more consistent way (Knill 1998; Knill and Lenschow 1998; Timmermans *et al.* 1998).

In the past, institutions were integrated in the analysis merely from the perspective of adequate design. Analysts coming from the top–down perspective asked for the optimal structural and organisational arrangements that would permit effective implementation of a certain policy (see Pressmann and Wildavsky 1973; Scharpf 1978). This thinking relies on the implicit assumption that national institutions would easily adapt to the suggested 'model' structure. Problems of institutional change were ignored. The bottom–up perspective assumes a similar malleability of existing institutional factors. Here, analysts are interested in the impact of varying institutional designs on the skills, resources and capacities of relevant actors. They ask for the perfect design facilitating the supply of implementing authorities with sufficient financial, legal and personal resources.

Without denying the importance of adequate institutional design, we argue that such a perspective remains incomplete as long as it ignores the problems associated with the process of adjusting the existing institutional arrangements to the defined 'ideal' model. The chapter by Favoino, Knill and Lenschow (3) drives home this point in discussing explicit attempts to improve the context for policy implementation through institution building within the EU Commission. They show that institutional reforms will only be successful if there is some minimum congruence with already existing institutional arrangements.

Most chapters in this book deal with environmental policies in the narrower sense. They show that problems of institutional adjustment are equally relevant here and not restricted to policies, which are explicitly directed at institutional change or reforms. As elaborated above, regulatory policies often require changes of well-established administrative structures, procedures and practices at the domestic level, and hence create pressures for institutional adaptation during the process of implementation. This 'by-product' of policy making is often overlooked in implementation research, either due to its problem-oriented focus on adequate policy design or due to an isolated reception and perception of certain policies in their specific context (including the interests and capabilities of implementers and target groups). Furthermore, it is often wrongly assumed that the institutional adaptation pressure of new instruments is negligible because of their less impositional nature. In reality many so-called new instruments are in fact 'hybrids' containing hierarchical elements; also the typically procedural character of new instruments easily amounts to a challenge for national administrations.

Linking EU policy making and effective implementation through the intermediate step of institutional adaptation is not only empirically but also analytically relevant. It is one of the few generally accepted findings in the otherwise diverse neo-institutionalist literature (Hall and Taylor 1996) that institutional change, regardless if required explicitly or implicitly, rarely takes place in a smooth and unproblematic way. Existing institutions 'matter', and they do so mainly by constraining the options for future changes and adaptations. Thus, an institution's normal life is characterised by persistence and continuity; fundamental or path-breaking changes are confined to exceptional situations or external shocks.

Institutional persistence increases with an institution's depth and breadth (Krasner 1988). Institutional depth refers to the extent to which institutions structure preferences and beliefs of actors by providing cognitive frames of reference. The final chapter by Knill and Lenschow shows, for instance, how the paternalistic state tradition with a strong emphasis on the rule of law in Germany pre-structures the administration's behaviour in the environmental field; instruments implying administrative discretion or a transparent relationship with the public are perceived as misfits in this regulatory framework and hence resisted. Institutional breadth, in turn, relates to the costs of institutional adaptation, including not only the number of additional institutional changes required as a result of comprehensive institutional linkages, but also the institutional impact on the distribution of power and resources between different actors. This is an aspect touched upon in the analysis of deficits in implementing the EU Environmental Impact Assessment Directive in several of the following chapters (see Börzel; Caddy, in this book), which argue that implicit requirements to establish broad institutional linkages between geographical and sectoral units have been one of the reasons for resistance.

The emphasis on institutional continuity and stability in the neo-institutional literature does not imply that institutions are entirely static. Indeed, institutions constantly adapt to external pressures.

However, the scope of these adaptations is constrained by the existing institutional arrangements; that is, the institution's 'roots and routes' (Olsen 1995, 6). Institutional change is expected to be incremental and path-dependent. Consequently, movement tends to occur on the level of 'second order changes' (Hall 1993), 'secondary aspects' (Sabatier 1993) or 'changes within the core' (Knill and Lenschow 1998). They do not challenge an institution's very identity.

Implications for implementation research
Applying neo-institutional theory to problems of effective implementation, we find that an institutional perspective may help to address conceptual deficits in two ways. First, it may reduce theoretical ambiguity by focusing on aspects of implementation which top–down and bottom–up approaches so far have both treated as a 'black box'. Second, an institutional approach allows for a more systematic account of the impact and malleability of 'context conditions' on implementation effectiveness.

It follows from these neo-institutional insights that, rather than being affected by the choice of the policy approach *per se*, effective implementation is basically dependent on the degree of institutional fit between existing institutional arrangements and the institutional implications emerging from European policies. Implementation is likely to be ineffective if the institutional implications of EU policies contradict strongly entrenched patterns of already existing institutions. Such contradictions may exist on the level of regulatory structures, hence they could affect institutional innovations as they are presently designed to ease the European policy formulation and implementation process, such as independent agencies or organisational networks. Contradictions may equally exist on the level of regulatory practices and procedures as implied in environmental policies. Let us repeat again, new instruments are not excluded from this possible problem as many of them assume high adaptive capacity of the institutional framework.

'Pure' new instruments, of course, should not assume certain structures on the ground but rather facilitate the adaptation of the policy tool to the respective 'context conditions'. The notion of context, however, remains unspecified in implementation theory and problematic in practice, as several chapters in this book show. In practice a policy's flexibility and regulatory discretion will be important only if the policy is applied to context factors that are very stable and inflexible; a flexible design is less significant in a context that would relatively easily adapt to the requirements of the policy instrument. We suggest that an institutional perspective would advance our understanding of the nature of context factors and their impact on the implementation process: one would need to proceed by first analysing the level of institutional embeddedness of the various relevant context factors and then compare the levels of context malleability with the respective degrees of actual flexibility implied in the policy. We may find, for instance, that a policy is highly flexible with respect to the exact administrative procedures selected to achieve the policy's objective while the policy is assuming at the same time that the administration is capable of choosing such an appropriate procedure. Turning to the actual context, we may face an administrative structure that has little capacity for independent decision making on the part of the implementing officials. In such a case, the so-called context orientation of the policy instrument has actually hampered effective implementation as the institutional dimension of the relevant context has been ignored.

Implications for European problem solving capacity:
'bounded innovation'
Applying an institutional perspective to policy implementation may also add some insights to the present theoretical and practical debate on the problem solving capacity of the EU multi-level system. In the past, this debate has primarily focused on the policy formulation phase. Decision traps were identified that hinder the adoption of optimal policy solutions and hence limit top–down problem solving (Scharpf 1985). This aspect of the theoretical discussion has not been further advanced in this volume. Nevertheless, the rather clear evidence that old as well as new policies may fall victim to such decision traps has been revealing. The argument that new instruments, due to their open and flexible texture, are less likely to be trapped between conflicting interests could not be confirmed.

One concern of this book is the linkage between effective implementation and problem solving. We have argued that it makes sense to focus on compliance with specified policy objectives as a pre-stage and pre-condition to actual problem solving in terms of policy outcomes. Following our theoretical and empirical considerations, new instruments are not necessarily superior to old instruments in this respect. Both instrument types may demand too high a level of institutional adaptation in order to set in motion a process of problem solving – instead, the policy may be resisted by its implementers and/or addressees.

This conclusion may yield a general policy dilemma for the problem solving capacity of the EU multi-level system: imposing the 'ideal' policy design from the top while ignoring the potential impact of existing institutions, may significantly reduce the chance for effective problem solving due to administrative resistance to adapting. Designing policy in conformity to existing institutions, however, may reduce the possibility to generate changes and solve problems (see Timmermans *et al.* 1998). New instruments may face the related dilemma: those measures that approach the issue of problem solving indirectly, by facilitating local learning processes, may impose a too minor (or indirect) challenge for triggering any reaction. Conversely, they may ask too much in terms of the local problem solving capacity and be ignored in practice. The latter case is most likely in low capacity and low mobilisation situations as indicated in the chapters on Southern and Central-East European states (Börzel, Caddy, Knill and Lenschow). To overcome these problems, policy makers have to develop policies that require something, but not too much from Member States. In other words, there exists a curvilinear relationship between the level of adaptation pressure implied in EU policies and the effectiveness of implementation (see Cerych and Sabatier 1986). Only if EU legislation fits into such 'bounded space for innovation', it – be it old or new – may contribute to problem solving in the EU.

Conclusion

In this book, and in this chapter in particular, we revisit a subdiscipline in public policy, namely implementation research that has become highly salient for EU environmental policy in recent years, but continues to suffer from theoretical weaknesses and ambiguities. EU policies are based on some of these ambiguous theoretical considerations. We have shown that the EU's shift towards a new approach in institution building and the choice of policy instruments may have been affected by a superficial analysis of the true character of the chosen measures and a unduly optimistic perspective of the anticipated effects.

We have identified in this chapter a 'black box' which both

top–down and bottom–up models in implementation research have in common, namely the institutional framework. We suggest that focusing on this black box will help resolve some of the ambiguities and contradictions in existing theory. Looking at institutional adaptation pressure helps us qualify the conditions under which a certain policy design is capable of solving the problem addressed as well as the conditions under which bottom–up 'learning' tools will actually find some resonance in the given institutional and political context. Hence, the institutional perspective advances top–down and bottom–up policy perspectives and offers a bridge that links arguments of an often polarised debate.

An institutional perspective to policy implementation may provide some additional insights to the present discussion on the problem solving capacity of the EU multi-level system. This debate has been primarily concerned with the European capacity to *formulate* and develop regulatory policies. However, the Community's capacity to solve regulatory problems is in a similar way defined by the extent to which its policies are actually *implemented*. Notwithstanding the dependency of implementation effectiveness on the prior formulation phase, we argue in this volume that additional insights can be gained from a separate analysis of the implementation phase. In this chapter we pointed out that European policies, regardless whether they are of the old or new type, only contribute to the problem solving capacity of the EU when they contain substantive but no fundamental institutional implications for existing arrangements.

References

Baier, Vicki E., James G. March, and Harald Sætren (1990). 'Implementierung und Ungewißheit'. In James G. March (ed.), *Entwicklung und Organisation: Kritische und konstruktive Beiträge, Entwicklungen und Perspektiven*. Wiesbaden: Gabler, 170–84.

Berman, Paul (1980). 'Thinking about Programmed and Adaptive Implementation: Matching Strategies to Situations'. In Helen Ingram and Dean Mann (eds), *Why Policies Succeed or Fail*. London: Sage, 205–27.

CEC (Commission of the European Communities) (1996). *Thirteenth Annual Report on Monitoring the Application of Community Law (1995)*. Luxembourg: Office for Official Publications of the EC.

Cerych, Ladislav and Paul Sabatier (1986). *Great Expectations and Mixed Preferences: The Implementation of European Higher Education Reforms*. Stoke on Trent: Trentham Books.

Collins, Ken and David Earnshaw (1992). 'The Implementation and Enforcement of European Community Environment Legislation'. *Environmental Politics*, 1 (4), 213–49.

European Parliament (EP), Committee on the Environment, Public Health and Consumer Protection (1996). *Working Document on Implementation of Community Environmental Law* (Rapporteur: Ken Collins), PE 219.420, Brussels.

Evans, Peter, Dietrich Rüschemeyer, Theda Skocpol (eds) (1985). *Bringing the State Back In*. Cambridge: Cambridge University Press.

Golub, Jonathan (1993). 'Recasting EU Environmental Policy: Subsidiarity and National Sovereignty'. In Ute Collier, Jon Golub, and Alexander Kreher (eds), *Subsidiarity and Shared Responsibility New Challenges for EU Environmental Policy*. Baden-Baden: Nomos.

Hall, Peter A. (1993). 'Policy Paradigms, Social Learning and the State. The Case of Economic Policymaking in Britain'. *Comparative Politics*, 25, 275–96.

Hall, Peter A. and Rosemary C. R. Taylor (1996). *Political Science and the Three New Institutionalisms*. MPIFG Discussion Paper 96/6. Köln: Max-Planck-Institut für Gesellschaftsforschung.

Hanf, Kenneth and Scharpf Fritz W. (eds), (1978). *Interorganizational Policy Making: Limits to Coordination and Central Control*. London: Sage.

Héritier, Adrienne, Christoph Knill and Susanne Mingers (1996). *Ringing the Changes in Europe: Regulatory Competition and the Transformation of the State*. Berlin: de Gruyter.

Ingram, Helen and Anne Schneider (1990). 'Improving Implementation Through Framing Smarter Statutes'. *Journal of Public Policy*, 10 (1), 67–88.

Jimenez-Beltran, D. (1996). 'The European Environmental Agency'. In Alexander Kreher (ed.), *The New European Agencies: Conference Report*. EUI Working Paper, RSC No. 99/49. Florence: EUI.

Knill, Christoph (1998). 'European Policies: The Impact of National Administrative Traditions on European Policy Making'. *Journal of Public Policy*, 18 (1), 1–28.

Knill, Christoph and Andrea Lenschow (1998). 'Coping with Europe: The Implementation of EU Environmental Policy and Administrative Traditions in Britain and Germany'. *Journal of European Public Policy*, 5 (4), 595–614.

Krämer, Ludwig (1992). *Focus on European Environmental Law*. London: Sweet & Maxwell.

Krasner, Stephen D. (1988). 'Sovereignty: An Institutional Perspective'. *Comparative Political Studies*, 21 (1), 66–94.

Lane, Jan-Erik (1995). *The Public Sector: Concepts, Models and Approaches*. London: Sage.

Linder, Stephen and B. Guy Peters (1989). 'Instruments of Government: Perceptions and Contexts'. *Journal of Public Policy*, 9 (1), 35–58.

Lipsky, M. (1980). *Street-Level Bureaucracy*. New York: Russell Sage.

Lübbe-Wolff, Gertrude (1996). 'Stand und Instrumente der Implementation des Umweltrechts in Deutschland'. In Gertrude Lübbe-Wolff (ed.), *Der Vollzug des europäischen Umweltrechts*. Berlin: Erich Schmidt Verlag, 77–106.

Mayntz, Renate (1983). 'Implementation von regulativer Politik'. In Renate Mayntz (ed.), *Implementation politischer Programme II*. Opladen: Westdeutscher Verlag, 50–74.

Olsen, Johan P. (1995). *Europeanization and Nation State Dynamics*. Working Paper 9/95. Oslo: ARENA.

Peters, B. Guy (1993). 'Alternative Modelle des Policy-Prozesses: Die Sicht "von unten" und die Sicht "von oben"'. In Adrienne Héritier (ed.), *Policy-Analyse. Kritik und Neurorientierung*, PVS Sonderheft, 24, Opladen: Westdeutscher Verlag, 289–306.

Pressman, J. and A. Wildavsky (1973). *Implementation*. Berkeley: University of California Press.

Sabatier, Paul A. (1986). 'Top–Down and Bottom–Up Approaches to Implementation Research'. *Journal of Public Policy*, 6, 21–48.

Sabatier, Paul A. (1993). 'Advocacy-Koalitionen, Policy-Wandel und Policy-Lernen: Eine Alternative zur Phasenheuristik'. In Adrienne Héritier (ed.), *Policy-Analyse. Kritik und Neurorientierung*, PVS Sonderheft, 24, Opladen: Westdeutscher Verlag, 116–48.

Scharpf, Fritz W. (1978). 'Interorganizational Policy Studies: Issues, Concepts, and Perspectives'. In Kenneth Hanf and Fritz W. Scharpf (eds), *Interorganizational Policy making: Limits to Coordination and Central Control*. London: Sage, 345–70.

Scharpf, Fritz W. (1985). 'Die Politikverflechtungs-Falle: Europäische Integration und deutscher Föderalismus im Vergleich'. *Politische Vierteljahresschrift*, (4), 323–56.

Timmermans, Arco *et al.* (1998). 'The Design of Policy Instruments: Perspectives and Concepts'. Paper presented at the 56th Annual Meeting of the Midwest Political Science Association, Chicago, 23–5 April.

Windhoff-Héritier, Adrienne (1987). *Policy-Analyse. Eine Einführung*. Frankfurt: Campus.

Part two

The impact of institutional innovations

3 *Marieva Favoino, Christoph Knill and Andrea Lenschow*

New structures for environmental governance in the European Commission: the institutional limits of governance change

Introduction

The Community's new approach to environmental policy, as it is developed in the 1993 fifth Environmental Action Programme (5th EAP) of the EU (CEC 1993a), implies a twofold strategy in order to address the increasing implementation deficit in the environmental field. Besides the development of new policy instruments and the reorientation of regulatory strategies and objectives, an important component of the new approach refers to institutional innovations at the European level. At the core of this latter strategy lies the reorientation in the mode of governance towards network-style and participatory forms of policy formulation (Lenschow 1999a). The Commission plans to rely on the participation and consultation of relevant public and private actors in the policy formulation process in order to improve the quality and legitimacy of policy design.

This shift in the policy formulation strategy corresponds well with the general reorientation from top–down to bottom–up approaches as described in this volume. Using a slightly different vocabulary, Christian Hey (1996) has described this development as a shift from 'active integration' implying a top–down process, led by the environmental Directorate General in the Commission (DG XI), 'which defines a set of policies and instruments for the achievement of [ambitious] environmental targets' (p. 6) for the respective policy sector, towards a more 'defensive' style that approaches the issue from the bottom up. The latter does not explicitly challenge the traditional priorities in other fields, but calls upon policy makers to assess the environmental impact of all policy initiatives and to limit environmental side-effects. The task of the environmental policy division would be to provide know-how, information and guidance rather than to 'commandeer' or to enforce. Similar to new policy instruments, the defensive strategy relies on processes of mutual awareness raising, consultation, coordination and joint evaluation. In advocating such a 'new governance' approach (see Kooiman 1993) in the environmental field, the Community strives to tackle potential implementation problems already during the stage of policy formulation.

Concretely, the 5th EAP established two major institutional innovations at the level of the European Commission for this purpose. The first element refers to the principle of *horizontal coordination* between the different Directorates General (DGs) of the Commission. In order to achieve a higher degree of coherence between actions taken in different European policy sectors, such as agriculture or transport, on the one hand and environmental policy on the other, the coordination mechanism between different DGs should accomplish more than avoiding the negative environmental externalities generated by sectoral policy initiatives. Coordination should result in a more systematic approach to EU environmental policy making by positively integrating environmental objectives into the policies developed in other sectors.[1] The second institutional innovation at the Commission level is based on the principle of shared responsibility as a rule for the interactions between the Commission and private and public actors operating on the local, national and supranational level. In order to incorporate formally the principle into the processes of formulation and implementation of environmental policy, the 5th EAP has established three participatory devices, the so-called *dialogue forums*. These include the General Consultative Forum on the Environment (GCFE), which brings together representatives from business, trade unions, consumers, professional associations, environmental organisations, regional and local authorities, the Environmental Policy Review Group (EPRG), in which national ministries and the Commission are represented, and the Network for the Implementation and Enforcement of EU Environmental Policy (IMPEL), whose members are representatives of the Commission and of national implementation authorities.

It is the objective of this chapter to investigate and explain the implementation of these institutional innovations on the Commission level. The effective formal and practical adoption of these innovations themselves can be considered as the necessary condition in order to achieve their overall objective of improving the implementation performance of EU environmental policy.

As will be shown, the implementation success of the different governance changes varies considerably between the two basic reform components (the establishment of horizontal coordination and the dialogue forums). While both the formal and practical implementation of shared responsibility in the context of the dialogue forums took place in a rather smooth and effective way, the picture is less rosy when it comes to horizontal coordination. With respect to the latter reform initiative, empirical findings reveal a puzzling variance in implementation success across DGs and hence policy sectors, with an overall picture of comparatively deficient implementation performance.

We argue that this variance in implementation success both across and within different reform initiatives can only be understood from a perspective taking account of the institutional compatibility of adaptational requirements within existing arrangements. To be precise, the mobilisation of actor coalitions in favour of effective implementation is likely to result in corresponding institutional adjustments only in cases where these adjustments can be achieved without challenging deeply entrenched policy legacies and regulatory traditions.

To illustrate the utility for this institutional perspective, we will first consider the explanatory power of alternative approaches. In doing so, we start from plausible assumptions derived from implementation theory (section two) and neo-institutional approaches (section three). As none of the hypotheses derived from this literature allows for a sufficient explanation of the variance found in our empirical cases, we illustrate the need for our more differentiated institutional perspective in section four. Section five summarises the results and draws general conclusions.

The explanatory scope of the support hypothesis

Notwithstanding the theoretical variety, which still characterises this field of inquiry, there is a certain consensus within the implementation literature that implementation effectiveness can be expected to increase with the extent to which a certain programme is supported by the implementers and actor coalitions addressed by the programme in question (Lipsky 1980; Mayntz 1983; Peters 1993). The

new forms of governance discussed in this chapter with their procedural and integrative approach explicitly apply the findings gained
in implementation research. We should therefore expect effective
implementation both in the case of the dialogue forums and with
respect to horizontal integration.[2]

In the case of the dialogue forums the institutional innovation
implies mutual benefits for all actors involved and hence broad support in favour of effective implementation. On the one hand, the
establishment of the GCFE provided an important opportunity for
public and private actors at varying levels (such as national regulatory authorities, business and environmental organisations) to
actively participate and potentially influence the making of EU
environmental policy. Moreover, the IMPEL network provided a
framework for implementers to exchange information among each
other and to give feedback to the policy making actors (Werner
1996). Equally, the institutionalisation of cooperative relationships
with these actors 'on the ground' implied advantages for the Commission. In particular, the dialogue forums can be seen as an important source of information and advice for the Commission that, as a
result of its scarce personnel resources, is highly dependent on external capabilities and resources. As pointed out by Mazey and
Richardson (1994), the Commission is very dependent on external
experts and groups for detailed information about diverse technical
standards, legislation and organisational structures throughout the
EU. Moreover, the inclusion of varying actors and interests during
the stage of policy formulation increases not only the legitimacy of
European policy making, but also the potential for a swift decision
making process in the Council. In light of these overall benefits
associated with the establishment of cooperative, network-type
exchange relationships (Marin and Mayntz 1991; Scharpf 1993),
the given actor constellation suggests a successful implementation of
both the formal and practical institutional innovations for setting up
the dialogue groups.

At first sight, a similar degree of support can also be assumed for
the introduction of horizontal coordination mechanisms between
the DGs of the Commission. In this context, support for effective
institutional adjustments emerged from basically three sources.
First, the integration of environmental policy consideration into
other policy sectors was strongly favoured by the environmental
Directorate (DG XI), as it implied a considerable strengthening of

the position of DG XI with respect to the internal decision making context within the Commission. Second, horizontal integration also found broad political support from other DGs. Many sectoral DGs had previously felt harassed by the often rather aggressive and missionary style of DG XI in imposing environmental standards on sectoral actors (Hull 1993). The new communicative channels were perceived as opportunities to influence the nature of *sui generis* environmental policy as much as DG XI hoped to influence sectoral policy (Wilkinson 1997). Third, horizontal coordination represents an issue that had been advocated by environmental organisations for many years. Corresponding reform initiatives at the Community level could therefore count on the strong mobilisation of these actors in favour of effective implementation. Such mobilisation was facilitated by the provision of additional institutional access points to influence European policy making in the form of the political commitment to integration and the establishment of new horizontal channels. Thus, Non-governmental Organisations (NGOs) would no longer solely depend on their relations with DG XI for presenting and advancing their interests, but could additionally address other DGs to advocate their concerns, if these DGs were required to take account of environmental issues when formulating their policy proposals.

In light of the general support and the new mobilisation potential in favour of both institutional innovations on the level of the Commission, one could have suggested effective implementation of both reforms. This would have been in line with the general support hypothesis formulated in the implementation literature. Empirical evidence, however, confirms this hypothesis only partially. While we observe effective implementation with respect to the establishment of the dialogue forums, horizontal coordination suffers from rather mixed and not altogether effective results.

Variance in the empirical case material

As indicated, the dialogue forums have been established as intended and contributed to 'greatly increased levels of dialogue between the Commission and a wide range of European bodies on issues connected to sustainable development' (CEC 1996, 102). The range of responsibilities and the institutional standing of the IMPEL network (see Werner 1996) and the Consultative Forum (see CEC 1997a)

have been widened. The latter had had an important say in formulating the recent Communication from the Commission on a
'Partnership for Integration' (CEC 1998). While the impact of the
dialogue groups on the state of the environment is impossible to test
– and may be evaluated critically – they appear to perform their role
as information channels and multipliers as intended. Hence, they
confirm the hypothesis that those measures that are attentive to the
interests of the 'actors on the ground' are implemented well.

The story looks a little different with respect to the effectiveness
of the new horizontal structures for coordination between DGs. The
first review of the 5th EAP noted regretfully that these 'measures so
far have had limited impact' (CEC 1996, 104). Two and a half years
later, Environment Commissioner Bjerregaard confirmed that the
internal measures to improve integration 'have not been particularly
effective' (EWWE 6/15, page 14, 1 August 1997). To complicate the
picture further, there has been great variance according to sectors.
Bjerregaard, for instance, noted that some progress had been
achieved in areas such as regional spending, development policy,
transport and energy.

In investigating the conditions for successful institutional innovation within the Commission further, we will focus on environmental
policy integration (as the measure for successful cross-DG coordination) in the two main EU spending policies, namely the Common
Agricultural Policy (CAP) and the European Regional Development
Fund (ERDF). Despite the uniform call to consider environmental
concerns in the policy formulation and to adapt the administrative
structures accordingly, the level of reform has been quite different.
In short, the legislative framework for regional development policy
has been relatively quickly adjusted to the demands of policy integration. By contrast, the 'greening' of agricultural policy has
occurred most resistantly, adjustments occurring merely at the margins of the main body of the policy.[3]

Greening the CAP

The greening of the CAP has occurred, primarily at the margins of
the main body of the policy, in the form of new funding opportunities for environment-friendly activities. The original framework of
the CAP, consisting of an environmentally problematic market price
support system, has been left in place (however, at declining prices).
Environmental degradation in the agricultural sector is the result of

the market failure to internalise the environmental cost of agricultural production (such as the exploitation and pollution of water and soil resources). Price guarantees are not made conditional on the implementation of the polluter pays principle (Baldock and Bennett 1991), for instance. On the contrary, the CAP regime operates to reinforce the market failures (OECD 1994, 110–14; Runge 1993, 96–7); by effectively coupling financial support to production output (and surplus) it contributes to environmental damage

Despite clear evidence of these environment-related market and government failures, reform attempts were limited prior to 1992. They consisted of adopting a few structural measures outside the CAP's guarantee section to support farmers in extensifying production or maintaining sensitive areas; the guarantee section itself was modified by introducing minor quantitative restrictions to reduce production.[4] Crucially, the motivation for these measures was economic (increasing budgetary constraints and the need to create a livelihood for farmers in peripheral areas) not environmental protection.

The 1992 MacSharry reforms (CEC 1992c; Grant 1995) resulted in a package that implied some environmental progress without destroying the traditional structure of the CAP. The price guarantee system – coupled to production – continued at a lower level of support and was now supplemented by a new system of direct income support – mostly de-coupled from production. In addition, accompanying measures were introduced, in part to reward farmers for providing   a   public   service   in   the   form   of preserving the rural environment (i.e. to address the second market failure), but also to induce farmers to reduce the environmental costs of their activities (i.e. to pay polluters for polluting less) and, of course, to address the surplus problem.

Critics point out that the accompanying measures were deficient from an operational standpoint because of the multiple objectives pursued. Also, they amounted to little more than 5 per cent of the budget for the guarantee section – hardly enough to 'green' the whole policy area. Hence, the assessment of the environmental improvements due to the 1992 reforms has been mixed. The Commission admits that '[o]n the whole ... rural policy in the Union still appears as a juxtaposition of agricultural market policy, structural policy and environmental policy with rather complex instruments and lacking overall coherence' (Agenda 2000 – Agriculture, 2).[5]

The recently agreed Agenda 2000 continues the incremental and 'add on' process of integrating environmental concerns in agricultural policy. Despite far-reaching commitments in the political leadership of the Commission, the level of *de facto* policy integration is marginal. Commission President Santer argued '[t]he starting point for the reform will be the idea that there must be a greater focus in European agriculture on quality, protection of the environment, animal welfare, [and] a return to more natural production methods' (EWWE 6/4, page 15, 21 February 1997). Similarly, DG VI under Commissioner Fischler was openly acknowledging the need for a more integrated approach (CEC 1997b). It convened an expert group under the leadership of agricultural economist Allan Buckwell to develop an integrated agricultural and rural policy, which will: 'ensure an economically efficient and environmentally sustainable agriculture and to stimulate the integrated development of the Union's rural areas, following the principles of consistency (with general EU goals), subsidiarity, targeting, de-coupling (from production) and simplification' (CEC 1997c, 6.1). These objectives were markedly different from the original goals of the CAP enshrined in Article 43 of the Treaty: productivity, fair standards of living, market stability, availability of supplies, reasonable consumer prices etc.

In contrast with these ambitious proposals, 'Agenda 2000' is more conservative in its choice of measures to implement the principle of environmental policy integration and continues previous gradual approaches to reform, focusing on modifications to the market system (hoping for indirect effects on the environment through cuts in guaranteed prices). New budgetary resources will be channelled to agri-environmental measures and higher co-financing rates. No active operational improvements are planned on the EU level, however Member States will be allowed (if they wish) to make direct payments to farmers conditional on their respect for environmental provisions.

Greening the Regional Development Fund
Environmental objectives did not feature explicitly in the original European Regional Development Fund (ERDF) guidelines (Regulation EEC 724/75 of the Council of 18 March 1975) and the original ERDF was implemented largely as a hand-out to Member States with regional problem areas.

Since the late 1970s the structure of the regional funds was modified several times (see Marks 1992; Hooghe and Keating 1994), not however with the intention to integrate other policy objectives. The 1988 reform paid some lip-service to the integration principle, without providing the necessary operational means (Lenschow 1998). These were introduced in the 1993 reforms of the Structural Funds. The reforms targeted the poor planning and monitoring performance, the limited eligibility criteria for environmental programmes or projects, and the tendency of supporting so-called end-of-pipe projects repairing environmental damage already done as opposed to preventing its occurrence. The new Regulations reinforced the integration principle by requiring 'development plans for Objectives 1, 2, and 5b to include an appraisal of the environmental situation of the region concerned and an evaluation of the environmental impact of the strategy and operations planned' (CEC 1993b, 29, referring to the new Framework Regulation's Article 7). Aside from providing a more operational framework for sustainable planning, this clause had the important institutional implication that national governments were now obliged to integrate environmental authorities in the preparation phase of regional programmes.

The legal evolution was paralleled by procedural changes beyond the linkage to DG XI, leading towards fuller integration. The Commission developed an 'aide memoire' for the Member States to clarify what information was to be supplied under the revised Regulations. While this profile has no legal standing it served to assist public authorities in fulfilling their legal obligations. It also facilitated the harmonisation of the national information submitted to the Commission. A list of indicators and a handbook were prepared with the intention of aiding the assessment of the environmental impact of the regional programmes and its costs. Hence, between 1988 and 1993 the policy evolved from a 'reminder' to comply with EC environmental law to a routinised procedure to protect the environment.

At the Member State level the practical application of the integration principle is still varied, as several highly publicised examples show (see Lenschow 1997; Long 1995). However, the horizontal coordination between DG XI and DG XVI has greatly improved in the planning as well as monitoring phase – a success story at least with respect to the implementation of the Commission's internal reforms.

In sum, considering that the Commission as a whole had agreed

on an integrated approach to policy making and that the commitment to pursue this objective had been declared throughout the
Commission including the leadership of the DGs involved in greening agricultural and regional policy, the varied levels of actual
integration are surprising. The general support hypothesis suggest-
ing the targeting of the policy addressees as the primary condition to
ensure effective implementation seems insufficient to account for
the differences just described.

Implementation from an institutional perspective

The explanatory limits of the support hypothesis developed in
implementation theory do not mean that our search for a sound
explanation of varying implementation performance has to start
from zero. Since both the establishment of dialogue forums and horizontal policy coordination refer to *institutional changes* in the
structure of EU environmental governance, an institutionalist
approach might provide a more promising starting point in order to
account for the varying levels of implementation effectiveness
revealed by our cases under study.

   Although the institutional literature is a growing and diverse field,
combining varying theoretical branches, there exists a general
consensus in acknowledging the structuring impact of existing institutional arrangements on political outcomes and institutional
development. Institutionalists generally emphasise that institutional
adjustments can hardly be understood in terms of 'effective adaptations' to changes in the institutional environment (March and
Olsen 1996), but are themselves crucially affected by existing
institutions. Institutionalists emphasise the stability and continuity
of institutions.

   As a general rule, institutional adaptation remains incremental or
path dependent, without challenging well-established core patterns
of existing arrangements (Thelen and Steinmo 1992; Krasner 1988).
Since existing institutions strive to link new elements by institution-
alising them within their framework (Zucker 1991), 'institutional
models are unlikely to be imported whole cloth into systems that
are very different from the one in which they originate' (DiMaggio
and Powell 1991, 29). An important mechanism favouring institutional persistence is the 'decoupling' of formal and informal structure and practice; i.e., the formal institutional arrangements are

adapted to the 'myths' of the changing institutional environment, while informal arrangements remain unchanged (Meyer and Rowan 1977; Brunsson and Olsen 1993, 9).

The institutional perspective therefore implies a rather sceptical expectation on the scope of effective institutional adaptation to external requirements, and hence effective implementation. Formal and practical compliance with adaptational requirements can only be expected as long as these pressures can be accomplished within existing arrangements without challenging established practices and structures. As soon as the gap between existing arrangements and external requirements becomes too big, we expect that implementation within the existing institutional framework yields ineffective results. New institutional elements will not be effectively incorporated into existing arrangements, but either be neglected or added to the periphery of the framework leaving the core of existing provisions unchanged (Wilson 1989, 225).

To what extent can we explain the varying implementation success of governance changes at the Commission level on the basis of this institutional perspective? Similar to the support hypothesis, the institutional approach provides us with a sound explanation of the effective implementation of the dialogue forums. As the required institutional innovations were basically compatible with the arrangements already in place, their incorporation into existing structures and practices was fully sufficient in order to achieve an effective formal and practical transposition of the reform requirements.

The reason for this high degree of institutional compatibility can be traced to the fact that the required changes basically implied the formalisation and institutionalisation of an already existing practice. Thus, the Commission had always developed its policy proposals in close cooperation with a broad range of public and private actors at the European, national and regional level. There exist numerous working groups, which are composed of national civil servants, Commission experts, representatives of interest groups, and external experts. Similar to the dialogue forums, the existing practice provided an important source of information for the Commission, while at the same time offering national bureaucrats and private interests the possibility of influencing the European policy making process (Siedentopf and Hauschild 1990, 448; Wessels 1990, 238).

The institutionalisation of varying dialogue forums facilitating the exchange of information between a broad range of actors from varying governmental levels follows the same logic as the already existing practice of formal and informal consultation procedures at the Commission level. The dialogue forums can be viewed as a further development of these procedures, which complement and formally confirm a practice, which was already in place. In light of this high compatibility of new requirements with existing arrangements, it is hardly surprising that the institutional adjustments to establish the dialogue forums took place in a rather effective way.

While the institutional approach provides a sound explanation of the effective implementation performance in the case of the dialogue forums, its theoretical expectations are only partly compatible with the empirical evidence found in the case of horizontal integration. In view of a high degree of institutional incompatibility between existing organisational structures and adaptational demands, one would expect an overall picture of ineffective implementation, with the incorporation of new elements into existing structures leading to a mere 'patching-up' of existing arrangements rather than towards the actual integration of new elements by effectively adjusting existing structures and procedures.

The institutional incompatibility can first be traced to the fact that horizontal coordination across different DGs implied a fundamental departure from the Commission's internal organisation principles. The internal organisation of the Commission is generally characterised by a high degree of sectoral segmentation, implying pillarised structures of a vertically integrated but horizontally fragmented organisation. While administrative segmentation does not necessarily pose insuperable hurdles to reaching effective forms of 'negative coordination' between different DGs, with each DG examining policy proposals from other sectors with respect to negative externalities for the sector under its jurisdiction (see Mayntz and Scharpf 1975; Scharpf 1993), the achievement of effective 'positive coordination' in the sense of common problem-solving across policy sectors, as it is intended by the horizontal integration approach of the Commission, requires considerable organisational changes in order to effectively overcome sectoral fragmentation.

Institutional incompatibility emerged not only from the 'misfit' of segmented administrative structures and the demand for positive coordination across policy sectors. It can also be observed at the level of substantive policy objectives. Thus, administrative fragmen-

economic, social and environmental objectives of the Community ... and increasing emphasis ... on diversification and extensification of agricultural production, and alternative uses of land' (CEC 1987, 5). The actual reconciliation of interests, however, proceeded to place the continued support for the farming sector first. Put somewhat cynically, genuine environmental measures were used to open new funding opportunities for farmers; furthermore, the environment created a rationale for generous compensation payments for farmers suffering from cuts in the guaranteed price agreements.

In sum, even under pressure, horizontal integration of agricultural and environmental policy was limited to activities outside the main body of the CAP, filling some gaps that had developed within this main body and pursuing environmental objectives to the extent that it fitted the traditional protectionist rationale of the policy. Environmental measures were rejected if they imposed financial costs on the farmers. With the continued mobilisation of the environmental interest, the nagging on the CAP will also proceed. But the negotiations of the Agenda 2000 are the latest example that movement is likely to effect the periphery rather than touch the core.

By comparison, the mobilisation for a 'greening' of the Regional Development Fund was more effective. Environmental interest groups discovered violations of several EU-funded projects with EU environmental law and blamed the Commission for ignoring its own commitments. Forming an effective alliance with inside-actors in the EU – DG XI, the environmental committee of the European Parliament, the Court of Auditors and several (donor) Member States – they succeeded in undermining the legitimacy of the Fund's operation and presented a threat of real sanctions[6] as well as a package of policy alternatives (for overviews of the entire campaign see Corrie 1993, Lenschow 1997, Long 1995). Not only relative powers of the ERDF administrators decreased but also institutional boundaries fell in the process of this campaign. Unable to hide behind thick walls as DG VI, DG XVI began to open its doors to colleagues from DG XI offering policy advice, DG XI actors in turn adopted less radical positions and improved their understanding of the operational regional policy.

Significantly, the regional policy case shows that defensive measures of opening channels of information and coordination became effective only in conjunction with the presence of mobilised actors pushing the doors wide open. This corresponds with findings in other chapters of this book, showing that new instruments may be ineffective in the absence of capable and already mobilised addressees. The comparison with the CAP case, in turn, shows that even mobilised actors may not go very far if institutional structures provide access only to the 'front garden' rather than the 'living room' of the policy.

Conclusion

In recent years, there has been a fundamental governance shift in EU environmental policy characterised by a general reorientation from top–down to bottom–up strategies in environmental policy making. In order to increase the overall implementation effectiveness of EU environmental policy, changes are not restricted to the design of so-called new instruments. They also include institutional innovations to increase participation of a broad range of actors already during the stage of policy formulation in order to improve the quality and legitimacy of European policy proposals. As these institutional innovations will only achieve their intended effects of improved implementation performance of EU environmental policy if they are implemented properly themselves, it has been the intention of this chapter to investigate the implementation performance for two basic innovations enacted in this context: the establishment of the dialogue forums and the principle of horizontal coordination.

Our analysis of the implementation performance of these measures both confirms and qualifies the theoretical considerations developed in chapter 2 of this book. First of all, our empirical evidence underlines the limited validity of theoretical assumptions developed in the implementation literature, namely that the mobilisation and stimulation of broad support provides a sufficient condition for effective implementation. In contrast with these assumptions, the failure of horizontal integration in the agricultural sector, in particular, demonstrates the limits of the support hypothesis.

Moreover, our analysis confirms the advantages to be gained from an institutional perspective in order to account for varying levels of implementation effectiveness. As revealed by the case of horizontal integration in the agricultural sector, even strong support in favour of effective implementation might not be sufficient to trigger institutional adjustments which imply a fundamental departure from well-established practices and structures. The agricultural case demonstrates the institutional limits of support building: existing institutional arrangements structure the distribution of resources and power between different actors involved in the implementation process. Depending on these opportunity structures, the influence of actor coalitions in favour of compliance might be outweighed by the strong position of vested interests in favour of the *status quo*. In other words: the possibilities for effective support-building are constrained by existing institutional arrangements.

In addition to these insights, our analytical findings allow for a further qualification of the institutional argument. In particular, our admittedly limited number of empirical cases indicates the need for a differentiated perspective on the level of institutional adaptation pressure exerted by new patterns of environmental governance. While the agricultural case of horizontal integration indicates that fundamental changes can hardly be expected even in instances of high support mobilisation, the actual adjustments in the field of regional policy reveal that strong support may lead to effective implementation in cases where the required changes imply substantial, but not fundamental, departures from existing arrangements. In order to understand varying levels of implementation success, we therefore need to apply a differentiated perspective on the degree of institutional compatibility between required changes and existing arrangements (Knill and Lenschow 2000). Depending on the stability and embeddedness of challenged institutions, the scope of institutional adaptation pressure might vary, and hence the opportunities for effective support-building.

Notes

1 Although some of the DGs can be characterised as cross-sectoral services, sectoral segmentation is a dominant structure of the Commission's internal organisation (Nugent 1995).
2 As in all chapters of this book, we define effective implementation as formal and practical compliance. We do not evaluate the actual impact of these new structures on improving the environment.
3 The policy evolution towards (more or less) environmental policy integration has been described at greater length elsewhere (Lenschow 1997, 1998 and 1999b). Here, we will therefore focus on the varied levels of innovation at the end of the process.
4 See CEC (1997a) for a brief history and overview of the relevant legislation.

5   This statement is confirmed by the criticism of the former EU environ-
    ment commissioner Bjerregaard, stating that EU governments make
    only slow progress towards integrating environmental considerations
    into sectoral policy making. Speaking at a conference organised in
    Bonn by the European Environmental Bureau to mark its 25th anniver-
    sary, Bjerregaard reiterated her disappointment with early papers on
    environmental integration prepared by EU energy, transport and agri-
    culture ministers, reiterating similar criticisms she had made the year
    before (ENDS Daily 18 May 1999).
6   For instance, the Parliament threatened to make use of its budgetary
    powers.

References

'Agenda 2000': Agriculture (1997). (full text)
     (http: //www.europa.eu.int/en/comm/dg06/ag2000/text/text_en.htm).
Baldock, David and Graham Bennett (1991). *Agriculture and the Polluter
     Pays Principle: A Study of Six EC Countries*. London, Arnhem: Institute
     for European Environmental Policy.
Brunsson, Nils and Johan P. Olsen (1993). *The Reforming Organization*.
     London: Routledge.
Commission of the European Communities (CEC), Directorate-General for
     Agriculture (1987). 'Environment and the CAP'. *Green Europe. News-
     letter on the Common Agricultural Policy*, No. 219. Luxembourg: Office
     for Official Publications of the European Communities.
CEC, Directorate General for Agriculture (1992). *CAP Working Notes
     1992: The Reform of the Common Agricultural Policy*. Luxembourg:
     Office for Official Publications of the European Communities.
CEC (1993a). *Towards Sustainability: A European Community Programme
     of Policy and Action in Relation to the Environment and Sustainable
     Development*. Luxembourg: Office for Official Publications of the Euro-
     pean Communities.
CEC (1993b). *Community Structural Funds. 1994–1999. Revised Regula-
     tions and Comments*. Brussels.
CEC (1996). *Progress Report from the Commission. On the Implementation
     of the European Community Programme of Policy and Action in Relation
     to the Environment and Sustainable Development. 'Towards Sustainabil-
     ity'*. COM (95)624 fin. Luxembourg: Office for Official Publications of
     the European Communities.
CEC (1997a). *Statements on Sustainable Development: The General Con-
     sultative Forum on the Environment 1993–96*. Luxembourg: Office for
     Official Publications of the European Communities.
CEC, Directorate-General for Agriculture (1997b). *Working Notes on the*

Common Agricultural Policy: Agriculture and Environment. Luxembourg: Office for Official Publications on the European Communities.

CEC (1997c). *Towards a Common Agricultural and Rural Policy for Europe.* Report of an Expert Group, convened by the Commission of the European Communities, Directorate General VI/A1 (http: //www.europa.eu.int/en/comm/dg06/new/buck_en).

CEC (1998). *Partnership for Integration. A Strategy for Integrating Environment into EU Policies. Cardiff – June 1998.* Communication from the Commission to the European Council, COM (1998) 333 fin. Brussels, 27 May.

Corrie, Heather (1993). 'Campaigning to Green the EC Structural Funds', mimeograph.

DiMaggio, Paul J. and Walter W. Powell (1991). 'Introduction'. In Walter W. Powell and Paul J. DiMaggio (eds), *The New Institutionalism in Organizational Analysis.* Chicago: Chicago University Press, 1–38.

Environment Watch: Western Europe (EWWE), (Cutter Information Corp.) various issues.

Grant, Wyn (1995). 'The Limits of Common Agricultural Policy Reform and the Option of Denationalization'. *Journal of European Public Policy*, 2(1), 1–18.

Hey, Christian (1996). *The Incorporation of the Environmental Dimension into the Transport Policies in the EU: Short Version of the EU Study.* Freiburg: EURES Institute.

Hooghe Liesbet and Michael Keating (1994). 'The politics of EU Regional Policy'. *Journal of European Public Policy*, 1(3), 367–93.

Hull, Robert (1993). 'Lobbying Brussels: A View from Within'. In Sonia Mazey and Jeremy J. Richardson (eds), *Lobbying in the European Community.* Oxford: Oxford University Press.

Jenkins-Smith, Hank C. (1988). 'Analytical Debates and Policy-Learning: Analysis and Change in the Federal Bureaucracy'. *Policy Sciences*, 21, 169–211.

Keeler, John (1996). 'Agricultural power in the European Community: Explaining the fate of CAP and GATT Negotiations'. *Comparative Politics*, 28(2), 127–50.

Knill, Christoph and Andrea Lenschow (2000). 'Adjusting to EU Environmental Policy: Change and Persistence of Domestic Administrations'. In James Caporaso, Maria Cowles and Thomas Risse (eds), *Transforming Europe: Europeanization and Domestic Change.* Ithaca, NJ: Cornell University Press.

Kooiman, Jan (ed.) (1993). *Modern Governance: New Government–Society Interactions.* London: Sage.

Krasner, Stephen D. (1988). 'Sovereignty: An Institutional Perspective'. *Comparative Political Studies*, 21 (1), 66–94.

Lenschow, Andrea (1997). 'Variation in European Environmental Policy

Integration: Agency Push within Complex Institutional Structures'. *Journal of European Public Policy*, 4(1), 109–27.

Lenschow, Andrea (1998). 'World Trade and the Greening of the CAP: Environmental Structural Assistance as a Tool to Survive Trade Liberalization'. In Jonathan Golub (ed.), *Regulatory Reform and EC International Environmental Agreements*. London: Routledge, 161–88.

Lenschow, Andrea (1999a). 'Transformation in European Environmental Governance'. In Beate Kohler-Koch and Rainer Eising (eds), *The Transformation of Governance in the EU*. London: Routledge, 39–60.

Lenschow, Andrea (1999b). 'The greening of the EU: The Common Agricultural Policy and the Structural Funds'. *Environment and Planning C: Government and Policy*. 17, 91–108.

Lipsky M., Michael (1980). *Street-Level Bureaucracy*. New York: Russell Sage.

Long, Tony (1995). 'Shaping Public Policy in the European Union: A Case Study of the Structural Funds'. *Journal of European Public Policy*, 2(4), 672–9.

March, James G. and Johan P. Olsen (1996). 'Institutional Perspectives on Political Institutions'. *Governance*, 9 (3), 247–64.

Marin, Bernd and Renate Mayntz (1991). *Policy Network: Empirical Evidence and Theoretical Considerations*. Frankfurt: Campus.

Marks, Gary (1992). 'Structural Policy in the European Community'. In Alberta Sbragia (ed.), *Euro-Politics: Institutions and Policymaking in the `New' European Community*. Washington, DC: Brookings Institution, 191–224.

Mayntz, Renate (1983). 'Implementation von regulativer Politik'. In Renate Mayntz (ed.), *Implementation Politischer Programme II*. Opladen: Westdeutscher Verlag, 50–74.

Mayntz, Renate and Fritz W. Scharpf (1975). *Policy-Making in the German Federal Bureaucracy*. Amsterdam: Elsevier.

Mazey, Sonia and Jeremy J. Richardson (1994). 'Policy Coordination in Brussels: Environmental and Regional Policy'. *Regional Politics and Policy*, 4(1), 22–44.

Meyer, John W. and Brian Rowan (1977). 'Institutionalized Organizations: Formal Structure as Myth and Ceremony'. *American Journal of Sociology*, 83(2), 340–63.

Nugent, Neill (1995). *The Government and Politics of the European Union*. London: Macmillan.

OECD (1994). *Agricultural Policy Reform: New Approaches. The Role of Direct Income Payments*. Paris: OECD.

Peters, B. Guy (1993). 'Alternative Modelle des Policy-Prozesses: Die Sicht "von unten" und die Sicht "von oben"'. In Adrienne Héritier (ed.), *Policy-Analyse. Kritik und Neurorientierung*, PVS Sonderheft 24. Opladen: Westdeutscher Verlag, 289–306.

Runge, Ford C. (1993). 'Trade Liberalization and Environmental Quality in Agriculture'. *International Environmental Affairs*, 5(2), 95–128.

Sabatier, Paul A. (1993). 'Advocacy-Koalitionen, Policy-Wandel und Policy-Lernen: Eine Alternative zur Phasenheuristik'. In Adrienne Héritier (ed.), *Policy-Analyse. Kritik und Neurorientierung*, PVS Sonderheft 24. Opladen: Westdeutscher Verlag, 116–48.

Scharpf, Fritz W. (1993). 'Positive und negative Koordination in Verhandlungssystemen'. In Adrienne Héritier (ed.), *Policy-Analyse: Kritik und Neuorientierung*, PVS Sonderheft 24. Opladen: Westdeutscher Verlag, 57–83.

Siedentopf, Heinrich and Christoph Hauschild (1990). 'Europäische Integration und die öffentlichen Verwaltungen der Mitgliedstaaten'. *Die öffentliche Verwaltung*, 43 (11), 445–55.

Thelen, Kathleen and Sven Steinmo (1992). 'Historical Institutionalism in Comparative Politics'. In Kathleen Thelen, Sven Steinmo, and Frank Longstreth (eds), *Structuring Politics: Historical Institutionalism in Comparative Analysis*. Cambridge: Cambridge University Press, 1–32.

Urwin, Derek W. (1991). *The Community of Europe: A History of European Integration since 1945*. London, New York: Longman.

Werner, Julia (1996). 'Das EU-Netzwerk für Umsetzung und Vollzug von Umwelrecht'. In Gertrude Lübbe-Wolff (ed.), *Der Vollzug des europäischen Umweltrechts*. Berlin: Erich Schmidt Verlag, 131–8.

Wessels, Wolfgang (1990). 'Administrative Interaction'. In William Wallace (ed.), *The Dynamics of European Integration*. London: Pinter, 229–41.

Wilkinson, David (1997). 'Towards Sustainability in the European Union? Steps within the European Commission towards Integrating the Environment into Other European Union Policy Sectors'. *Environmental Politics*, 6(1), 153–73.

Wilson, James Q. (1989). *Bureaucracy: What Government Agencies Do and Why They Do It*. New York: Basic Books.

Zucker, Lynne (1991). 'The Role of Institutionalization in Cultural Perspective'. In Walter W. Powell and Paul J. DiMaggio (eds), *The New Institutionalism in Organizational Analysis*. Chicago: Chicago University Press, 83–107.

4 *Rasmus Dilling*[1]

Improving implementation by networking: the role of the European Environment Agency

Introduction

The European Environment Agency (EEA) has been a recent institutional innovation on the EU level to support and improve the formulation and implementation of EU environmental legislation. It was established in 1990[2] and started its activities in 1994, after the Council had decided to locate it in Copenhagen. The main task of the EEA is to provide the Commission and the Member States with objective and comparable information on the environment. In this way, the Member States and the Commission should be enabled to take the appropriate measures to protect the environment, to assess the results of such measures and to ensure that the public is properly informed about the state of the environment. In this chapter I will investigate the effective implementation of the EEA's operations themselves and suggest ways to further improve its institutional and functional design.

In view of the persisting implementation deficits in EU environmental policy and the announced review of the EEA's function,[3] it has often been suggested that the regulatory powers of the EEA should be significantly increased. Thus, rather than being responsible for the provision and exchange of environmental information only, the EEA should be given executive powers with respect to environmental inspection and control comparable to the regulatory competencies of the European Commission in the field of competition law. However, in the light of the current political situation such transformations of executive powers from the Member States to the EEA are unlikely to take place in the near future. Moreover, this option would imply far-reaching institutional repercussions on well-established regulatory traditions at the domestic level. It is highly questionable that such fundamental institutional adjustments will take place in a smooth and swift way; hence, increasing the risk that the effectiveness of regulatory changes suffers from the inertia of domestic regulatory traditions. Therefore, the challenge with respect to the review of the EEA's activities will be to find solutions which are politically more realistic in order to improve the implementation of EU environmental legislation.

In the following, I argue that rather than increasing the EEA's regulatory powers, one of the major potentials for a more effective and consistent implementation of EU environmental policy throughout Europe lies within the present framework of the EEA – in the concept of networking. In other words, the EEA may contribute to improving the implementation effectiveness of EU environmental policy by making use of existing political and institutional capacities. This way, the proposed reforms may better fit within 'the bounded space of innovation' (Knill and Lenschow, chapter 2, in this book) by explicitly taking account of the political and institutional capacities for regulatory adjustment at both the European and domestic level.

Networking is understood as the informal interaction and horizontal cooperation of public and private actors across all levels to promote the generation and exchange of information and to avoid the duplication and overlapping of work. In contrast to formal and hierarchical 'command-and-control' regulation, networks are driven by the voluntary cooperation and mutual interest of participating actors (see Ladeur 1996a, 12; Majone 1995, 13 and 22). The promotion of informal networks allowing for the participation of all public and private actors involved in the formulation and implementation of EU environmental policy plays a crucial role in the Community's 'new approach' to environmental regulation, which emphasises public participation, voluntary regulation and self-regulation in favour of classical forms of hierarchical 'top–down' approaches.

I suggest that the EEA has the potential to play an even more central role in the promotion and development of horizontal networking structures; this would allow for an improvement of the mutual exchange and provision of environmental information. Focusing on the institutional role herein for the EEA, the success of further networking depends on the improvement of some basic requirements towards the EEA. These relate mainly to the flexibility and accountability of the Agency and should be incorporated into the founding

Regulation of the EEA. As described later, the concerns relate to the objectives of the EEA and to procedural aspects such as the access to information held by the Agency and the judicial review as well as the political accountability of the EEA.

In this chapter, I will first present the new regulatory approach in EU environmental policy and the role of networking in this context. On the basis of the EEA's current organisation and structure, I will then investigate the potential of the EEA to stimulate and participate in the development of networking.[4]

Networking as part of the 'new approach' to environmental regulation

In recent years, a strategic shift has been observed in EU environmental regulation towards more horizontal and transnational forms of governance; based primarily on a higher integration of the national administrations but also on an emerging tendency to integrate private actors in the formulation and implementation of EU environmental policy. The emergence of these new regulatory strategies should be understood against the background of implementation and compliance failures associated with traditional concepts of hierarchical governance, relying on command-and-control regulation (Bailey 1997; Collins and Earnshaw 1992; Commission 1996).

The main reasons for the implementation failures of the traditional approach were linked to its inadequacy in dealing with highly varying national conditions. These included the wide range of practices and structures of national administrations in charge of implementing Community law, differences in national legal and political cultures, and the varying priorities given to environmental policy across Member States (see Knill and Lenschow in their introductory chapter to this book). Moreover, the traditional approach was considered inadequate given the peculiarities of the policy area (including the scientific and technological complexity and lack of adequate information on the state of the environment) and lack of finances, qualified staff, equipment and other resources.

Besides the promotion of new instruments leaving more leeway for the Member States to implement European legislation in the light of domestic requirements, an important response at Community level to the implementation problems was to improve the quality of and access to environmental data and information (Davies 1994, 314). In this context, the Commission intended to increase support for its regulatory activities by improving transparency and public participation. Thus, the Commission emphasised the importance of public access to environmental information and improved legal standing for private actors and interest groups in national courts (Commission 1996; see Kimber, chapter 8, in this book). The Community also initiated a further integration of the national administrations and private parties (the regulatees) in implementing the EU environmental law.[5] Both in the establishment of the EU and in the mobilisation of the public, national administrations and regulated private parties, the Community has introduced a more transnational and horizontal administrative approach based on networking. The Community thus, in principle, down-played its hitherto regulatory role and now tends to act more as a coordinator in networking among Member States (Dehousse 1997, 255).

The advantages associated with the concept of networking relate to two features. First, networking allows for the better distribution of environmental information. Given that environmental regulation and control are becoming increasingly complex, it has to be recognised that the lack of enforcement and implementation in the Member States is not usually a consequence of bad intentions of national administrations or private enterprises, but a matter of lacking administrative capacities as well as administrative and societal awareness. In many cases, corresponding information and resources are not sufficiently available or are badly coordinated. In this context, the development of exchange networks has an important potential for the better distribution of information and expertise across different national authorities as well as the private actors affected by European legislation.

Second, and following the first factor, networking plays an important role in managing the increasing complexity of environmental regulation.[6] Traditionally, environmental regulation was based on common shared experience and knowledge, allowing the regulator to establish norms or issue authorisations on the basis of sound scientific evidence with respect to the impact of the activities. To a large extent, this traditional approach no longer responds to the needs of either the regulator or the regulated. Increasing complexity has led to increasing uncertainty about the expected impact of environmental pollution and the regulatory means of coping with these problems. This regulatory uncertainty indicates that the traditional hierarchical relationship between public and private actors is no longer adequate. The answer could lie in a more horizontal administrative approach, which largely integrates the individual private parties (the regulatees) in the administrative decision making by developing individual norms and criteria, setting up self-monitoring regimes, and by networks linking these norms and requirements with other parties sharing the same concerns. This would be in line with the above described new transnational governance introduced by the Community, albeit in a more elaborate form. These interactions between the parties will increase common knowledge and could reduce uncertainty. Thus, networking not only allows for a more efficient division of labour and exchange of information and other resources, but it can also stimulate and promote the quality of the outcome and the networking itself due to the parties' credibility and reputation in the repeated transactions (Bailey 1997; Ladeur 1996a, 1996b, 1998; Majone 1995, 22; Majone 1997, 272).

This horizontal administrative approach indicates a more open process of standard setting with more emphasis on procedural and methodological criteria than substantial norms (Ladeur 1996b, 23). It must be recognised that this approach could lead to an unequal treatment of similar activities Community wide and therefore could come into conflict with the intentions of the internal market. The new administrative approach should therefore be conducted as a supplement to the more substantial norms, for example, in areas with high scientific uncertainty. The unequal treatment of similar activities already follows from the dissimilar administration of existing procedural Community norms in the Member States. This has been significant in the administration of the Directive on Environmental Impact Assessment,[7] the Directive on Free Access to Environmental Information[8] and will probably also be the consequence of the administration of the Directive on Integrated Pollution Prevention and Control.[9]

To conclude, although classical forms of environmental regulation still play an important role in Community environmental policy, these concepts have increasingly been supplemented by a new approach towards less hierarchical instruments and horizontal forms of networking aiming at the far-reaching integration of public and private actors. I will take a closer look at the potential role of the

EEA in this context. As a background for this investigation, the following section gives a brief overview of the EEA's current structure and organisation.

The European Environment Agency[10]

It is not my intention to discuss the more constitutional aspects and problems in relation to the creation of independent agencies in the Community context (see Lenaerts 1993; Everson 1995). However, it is important to understand that the creation and legitimisation of the EEA is partly linked to the above-mentioned emergence of a decentralised Community environmental policy based on transnational governance, which is again linked to the fundamental crisis deriving from the lack of legitimisation and public accountability of the traditional Community structures (Dehousse 1997, 246 and 257). The transfer of powers from the Commission to an independent agency where each Member State, the Commission and the European Parliament have principally the same influence and where publicity is enshrined as a major objective, improves the accountability towards the EU institutions, the Member States and the public, and increases the overall acceptance and legitimisation of the agency's role within a concept of horizontal networking rather than hierarchical control.

More generally, specialised independent agencies are normally regarded as being able to operate very efficiently in rapidly expanding and highly specialised fields – for instance, in the environmental area. They are also considered as being able to operate more smoothly than the more traditional EU institutions given their independent nature, political neutrality, single-orientated purposes and non-dominant influence on the various participants in the network structure (Everson 1995, 185; Majone 1994, 4). Likewise, the agencies also differ from the various committees assisting the Commission (comitology) with regard to the fact that the Member States are able to exercise more influence on decision making in an independent agency, such as the EEA, than in a more traditional committee of the Commission (Vos 1997).

The European Communities formally established the European Environment Agency (EEA) and the European Environmental Information and Observation Network (EIONET) with Regulation 1210/90 of 7 May 1990, based on article 130s (EC). The Agency opened its activities on 31 October 1994; after the Council had decided to locate it in Copenhagen.[11]

The management of the Agency consists of a management board which includes a representative of each Member State, two representatives of the Commission, and two scientists chosen by the European Parliament (art. 8(1)). Each member has one vote (art. 8(2)). Based on principal areas of activity in the Regulation (art. 3), the management board adopts annual and multi-annual work programmes concerning the more specific priorities of the Agency (art. 8 (4 and 5)). The Agency is headed by an executive director who is appointed by the management board (art. 9). The board and the executive director are assisted by a scientific committee composed of nine members who are particularly well-qualified in the field of the environment (art. 10). The Agency has a legal personality of its own (art. 7).

The main task of the EEA is to provide objective, reliable and comparable information – so-called best available information (BAI) – which will enable the Community and the Member States to take the requisite measures to protect the environment, to assess the results of such measures; and to ensure that the public is properly informed about the state of the environment (arts 1.2 and 2(ii)).

In order to carry out this task the EEA sets up and coordinates the environmental information and observation network (EIONET) which is primarily based and dependent on information provided by the Member States (art. 4). Each Member State designates a 'national focal point' which will be in charge of the cooperation with the EEA and the national coordination of activities related to the EEA work programmes. These 'points' transmit the information from the national level, i.e. from the main component elements and the national reference centre of each Member State, to the Agency. The Member States can, among their own national institutions, propose so-called 'topic centres'. These are institutions with which the EEA will contract directly in order to execute the tasks identified in the Agency's multi-annual work programmes. The topic centre will carry out its specific task in a precise geographical area and will also cooperate with other institutions which form part of the network.

It must be mentioned that the Community has for many years recognised the importance of the integration of the best available environmental information. Thus, in 1985, as a consequence of the Third Environmental Action Programme, the Community established an environmental network of its own, the so-called CORINE-Programme (Coordinating and Ensuring the Consistency of Information on the State of the Environment in Europe), which is now continued through the activities of the EEA, especially in the EIONET context.

Besides the EIONET network, the different network structures described in the Regulation are as follows: First of all, the EEA shall seek to cooperate with EU institutions and programmes; not only with the Commission, the Council and the European Parliament, but also with the Joint Research Centre (JRC) and the Statistical Office (EUROSTAT) (art. 15(1)). Second, the EEA is intended to promote the incorporation of EU environmental information into international environmental monitoring programmes and to cooperate with international organisations and participate in international programmes in order to exchange information and experiences, and also to avoid duplicating work and efforts (arts 2(v and x) and 15). Thus, agreements have been made with the Organisation for Economic Cooperation and Development (OECD), the United Nations Environment Programme (UNEP), the World Health Organisation (WHO), and the US Environmental Protection Agency (EPA). Third, the EEA is also open for membership to other countries, i.e. non-members of the Community (art. 19). Finally, the EEA is mandated to participate in more informal networks according to article 3 of the Regulation; the EEA can include all elements enabling it to fulfil its objectives.

From the various networks systems the EEA obtains immense amounts of information on the state of the environment and it is notable that the list of providers is in principle endless. Thus, the Agency is also open for information provided by alternative sources such as NGOs, private parties, academics, etc. However, this raises some concerns due to its present limited capacity. Thus, it might be seen that the Agency as it currently stands is not capable of guaranteeing the same qualitative examination of all the incoming data and that potential valuable information might therefore be lost. In addition, the discretion of the Agency in its assessment of the incoming data raises some concern in relation to ranking the information in priority and importance – what is the best available information? Thus, its discretionary powers can come into conflict with other interests which highlight the importance of access to information and a genuine system of review. These aspects will be discussed in the next section.

In the light of the far-reaching activities of EEA within the different networks mentioned and its independent status, one could thus conclude that the structure and tasks of the Agency are well suited to playing an important role within the networking approach in environmental regulation. However, as will be shown in the following section, there exist important legal and procedural limitations which need to be improved in order to realise the Agency's full networking potential.

Improved networking potential of the EEA

A closer look at Regulation 1210/90, the legal framework concerning the EEA's activities, reveals several constraints which limit the Agency's potential in order to promote the exchange of information between different public and private actors involved in the formulation and implementation of environmental policies. Specifically, problems can be observed with respect to four issues: namely, the objectives of the EEA, access to information, judicial review, and accountability. All of these areas represent actual or potential obstacles to the further development of the EEA's networking capabilities.

Before turning to the analysis, it should be stated that the EEA of today is only in its starting phase and that the conflicts are not all of practical significance in the current daily work of the Agency. However, it is important to emphasise that these areas all represent obstacles to the further development of an independent EEA and the further development of networking and are therefore of importance for the efficiency of the system.

The objective
The objectives in article 1 raise some difficulties and therefore also some uncertainties concerning the aim of the EEA. The objective of the EEA is to achieve the aims of environmental protection and improvement laid down by *the Treaty and by successive Community action programmes on the environment,* by providing *the Community and the Member States* with objective, reliable and comparable information at European level enabling *them* to take the requisite measures to protect the environment, to assess the results of such measures, and to ensure that the public is properly informed about the state of the environment (art. 1 (2)). In legal terms this means

that the EEA can participate only in networking in promoting *EU environmental policy* and is therefore committed only to supporting the Member States in achieving Community policy and not their own environmental policies – local, national and and or international. This finding cannot be unintentional, since the original article 1 of the proposal of the Regulation actually included the support of environmental goals at *international, national, regional and local levels,* albeit the scope of the objectives was narrowed down, as shown in the final Regulation.[12]

This finding seems to be in contradiction with the intentions of the establishment of the EEA.[13] The objective should be to improve environmental conditions in general, with no geographical limitation and for the benefit of both Community and national environmental policies. It is also remarkable that third countries joining the EEA will, according to article 19, have to participate in fulfilling EU environmental policy rather than focusing on their own policies.

It is worth noting that the objective stated in article 1.2 not only restricts the possibility of Member States and other participants in fulfilling their own environmental goals, but also excludes the EEA from participating in networks not fulfilling specific Community goals. Furthermore, the intention in article 1 of only providing the Member States and the Community with information, enabling *them* to inform the public, and not the various other actors, could reduce the motivation of the participants to interact in networking. Thus, the EEA risks not obtaining valuable information and not participating in relevant networks.

Therefore, in order to provide the EEA with the best possible tools for participating and operating in all kinds of relevant networks, the objectives in article 1 should be extended in order to ensure the support of environmental goals at all levels – at the Community level, at the national, regional, local levels, at levels related to industrial branches, NGOs, etc. – and also to ensure that the information is not only for the benefit of the Community and the Member States but also for the benefit of all actors and participants.

Access to information
Direct access to information at the EEA – and not only at the Community and the Member States – is of importance for the following reasons. First of all, the different interpretations and applications among the national administrators concerning access to

information (see Kimber, chapter 8, in this book) highlights the importance of access for the European public in general to information from more independent institutions such as the EEA. Second, related to the independence of the EEA, this finding is also linked to the matter of impartiality, since the parties involved in projects are often public enterprises; this could give rise to the fear of an interfering of interests when the relevant authority examines a request for access. A third argument for direct access to information at the EEA is simply that it will intensify the comparability of data and information. The opportunity to obtain all kinds of relevant information and data in relation to a particular project can only be obtained by the possibility of 'shopping' at different authorities and institutions. Furthermore, although the Directive on the Freedom on Access to Environmental Information states that any refusal of a request towards a Member State has to be justified by the national authority and the decision has to be linked with adequate judicial or administrative review (art. 4), it must be recognised that time does not always allow for long-term judicial discourse in the environmental area.

Examining the current legal context, it is notable that the task of informing the public is exclusive in the domain of the Community and the Member States (art. 1). This provision must be read together with article 6, which states that the environmental data from the EEA may be published and made accessible to the public – but the article does not specify by which institution. As described above, the legitimisation and proper functioning of the EEA is linked closely to its role as an independent provider of reliable environmental information. Article 1 should therefore be reviewed in order to ensure that publicity is provided by the EEA, the Community and the Member States. This would reflect the general intentions lying behind the establishment of the Agency and also the reality of the EEA, given that one of its main activities since its establishment has been to produce general public information.

The issue of publicity is linked to the question of *the right* of access to the information and networks of the EEA. The Regulation provides the EEA with autonomous powers and the discretion to assess and select the incoming information, to operate and control the networks and to define areas of priority, which can be found in the annual and multi-annual programmes (art. 8). It must be recognised that the participants and actors in certain situations will have other interests than the EEA. Therefore, the Regulation must provide the public with a clear and firm legal right to access to information and link this right to a judicial and/or administrative review of the activities of the EEA; for a review concerning the Agency's assessment of data, operation of the networks and administration in general see the following section on judicial review. However, this would presuppose an adoption and/or an improvement of procedural and administrative norms – in the Regulations establishing the Agency, directly in the EU Treaty, in new EU administrative legislation or in norms of their own, developed through practice and confirmed by the EU Ombudsman and and or the ECJ.

The right of access to information seems to be provided by article 6.2 of the Regulation, which states that 'environmental data ... shall be made accessible to the public, subject to compliance with the rules of the Commission and the Member States on the dissemination of information, particularly as regards confidentiality'. However, this provision also raises some legal uncertainties.

First, since the objective of the Agency is to provide only *the Community and the Member States* with information enabling *them* to inform the public (art. 1), uncertainty emerges as to whether the right of access relates only to the Community and the Member States and therefore not to the Agency itself. Consequently, any application concerning access could be rejected by the Agency and would have to be addressed to the Community institution or Member States instead. Moreover, referring to the rules of the Member States as a unity is problematic since the legal systems regulating access to information throughout the Community still differ greatly – even after the adoption of Directive 90/313 on the Freedom on Access to Environmental Information (see also Kimber, chapter 8, in this book) which, notably, also allows the single Member State to apply even more favourable measures to ensure access to information due to the legal basis in article 130s (EC), and therefore encourages different legal systems. Thus, by referring to the Member States and the Commission, article 6 refers in practice to 16 different administrative systems. It would not be possible for the EEA to operate within such different systems; thus, realistically, a workable interpretation of article 6 would lead to the conclusion that any request for access to information has to be addressed directly to – and examined by – a national authority or the Commission, and not the Agency itself.

Second, however, *if* it is assumed that article 6.2 provides the public with a legal right to access directly to the EEA itself, the legal weakness of the right becomes notable since the extent and application of the right is linked to and dependent on the rules of the Commission and the Member States. It may be criticised that such an important feature as access to information can be regulated according to secondary Community legislation, national legislation and especially by referring to the rules of the Commission – these rules are based only on a declaration and are to a large extent therefore subject to the political attitude of the Commission.[14] This means that access to information at the EEA could change as Community and national policies change, which would be in contradiction with the fundamental importance of ensuring the right of access, and also with the fundamentally independent structure of the Agency.

Furthermore, *if* direct access to the Agency is assumed, it raises the question of how article 6 should be interpreted. Should the Agency with reference to the various national administrative systems use the lowest or highest common denominator – if this is even possible? In addition, how should the reference to confidentiality be governed? The Agency argues, that having been granted legal personality and legal autonomy, the Agency is not bound by the code of conduct by the Council and the Commission and therefore has to adopt its own set of rules.[15] However, this interpretation seems problematic. The legal status of the Decision is secondary since the Regulation does not authorise the Agency to deviate from article 6 of the Regulation: dissemination of information has to comply with the rules of the Commission and the Member States. Therefore, without any specific delegation in the Regulation, the Decision must merely be regarded as an internal code of conduct and the Agency has to administer the Decision and conduct its policy on access to information in conformity with the rules of the Commission and the Member States. Thus, the Decision does not ease the difficulties arising from article 6 of the Regulation concerning access to information.

As described above, the legitimisation and proper functioning of the EEA is closely linked to its role as an independent provider of reliable environmental information. The uncertainties and restrictions currently governing the EEA's information policy tend to jeopardise the accountability of the Agency, and hence its capability for effective networking. At present, public and private actors participating in the EEA's information networks face considerable uncertainty regarding the extent to which the EEA makes use of the environmental information it receives. To what extent will these data be interpreted as confidential by either the Agency, the Member States, or the Commission? To what extent will network participants have access to the data held by the EEA?

Therefore, a clarification of these aspects to ensure firm and uniform criteria related to the right of access to information and the confidentiality of the data is needed. This finding does not apply only to the regulation itself but also to the general issue of openness and access to documents in the EU.

In this respect it is noteworthy that the new Treaty of Amsterdam introduces a new principle of a right of access to documents of the European Parliament, the Council and the Commission. The general principles and limits shall be determined by the Council within two years of the entry into force of the new Treaty.[16] This introduction of a right to access combined with a future secondary EU legislation seems promising and is a step in the right direction. However, due to the controversies related to the various administrative cultures among the Member States and also the importance of the subject for all parties concerned, it must be recognised that the road towards uniformity may be long. Also of interest, the institutions concerned do not include external bodies, such as the agencies.

Furthermore, the introduction of overall administrative norms at Community level could be promoted by the EU Ombudsman institution and that the Ombudsman is entitled to review the performance of the Agency (European Ombudsman 1995, 10).

Judicial review

The Agency is a legal person in its own right which is a logical consequence of its independent status (art. 7). This means that the Agency can autonomously participate in legal actions. Therefore, any private or legal person with legal capacity and interest is in this respect able to take legal action against the Agency in relation to its activities.

The Regulation provides the EEA with autonomous powers and the discretion to assess and select the incoming information, to operate and control the networks, and to define areas of priority due to the annual and multi-annual programmes. As already stated, it must be recognised that the participants and actors in certain situations will have other interests than the EEA. Therefore, the

Regulation must provide the public with a clear and firm legal right to judicial review of the activities of the EEA; a review concerning the Agency's assessment of data, operation of the networks and administration of requests on access to information.

Concerning the jurisdiction, the ECJ is designated as the venue for legal disputes (Breier 1995, 520). However, the ECJ has jurisdiction only in relation to contractual liability, if agreed, and in relation to non-contractual liability if the dispute is related to compensation for any damage (article 18 (1 and 2) and article 178 and 215 (2) (EC)). The non-contractual aspect is of interest for the present discussion because one can imagine a request of access to information raised by a person without any contractual relation to the Agency and without any directly linked economic interest. By leaving out any claim of compensation and seeking purely recognition for right to access, a plaintiff could eventually successfully, according to international private law, pursue the case in a domestic court. Thus, the Agency could risk legal proceedings in the country of domicile of the plaintiff, which – due to the international work of the Agency – could be both in and outside the EU. In order to avoid this uncertainty, the ECJ should be empowered with a firm jurisdiction covering all the activities of the Agency.

A judicial review of the Agency's actions can be divided into a substantial review of the Agency's discretion in its evaluation of the incoming data, on the one hand, and a procedural review of the Agency in relation to the administrative norms for the operation of networking – like access to information – and in relation to the criteria and guidelines for the evaluation itself.

Considering the substantial review, one could argue that the Agency does not make any reviewable decisions in simply recommending certain information for the policy makers. Instead, the reviewable decision takes place when the policy maker issues the policy based on specific chosen data. Then, the review of the validity of the act can take place, which could also include the validity of the applied data. Although a substantial review therefore seems unlikely at the present stage, it would, however, be wrong to consider the EEA as a purely neutral, inactive and information gathering institution in relation to the European decision making process. It is generally recognised that the role of information in contemporary policy making is not only instrumental but also constitutive – information is not only a necessary input into the policy process; under some conditions, the information constitutes policy (Majone 1996, 1997; Shapiro 1996, 101). Thus, it must be recognised that the EEA – even as a 'pure' information gatherer and provider – has a significant potential influence on the European decision making process. The Agency has or can have a potential influence on the content and coherence of the information provided due to its influence on the priority setting, evaluation of data and administration of networks since the moderate Regulation makes it possible for the Agency to act with a considerably high level of discretion.[17]

In this light, the judicial review of the Agency's activities should at least be linked to procedural aspects. However, such judicial review could for the time being cause some difficulties since the Agency is without any major criteria concerning its administration of the incoming data and also on its administration of requests on access to information. A clarification would presuppose an adoption and/or an improvement of procedural and administrative norms in the Regulation establishing the Agency, directly in the EU Treaty, in new EU administrative legislation, or in norms of their own developed through practice and confirmed by the EU Ombudsman and/or the ECJ.[18]

Although the EEA's scientific committee is supposed to make up guidelines for the evaluation of data, these should not only be guidelines for the use of the Agency but also for the use of the national authorities and the national focus points, which also evaluate the information before they transfer the data to the Agency. In this sense, a certain uniformity will develop in the criteria for the evaluation of data.

Accountability

The question of accountability is strongly linked to issues of control over and influence on the Agency and its activities. Given the transnational character of the EEA, accountability has to be analysed from the perspective of different actors, which might have a different interest in controlling and influencing the activities of the EEA. Different actors include the Community institutions and the Member States, as well as other public and private actors involved and affected by the networking activities of the Agency.

With respect to the influence and control potential of Community institutions, it is notable that the Commission is exclusively entitled to propose the executive director of the EEA (art. 9(1)), give its opinion on the annual and multi-annual work programmes before they are adopted by the management board (art. 8(4 and 5)) and to appoint two members of the board (art. 8 (1.1)). In addition, the European Parliament appoints two members of the management board (art. 8 (1.2)).

In budgetary terms, the EEA falls under the so-called 'non-compulsory' part of the EU budget. Through the budgetary procedures, and especially through the preliminary draft budget, the Commission, the Council, the European Parliament and the Court of Auditors can exercise potential influence on the work of the Agency (arts 11–14). Additionally, the management board appoints a financial controller to monitor the budgetary performance of the Agency (art. 13(2)).

Accountability towards the Member States is mainly to be found in the composition of the management board of the Agency where each Member State is represented by one member. However, Member States from the sphere of so-called third countries are also represented but do not have any voting right.[19]

Accountability towards the public relies on the transparency of the Agency in general and is closely linked to the above-mentioned aspects of access to information and judicial and/or administrative review. As pointed out above, there currently exist significant procedural deficits with respect to these matters, hence implying that the Agency's accountability is not very well balanced between the Community institutions and the Member States, on the one hand, and other public and private actors on the other. Potential short-term improvements in the EEA's public accountability could be achieved by the institution of the EU Ombudsman and the introduction of public hearings as a general element into the decision making process of the Agency.

The strong political influence exerted by both the Commission and the Member States on the activities of the Agency is in contradiction to the EEA's status as an independent body. Even if in the light of the present situation this political bias on the Agency has to be accepted, it should at least be required that the accountability of the Agency towards different interests and actors is more equally balanced. Otherwise, the legitimacy of the EEA will be weakened, and hence reduce the ability of the Agency to interact and cooperate with as many public and private actors as possible.

Conclusion

This chapter has analysed the potential of the EEA for improving the problems of ineffective and inconsistent implementation of EU environmental policy. In contrast to the suggestion that the Agency could best achieve this potential by increasing its regulatory powers, it has been argued that the most important role of the EEA has to be seen in its networking capacities; i.e. the promotion and establishment of exchange networks among different public and private actors. Given the reliance on such moderate rather than revolutionary challenges to the existing regulatory framework, the actual implementation of reform proposals is less likely to suffer from political resistance and institutional inertia of well-established regulatory traditions.

The promotion of networking, allowing for the participation of all public and private actors involved in the formulation and implementation of EU environmental policy, plays a crucial role in the Community's 'new approach' to environmental regulation. This emphasises public participation, voluntary regulation and self-regulation in favour of classical forms of hierarchical 'top–down' approaches. Nevertheless, this analysis has shown that even procedural innovation is a complex task with the risk of poor implementation.

The EEA has significant potential to stimulate, promote and establish the exchange of information and knowledge in the context of various informal networks. However, in reviewing the current legal framework governing the activities of the EEA considerable hurdles have been found which might reduce the EEA's ability to realise its full networking potential. Problems exist with respect to four areas, namely, the restricted definition of the objectives of the EEA, the ambiguous rules concerning public access to environmental information held by the Agency, the limited opportunities for judicial and administrative review of the Agency's activities, and the unbalanced accountability of the Agency in favour of the Commission and the Member States, which considerably reduces its independent status. With respect to all of these aspects, substantial amendments to the procedural and legal framework of the Agency are necessary in order to secure its political credibility and legitimacy – both of which are necessary conditions for successful networking.

Notes

1 I would like to thank both editors of this book for their very helpful suggestions and comments on this chapter. I would also like to thank Professor Karl-Heinz Ladeur at the European University Institute and Universität Hamburg for his comments and his support of my work.

2 Regulation EEC No. 1210/1990 on the Establishment of the European Environment Agency and the European Environment Information and Observation Network (EIONET). OJ No. L 120, 11.5.1990, p. 1 (the Regulation).

3 The review was postponed until the end of 1997, see Commission Proposal, COM (95) 325 final, 7 July 1995, European Parliament Resolution A4 234/95, OJ No. C 287, 30.10.95, p. 233 and Council Conclusion adopted 9 November 1995, doc. 11175/95 (Press 310). On 13 June 1997, the Commission forwarded a proposal for amending Regulation 1210/90. The proposal does not contain any changes in relation to the discussions in the present chapter, Proposal for a Council Regulation (EC) amending Regulation EEC No 1210/90 of 7 May 1990 on the establishment of the European Environment Agency and the European environment information and observation network, COM (97) 282 final.

4 This chapter will not focus specifically on the Agency's role in enforcement networks such as the 'European Union Network for the Implementation and Enforcement of Environmental Law' (the IMPEL Network – formerly 'Chester Network') but, rather, focus on networking in general (concerning enforcement networking, see Collins and Earnshaw 1992, 238; Davies 1994, 339).

5 The emergence of transnational governance based on networking is visible in various forms. Note, for instance, the Commission's CORINE network (now EIONET network) for information exchange, the IMPEL network for enforcement, or the adoption of the Directive 96/61 concerning Integrated Pollution Prevention and Control (IPPC) OJ No. L 257, 10.10.96, p. 26. Moreover, the Community increasingly integrates private parties into the implementation phase. See, for instance, the voluntary programmes on an ecolabel award scheme and on eco-audit and eco-management (Wright and Bouma, chapters 5 and 6, in this book).

6 The management of complexity, the administrative context and the linked relationship between public and private law, see Ladeur 1996a, 1996b and 1998. Complexity relates to the increasing amount of regulation and to the increasing technicality in the regulations, which again is linked to the increasing need for scientific expertise.

7 Directive 85/337 on Environmental Impact Assessment (EIA), OJ L 175, 5.7.1985, p. 40.

8 Directive 90/313 on the Freedom on Access to Environmental Information, OJ L 158, 23.6.1999, p. 56.

9 Directive 96/61 concerning Integrated Pollution Prevention and control (IPPC), OJ L 257, 10.10.96, p. 26.

10 General literature on the Agency; see Ladeur 1996a and 1998; Kreher 1996, 1997 and 1998; Bailey 1997; Breier 1995; Davies 1994.

11 OJ C 323, 30.11.1993, p. 1.

12 The proposal; OJ No. C 217, 23.8.1989, p. 7 and COM (89)303 final, 12.7.1989, p. 2.

13 See Preamble p. 9 (enabling the Member States to protect the environment) and p. 15 (the Agency is open for third countries) and article 2(ii); the task of the EEA is – among others – to provide Member States with information for framing and implementing environmental policies.

14 It is notable that Directive 90/313 on the Freedom on Access to Environmental Information relates only to the public authorities in the Member States and therefore does not include the Community institutions or the EEA as an independent institution. The Council and the Commission adopted a Code of Conduct in late 1993, followed shortly thereafter by the adoption of separate decisions of the two bodies of the implementation of the Code. (Declaration 93/730 on a Code of Conduct concerning public access to Council and Commission documents and the Council's Decision 93/731 of 20 December 1993 on public access to Council documents, OJ No. L 340, 31.12.93, p. 43; Commission Decision 94/90 of 8 February 1994 on the public access to Commission documents, OJ No. L 46, 18.2.94, p. 58.)

15 The Agency has adopted Decision of 31 March 1997 on public access to its documents, OJ No. C 282, 18.9.97, p. 5. The Agency indicates that these rules follow closely those adopted by the Council and the Commission but will be applied on an independent basis. The Agency is determined to grant access in the widest possible way without requiring proven interest by the applicant (arts 1 and 2). The access can be refused under certain conditions following article 5 which, for reasons of coherence, is drafted in exactly the same way as the exceptions in the code of conduct adopted by the Council and the Commission, Preamble 8. Any refusal can be review by the chairperson of the management board, article 4 and in case the refusal is sustained, the applicant will be informed about the possibility of referring the case to the Ombudsman pursuant to article 138e (EC).

16 Treaty of Amsterdam, new article 255 in the Treaty on the European Communities (TEC) (former art. 191a, i.e. art. 12 Treaty of Amsterdam and following Annex Part B). The openness will also be strengthened by an amendment to the second paragraph of new article 1 of the TEU (former art. A, i.e. art. 12 Treaty of Amsterdam and following Annex Part A).

17   The priority setting follows the wide criteria in article 3 (2) of the Regulation and – more specifically – the annual and multi-annual work programmes which the management board adopts after consultation of the scientific committee, article 8 (4).

18   The Agency Decision of 21 March 1997 on access to its documents gives some – but few – criteria on the administration on access to information. This administration is linked to a administrative review by the chairman of the management board and further information on the possibility of referring the matter to the Ombudsman pursuant to article 138e (EC).

19   Article 3.2 of Protocol 31 to the Agreement on the European Economic Area, OJ No. L 253, 29.9.1994, pp. 32 and 34; Decision of the Joint Committee of the European Economic Area No. 10 and 11/94 of 12 August 1994 amending Protocol 31 to the Agreement of the European Economic Area, on Cooperation in Specific Fields Outside the Four Freedoms.

References

Bailey, Patricia M. (1997): 'The Changing Role of Environmental Agencies', *European Environmental Law Review*, May, pp. 148–55.

Breier, Siegfried (1995): 'Die Organisationsgewalt der Gemeinschaft am Beispiel der Errichtung der Europäischen Umweltagentur', *Natur und Recht*, Heft 10 and 11, pp. 516–520.

Collins, Ken and David Earnshaw (1992): The Implementation and Enforcement of European Community Environment Legislation, *Environmental Politics*, Vol. 14, No. 4, pp. 213–49.

Commission of the European Union (1996): *Implementing Community Environmental Law*. Communication to the Council of the European Union and the European Parliament, 22.10.1996.

Davies, Peter G.G. (1994): 'The European Environment Agency', *Yearbook of European Law*, Vol. 14, pp. 313–49.

Dehousse, Renaud (1997): 'Regulation by Networks in the European Community: The Role of European Agencies', *Journal of European Public Policy*, Vol. 4, No. 2, pp. 246–61.

European Ombudsman: *Annual Report 1995*. Luxembourg: Office for Official Publications of the European Communities.

Everson, Michelle (1995): 'Independent Agencies: Hierarchy Beaters?', *European Law Journal*, Vol. 1, No.2, pp. 180–204.

Kreher, Alexander (ed.) (1996): *The New European Agencies: Conference Report*. EUI Working Paper, RSC No. 96/49.

Kreher, Alexander (1997): Agencies in the European Community. A step towards Administrative Integration in Europe, *Journal of European*

Public Policy, Vol. 4, No. 2, pp. 225–45.

Kreher, Alexander (ed.) (1998): *The EC Agencies between Community Institutions and Constituents: Autonomy, Control and Accountability: Conference Report*. European University Institute, Florence.

Ladeur, Karl-Heinz (1996a): *The New European Agencies: The European Environment Agency and Prospects for a European Network of Environmental Administrations*. EUI Working Paper, RSC No. 96/50.

Ladeur, Karl-Heinz (1996b): *Network as a Legal Concept*, Paper for the Conference Social Regulation through European Committees: Empirical Research, Institutional Politics, Theoretical Concepts and Legal Developments, European University Institute, Florence, 9 and 10 December.

Ladeur, Karl-Heinz (1998): 'Proceduralisation and the Management of Complexity in Public Organizations: The Case of the European Environment Agency'. In Alexander Kreher (ed.), *The EC Agencies between Community Institutions and Constituents: Autonomy, Control and Accountability: Conference Report*. European University Institute, Florence, pp. 143–63.

Lenaerts, Koen (1993): 'Regulating the Regulatory Process: "Delegation of Powers" in the European Community', *European Law Review*, Vol. 18, pp. 23–49.

Majone, Giandomenico (1994): *Independence vs. Accountability? On-Majoritarian Institutions and Democratic Government in Europe*, EUI Working Paper, SPS No. 94/3.

Majone, Giandomenico (1995): *Mutual Trust, Credible Commitments and the Single European Market*, EUI Working Paper, RSC No. 95/1.

Majone, Giandomenico (1996): 'New Agencies in the EC: Regulation by Information'. In Alexander Kreher (ed.), *The New European Agencies: Conference Report*. EUI Working Paper, RSC No. 96/49, pp. 5–11.

Majone, Giandomenico (1997): 'The New European Agencies: Regulation by Information', *Journal of European Public Policy*, Vol. 4, No. 2, pp. 262–75.

Shapiro, Martin (1996): Agencies in the European Union: An American Perspective. In Alexander Kreher (ed.), *The New European Agencies: Conference Report*. EUI Working Paper, RSC No. 96/49, pp. 101–4.

Vos, Ellen (1997): 'The Rise of Committees', *European Law Journal*, Vol. 3, pp. 210–29.

Part three

The impact of new instruments

5   Robert Wright[1]

Implementing voluntary policy instruments: the experience of the EU Ecolabel Award Scheme

Introduction

There can be no doubt whatsoever that the policy profile of 'the implementation problem' in EU environmental policy has been increasing steadily from the 1980s. In 1984 the Commission published the first of its annual reports to the European Parliament on the application of Community law. Each year these annual reports would go on to provide statistics concerning the perilous state of the implementation of EU environmental law. In 1987, the Fourth Environmental Action Programme (4th EAP) was adopted by the Council, and for the first time in a Community environmental action programme, specific reference to the importance of ensuring effective implementation was made. In adopting the 4th EAP, the Council specifically referred to 'the particular importance it attaches to the implementation of Community legislation'.[2] In 1990, the European Council adopted the 'Declaration on the Environmental Imperative' at the Dublin Summit, wherein a commitment to improving the implementation of EU environmental policy was made.

It was against this backdrop that the Fifth Environmental Action Programme (5th EAP) was written and presented by the Commission in 1992 and adopted in 1993 by the Council. Quite simply, the 5th EAP set out in detail a new approach to EU environmental policy which was aimed (amongst other things) at overcoming the implementation problem. One of the ways in which this was to be attained was by broadening the use of policy instruments. Rather than relying solely on top–down regulatory instruments, EU environmental policy would make use of voluntary policy instruments, which did not require implementation through the variously complex links of the more traditional 'regulatory policy chain'. Relying on this 'regulatory chain' whereby environmental policy has to be drafted, adopted, transposed, practically implemented, enforced and monitored was quite correctly viewed as having contributed greatly to the implementation problems undermining EU environmental policy. A new voluntary approach could help overcome and circumvent the sort of implementation problems that had been dogging EU environmental policy for so many years. Or, so it seemed at the time.

As this chapter shows, the operation of what we shall hereafter call 'the voluntary approach' to EU environmental policy has been far from straightforward or problem free. By focusing on the implementation to date of the EU Ecolabel Award Scheme as set out in Council Regulation 880/92,[3] I will show in fact that many of the traditional implementation problems associated with top–down policy instruments have persisted. Despite not requiring the full mechanics of the more traditional 'regulatory chain', the operation of this scheme has been extremely problematic. Why is it that a policy instrument such as the EU Ecolabel Award Scheme which is voluntary, has faced the sort of problems which are normally associated with the more traditional application of the top–down legislative approach?

In order to answer this question, this chapter is made up of three sections following this introduction. First, I shall discuss the problematic aspects of 'traditional regulation': specifically, what are the deficits in the use of legislative instruments which the application of a voluntary approach attempts to redress? In order to answer this question I shall briefly discuss the nature of the voluntary approach itself, and develop a brief comparative analysis of the strengths and weaknesses of both approaches. It will be shown that there is no dichotomy between these approaches to EU environmental regulation. Rather we must recognise that most policy instruments, which appear to be voluntary, are in fact 'hybrids' that contain aspects of both approaches. Attempting to solve the sort of implementation deficits which result from a reliance on the legislative approach to regulation alone can therefore not be sought by simply developing and applying a voluntary approach without recognising its inherently regulatory aspects. If the implementation problems of traditional regulation are not to be repeated, policy makers must succeed in combining the strengths of both the voluntary and the legislative approach.

As we shall see in the second section of our analysis, a successful combination was not achieved in the case of the EU Ecolabel Award Scheme, given that its operation was undermined by the combined weaknesses of both approaches, rather than a combination of their strengths. The third section will conclude by discussing the revision of the scheme which was started in 1996, and assess its attempts to overcome the sort of problems which have been experienced in its implementation. This will allow us to implicitly evaluate the capacity of EU voluntary policy instruments to overcome traditional implementation deficits.

The 'legislative approach' *versus* the 'voluntary approach'?

This section is divided into two. First, I shall provide an overview of the sort of implementation problems that have developed with regard to the legislative approach. Second, I shall develop a comparative analysis of both approaches in order to assess their strengths and weaknesses as well as understand whether or not the use of voluntary instruments is capable of overcoming the implementation deficits experienced in more traditional regulatory policy.

The implementation deficit in the context of EU environmental policy

Interest among policy analysts in what has come to be termed as the 'implementation problem' has been steadily growing over the last two decades ever since Pressman and Wildavsky (1973) noticed that the implementation of policy is neither easy or straightforward and that it is a very complex process, which cannot be underestimated by policy makers. A new focus on the 'complexity of joint action' and the fact that implementation is conducted at 'arm's length', not only came together to form a springboard for a growing emphasis among policy analysts on policy implementation problems, but also helps describe and explain the sort of problems that face the implementation of EU environmental policy.

It has been generally recognised by both the Commission and various analysts of EU environmental policy that the first stage or phase of EU environmental policy up until the 4th EAP was marked by an exclusive focus on passing legislation and creating a legal framework: quite simply, policy formation was concentrated on at the expense of policy implementation (European Parliament, 1992;

House of Lords, 1992; European Commission, 1992; Macrory, 1992). In many ways this was only to be expected given that it takes considerable time for implementation problems to be noticed, and then even more time for them to be placed on the policy agenda. Mazmanian and Sabatier (1983) and Sabatier (1986) note for example that 'policy-oriented learning' can only take place over an extended time span of 10–15 years. In other words, implementation analysis takes time to develop, and it is only as a result of sustained analysis of the implementation of EU environmental legislation, that both deficits and underlying factors have become well documented.

The Commission's own statistics have consistently illustrated the extent of the implementation problem facing EU environmental law. According to the Annual Report on the implementation of Community law for 1995, many Member States had notified implementing measures for only 83 per cent of environmental directives applicable, meaning that in some cases as many as 22 directives had not been transposed into national law.[4] On average, implementation measures for 91 per cent of applicable directives had been notified. In the same year, the Commission had registered a total of 265 suspected breaches of Community environmental law based on complaints from the public, parliamentary questions and petitions and cases detected by the Commission. This amounted to 20 per cent of all infringements registered by the Commission for 1995. By 1996, over 600 environmental complaints and infringement cases were outstanding against Member States, with 85 awaiting determination by the European Court of Justice.[5] It is therefore not difficult to see that implementation problems particularly affect EU environmental policy. There is a wide variety of difficulties facing the successful implementation of EU environmental policy, which I shall now briefly outline.

The initial problems concern ambiguous or poorly drafted legislation which partially result from the fact that the adoption of EU legislation emanates from a political bargaining process in the Council. The first aspect of the implementation problem therefore rests with the formation of policy. Quite simply, if a Directive is poorly drafted, it will not be successfully implemented. Unfortunately the likelihood of poorly drafted legislation in such a complex policy process as the EU's is quite high. There are considerable problems in making a single piece of environmental legislation applicable to the variety of differing environmental conditions which exist across the

EU. Then, once they have been adopted, EU environmental Directives have to be transposed into national law. Transposition of legislation often takes a lot of time. Even when Member States are not reluctant to transpose directives, the process itself can be difficult and time consuming. For example, transposition very often requires the enactment of a variety of national implementing measures. In federal and quasi-federal policy systems such as Germany and Italy, many implementing measures are required to be enacted by regional levels of government. This can lead to a bewildering proliferation of implementing texts at national and regional level. As a result, transposition across Member States is therefore usually uneven with a mixture of good and bad implementers. Regarding this point, the House of Lords (1992) has noted that:

> the rigour with which Member States enforce Community law thus in general reflects national enforcement policies, the vigilance and competence of national regulatory agencies and the legal remedies and sanctions available under national law. It is also dependent on the degree to which accurate information about environmental media is collected and handled. Given these variables, it is inevitable that enforcement and its effectiveness will differ across the Community not merely between but within Member States. (House of Lords, 1992: 28)

The legislative and the voluntary approach in EU environmental policy: comparative strengths and weaknesses

Considering the above aspects together helps us understand and appreciate that implementing the legislative approach to EU environmental policy is an extremely complex and problematic process. The difficulties faced in preparing legislative proposals, the difficult choice of what form Community legislation should take, the political nature of adopting the proposals, the high chance of faulty transposition into national law, Member States' reluctance or inability to correctly implement and enforce the legislation, the inevitability that it will be implemented and enforced across the EU in an uneven fashion, the time-consuming and costly nature of the formal procedures of enforcement, and the inability of the Commission to monitor all of this, mean that the 'transaction costs' involved with organising the implementation of the legislative approach are particularly high.[6] This is especially the case where implementation takes place in a 'multi-organisational' setting requiring coordinated participation of multiple organisations, which in turn depends on 'combined information, abilities and actions of a variety of partially-autonomous but interdependent units' (O'Toole, 1993: 33).

Besides the particular difficulties emerging from the nature of the EU policy making process, the legislative approach faces more general problems which might contribute to European implementation deficits. First, the setting of standards is not very suited to policy which aims to fix demanding targets which can incrementally and progressively move economic activities 'towards sustainability'. As von Weizsäcker (1990: 202) notes:

> Once a given standard is reached there is little incentive left for polluters to go further in emission reduction. And, if standards are coupled with 'best available technology' stipulation, polluters often have little interest in progress in pollution prevention technologies because such progress leads to additional costs and no benefits to the firm.

Second, uniform legislation, is likely to suffer from the 'lowest common denominator' syndrome, whereby 'average' positions attempt to accommodate the less able environmental achievers, but in doing so, also constrain the more potentially able achievers. Legislative policy instruments on their own are therefore unlikely to be flexible enough to fulfil the long-term goals of environmental protection and sustainability.

Third, the reliance on statutory instruments with a real implementation time of several years has increasingly lost policy credibility. Given that the average EU Directive has a timespan which may go beyond that of a polluter's activity, that same polluter may estimate that they can violate a Directive with impunity simply because by the time the Directive has been implemented and enforced, their activity may have ceased. Pollution which takes place over a smaller timespan than a particular piece of legislation may easily avoid the regulatory net. This is a particularly relevant point given that many environmental problems can develop and change faster than the regulation designed to solve them.

It is very much with these problems in mind that the Commission developed a new policy strategy, which relies less on the legislative approach. The problems associated with this approach could not simply be overcome by improving the way in which environmental legislation is made and implemented.[7] They had to be *circumvented* by supplementing the legislative approach with the voluntary approach. Quite simply, applying a voluntary approach has the potential for lowering the 'transaction costs' mentioned above and transcending traditional implementation problems. As Scharpf (1993: 129) states 'the famous Coase Theorem demonstrates that all welfare gains achievable through ideal hierarchical co-ordination can also be captured through voluntary contracts between autonomous and purely self-interested actors'. Hence, regulation does not have to take a statutory or legislative form: 'it can also be achieved by delegating responsibilities to private or semi-private bodies, in which case one speaks of self-regulation' (Majone, 1996: 23).

What are the advantages of the voluntary approach in the overall context of a complex and difficult process of European policy making? The straightforward answer is that the voluntary approach presents clear advantages for both policy makers and implementers alike. First, it can help fulfil environmental objectives in a cost-effective manner in so far as it encourages industry to modify its behaviour more profoundly over time by offering incentives instead of simply depending on the implementation of 'hard law' which in any case creates the need for costly bureaucratic intervention. Second, sectoral-based voluntary agreements can offer a more sound and feasible basis for environmental policy in that they are specifically related to identifiable and relevant target groups and can also be based on more complete and feasible information gathered from their particular sector. In this way sectoral-based voluntary agreements can lessen the need for the sort of detailed and complex legislation that has contributed to the implementation gap and avoid the sort of problems associated with applying vague and 'holistic' legislation which is unable to take account of sectoral and national characteristics. Third, by developing more realistic targets instead of setting down unrealistic blanket standards, it gives business more chance of being able to comply with policy objectives. Moreover, the costs of reneging from voluntary deals can be born directly by the guilty parties for whom reputation is an important asset in sectoral networks. Fourth, the voluntary approach can help apply existing legislation at the 'street level' and therefore lessens the need for complex implementation and monitoring processes. Overall, the voluntary approach can be more suited to the complex nature of contemporary environmental policy making than a purely top–down legislative approach, which in any case has proven to be time consuming, costly and burdensome.

On the basis of the above points, we could conclude that the voluntary approach is much less likely to lead to traditional implementation deficits and has more capacity to overcome and circumvent implementation problems than 'programmed implementation', which since the late 1970s has assumed 'that implementation problems can be made tolerable, if not eliminated, by careful and explicit pre-programming of implementation procedures' (Berman, 1980: 205). The voluntary approach seems more suited to resolving such problems because it is based on more 'adaptive implementation', meaning that it 'allows policy to be modified, specified and revised – in a word, adapted – according to the unfolding interaction of the policy with its institutional setting' (p. 210). It can lead to more flexible and effective self-regulation which may be better suited to fulfilling regulatory aims and objectives.

Notwithstanding these advantages, however, it should not be overlooked that also the voluntary approach suffers from certain weaknesses, which are avoided by applying a legislative concept of regulation. Thus, surveys show that unless there is some form of democratic accountability and monitoring by governing institutions, or involvement by other actors such as environmental and consumer NGOs, they will lack credibility and be distrusted by the public.[8] Moreover, complete reliance on voluntary policy instruments is too dependent on market variables. Just as companies act to improve environmental performance in order to benefit from potential market incentives, so they also act to save money, which means being far less environmentally pro-active when market downturns dictate. In periods of recession therefore, environmental policy may all but disappear if it relies too much on a voluntary approach. Of course there is also the 'free riders' problem: some actors will take advantage of the short term losses experienced by competitors involved in voluntary policies, or enjoy the same benefits from the costs incurred by their participants. Finally, reliance on the voluntary approach will lead to a very uneven playing field, which has very important implications also for other policy areas.

The legislative approach, by contrast, contains a set of recognisable policy objectives and can therefore be relatively straightforward to interpret and enforce. Their uniformity means that legislative instruments help create a 'level playing field' upon which all policy actors face the same set of constraints and opportunities. In this way they help complete the internal market. Compliance can also be determined and demonstrated. Despite these apparent advantages, it is still far from certain whether they are suited to the particular requirements of environmental regulation?

Table 5.1 provides a succinct summary of the various strengths and weaknesses of both approaches, indicating that – taking both concepts from an ideal-type perspective – they are characterised by opposing strengths and weaknesses; hence indicating that the choice of adopting one approach over another is far from simple.

Table 5.1 *Strengths and weaknesses of the legislative and voluntary approaches to environmental regulation*

Strengths	Weaknesses
Legislative approach	*Legislative approach*
1 Consistency and uniformity	1 Potential of confrontation and resistance in policy formulation and implementation
2 Clear objectives	2 Requires much 'enacting' legislation
3 Easy compliance and monitoring	3 Static and inflexible
4 Guarantees regulatory activity	4 No encouragement to go beyond minimum requirements: reactive
	5 Costly and burdensome administration
Voluntary approach	*Voluntary approach*
1 Less confrontation and resistance in policy formulation and implementation	1 Can lead to inconsistency
2 Low legislatory requirements	2 Problematic monitoring
3 Flexibility	3 Does not guarantee regulatory activity
4 Target-/context-orientation	4 Problem of 'free riders'
5 Encourages innovation by incentives	
6 Based on technically specialised knowledge	

In view of this constellation of mutual advantages and disadvantages, it becomes evident that the voluntary approach is no panacea to EU environmental policy's implementation deficit. In this light, the crucial question seems not to replace the regulatory approach by voluntary concepts, but to reform existing regulatory concepts by making use of synergy effects between of the strengths of both ideal-type concepts.

This aspect is further underlined by the fact that the application of a particular approach is unlikely to fit neatly into any of the above 'ideal-type' scenarios. The distinctions between both approaches are not so strict, and their inherent strengths and weaknesses will depend on how they are operationalised in the EU environmental policy context. Thus, it has to be emphasised that both concepts are still *regulatory* approaches: they simply apply different means for the attainment of very similar ends. Any policy which attempts to make regulation work better must therefore be viewed as forming part of a strategy of 'regulatory reform' (Majone, 1990 and 1996), rather than amounting to de-regulation. Any debate about the application of voluntary concepts simply concerns seeing how policy can 'achieve the relevant regulatory objectives by less burdensome methods of governmental intervention' (Majone, 1990: 3). Just as the 'primary rationale for regulation ... is to remedy various kinds of market failure' (Kay and Vickers, 1990: 225), so the rationale for re-regulation is to remedy regulatory failure, which would include for example, poor or ineffective implementation. The Commission's attempts to improve environmental law-making provides an example of regulatory reform just as much as the application of a more voluntary approach to environmental regulation. It is therefore mistaken to see the legislative and the voluntary approach as diametrically opposed to one other: each is but one side of the regulatory coin.

Indeed, our focus on the EU Ecolabel Award Scheme provides a very good case study of how environmental policy instruments can contain aspects of both approaches, but also suffer from implementation problems resulting from a failure to successfully integrate or combine the aspects of both. It shows that in the reality of the EU policy making process, there is no strict dichotomy between the legislative and voluntary approach, just as there is no strict dichotomy between 'top–down' or 'bottom–up' implementation, or 'programmed' and 'adaptive' implementation (or indeed 'de-regulation' and 're-regulation'). Features of both are always present in policy making. The implementation experience of the EU Ecolabel Award Scheme provides an excellent case not just of how difficult it is to achieve a successful combination of the strengths of both approaches, but also of the implementation problems that can result from the failure to do so.

The EU Ecolabel Award Scheme: legislative or voluntary?

This section briefly traces the background to the EU Ecolabel Award Scheme, and provides an overview of the principles and guidelines which underpin the scheme, as well as the implementation problems it has faced up to 1997. As we shall see, it is a hybrid policy instrument. During its first five years it faced many implementation problems, which are similar to those normally associated with the more traditional legislative approach. This can be explained by the fact that although it is a voluntary policy instrument emanating from the new approach set down in the 5th EAP, it has also developed very much within a more traditionally regulatory context. However, despite this more traditionally regulatory appearance, which is marked not only by the fact that it is based on EU legislation, but also by the central role played by institutions such as the Commission, regulatory committees and Member State competent bodies, it must still be seen as emanating from the voluntary approach. It aims to promote and develop more environmentally aware behaviour in a gradual way over time by using pro-active incentives, and is recognised by the 5th EAP as being an important market-based tool which can 'target' industry and help promote shared responsibility among economic and social actors. No market actor has to participate in the scheme in any way whatsoever unless it chooses to do so. Indeed, even if business actors decide to become involved in the preliminary and preparatory phases, they can withdraw from the scheme later on and do not have to apply for labels for product groups for which criteria have been developed in those early phases.

Background and content of the Ecolabel Award Scheme
The idea to develop a European-wide Ecolabel was prompted by the existence of the *Blauer Engel* Scheme in Germany which had been set up in 1978. It also originated from the perceived need to harmonise the variety of national labels, which could be seen as

creating obstacles to the smooth and effective operation of the single market.[9] Moreover, concern expressed about contaminated products after the Chernobyl disaster in 1986 provided salient demands for government action to provide better information on product safety.[10] Finally, a public policy response to the multiple growth of unaccountable private ecolabels with a potential for misleading consumers, was deemed necessary. In this way the EU Ecolabel is an example of both a consumer and an environmental policy output.

Many problems were experienced during the drafting of the Commission Proposal[11] relating to the extent to which the scheme would be centralised and coordinated in the Commission, as well as how its relationship with diverging national priorities would be established and harmonised. For example, the main interest groups representing industry, consumers and environmentalists called for a more decentralised system.[12] The European Parliament insisted that a mechanism be included for the full involvement at the earliest stages of all social groups and stakeholders in the scheme. As a result, the Council adopted a regulation in March 1992, whereby competent bodies at Member State level and the various interest groups at the European level were given more of a substantial role than was initially envisaged. From the beginning therefore, there were 'identity problems': namely, was it to be more 'top–down' regulatory in appearance, or 'bottom–up' voluntary?

Council Regulation 880/92/EEU itself, which sets up the Ecolabel Award Scheme, has three objectives. First and foremost, it is intended to promote products, which have a reduced environmental impact during their entire life cycle. Second, it is designed to inform consumers about both the quality and the environmental impact of the product both of which are intended to reinforce each other to form what can be termed as a 'sustainability cycle'. In other words, as consumers reward the more environmentally friendly producers, so those producers compete to manufacture the least damaging products and therefore potentially increase their market share. The third objective of the scheme is to eventually overcome the competition of national awards. Its more general aim is to:

> gradually allow an improvement of products by giving a recognition bonus to those which are more favourable to the environment. The best information for the consumer is an essential element in his or her purchasing decision. The Ecolabel will make an effective contribution to performing this task at Community level in the joint interests of

consumers and the environment. The European Ecolabel will avoid competition between different national labels which could send out contradictory signals to consumers in the wider market.[13]

The scheme is valid for all products apart from food, drink and pharmaceuticals. Products imported into the EU from third countries are also eligible for the award. The criteria developed refer to product groups rather than single products: that is, products defined as serving similar purposes. The scheme is also governed by a set of policy, procedural and methodological guidelines. These guidelines are not legally binding. Instead they were designed to assist the Commission 'in its task of systematically monitoring the work carried out by the parties involved in the establishment of product groups and ecological criteria and… assist as a lead competent body by providing a framework to organise and conduct its activities through a systematic and objective approach'[14] Taken together they illustrate an attempt by the Commission to set down the 'rules of the game' governing the operation of the EU Ecolabel.

The rules governing the scheme are made up of three sets of principles and guidelines. First, the policy principles outline the policy objectives and aims and provide the underlying rationale for the scheme. Second, the procedural guidelines set down the practical mechanisms which operate the scheme. Third, the methodological guidelines underpin the way in which ecolabelling criteria should be developed ecologically. We shall now outline and examine the problems that have been experienced in the implementation of these principles and guidelines, which have caused difficulties for the operation of the scheme itself.

Implementation problems: ambiguity, complexity, inconsistency and confusion

With regard to the policy principles which frame and determine the very nature of the Ecolabel Scheme as a policy instrument, one generic problem has never been resolved, but has proven to be important in helping explain some of the difficulties that have been experienced the scheme's implementation. That is, there has been a certain amount of ambiguity concerning whether it is primarily an environmental or a consumer policy instrument, or even a product policy instrument. There are many aspects of the scheme that would lead us to conclude that it is in fact all three of these: it aims to limit environmental damage and guide production and consumption patterns in a more sustainable direction; it aims to provide consumers with information and insists that ecolabelled products must be fit for consumer use; and, it has important implications for product design. Given these features, there has been a lack of clarity among the principal actors as to what the aims of the scheme actually are, which has led to policy confusion.[15] More specifically, the ambiguity has hampered the development of consensus and development of a cohesive stakeholder approach which has led to varying degrees of fragmentation and even conflict.[16]

Complexity and rigidity   More explicitly, one central element of the policy principles relates to the scheme's methodology when it is stated that criteria development must follow a 'cradle to grave' approach, which means that consideration should not be limited to the intrinsic characteristics of the product, but also to how the product is actually produced. Moreover, all stages of the product's life must be taken into account: namely, pre-production, production, distribution, utilisation and disposal. In addition, all environmental aspects for each stage must be considered when developing the criteria's parameters. Gradually, (but with difficulty) a methodological framework based on Life Cycle Assessment (LCA) was developed in order to operationalise the 'cradle to grave' approach. However, it did not solve the problem of actually making the scheme's methodology work successfully. A number of problems persisted partly because its role as a 'decision support tool' was exaggerated. It was not the methodology itself which led to the problems, but rather the original (political) decision to develop such an extensive analysis of the product's life cycle and at the same time the attempt to include all of the environmental aspects. At its most simple level, the scheme tried to do too much too soon and this directly led to early implementation problems.

First, the length of time required to develop and apply the 'cradle to grave' approach using an as yet untried methodology, created problems in completing the scheme's various procedural guidelines. For example, it took three years for Germany to complete the LCA studies for detergents. Given that the Commission had hoped to award the first labels by the end of 1992, the sense of failure that set in from the very start was tangible. It also became apparent that application of LCA as a scientific methodology was not free from political disputes. For example, Ireland objected to the exclusion of peat-based soil improvers from the soil improvers product group due to the importance in Ireland of the peat industry and Denmark was accused of developing LCA in a way that was biased towards specific manufacturing conditions in Scandinavia. Political rivalries between Member States therefore undermined the objective application of LCA methodology. Also, because there were no uniform definitions of LCA, many disputes developed regarding technical data and the compatibility of ecological and fitness for use criteria. In most cases, industry argued that ecological criteria would undermine product quality and therefore decrease their market share. The misplaced faith in the use of LCA therefore helped drag the scheme into a maze of political and technical difficulties from which it did not recover.

Confrontation and resistance   The inclusion of production process characteristics created immense problems. European industry was dissatisfied that criteria took into account production process characteristics as it obliged manufacturers to continue modifying production techniques which would in any case be revised every three years. As a result, the Confederation of European Paper Industries (CEPI) withdrew from the development of criteria for the fine paper product and a bizarre situation developed whereby the long process of criteria setting continued even though industry had clearly stated that it would not participate in the scheme.

Even greater problems developed with the North American paper industry who argued that there had been a lack of transparency and equality of treatment in comparison to European industry.[17] Moreover, it complained that the criteria were discriminatory against non-EU traders and so represented a trade barrier and an infringement of the GATT principles, as they referred to characteristics of a production process, which were not present in North America and so would not be able to be met by North American industry meaning that their access to European markets would be closed. This issue brought to the fore a problem, which would persist and gain greater importance as the scheme developed: namely, doubts over the compatibility of the EU Ecolabel with the GATT.[18] The relevance of this is that these doubts have not only created policy uncertainty but have opened the scheme to accusations that the criteria were based on political choices rather than a sound scientific basis and this situation undermined the credibility of the scheme as a serious environmental policy instrument. In total therefore, over-reliance on an untested and highly time-consuming methodology whose application has led to doubts about the scheme's credibility, has had a negative effect on the operation and implementation of the scheme.

Inconsistency and lack of uniformity   Another policy principle states that the scheme's ecological criteria should help achieve high levels of environmental protection – a principle which conforms with the aims of the 5th EAP and article 130r of the Treaty. To ensure adequate environmental protection, criteria from product group selection are identified: for example, environmental relevance; use of natural resources; interest among consumers; and, interest from industry and other relevant groups. These aspects also help ensure market relevance which is essential if ecolabelled products are to make any impact on existing production and consumer patterns.

In many ways, this principle was not implemented properly; in the sense that the selection of product groups for inclusion in the scheme at the start was haphazard and mainly influenced by the Member State competent bodies who were later accused of selecting product groups which were relevant primarily to industries in their own countries. Furthermore, the technical difficulties and potential for Member State rivalries and industry–environment conflicts were largely overlooked. The fact that LCA and the 'cradle to grave' approach were unrefined as a methodology was therefore not the only reason that there were long delays in the completion of studies and draft criteria. Another important reason lay in the fact that some of the product groups had been badly selected. In 1995, the Commission refined its approach to this problem, by setting down a more explicit matrix of goals which were to determine product group selection. Moreover, in the summer of 1995, product group selection and feasibility studies were opened up via calls for tender published in the *Official Journal*.

Over-specialisation and lack of innovation: 'environmental elitism'
Another important policy principle which also led to conflicts, concerns limiting the market share of ecolabelled products to approximately 10–15 per cent, in order to ensure that ecolabelling is selective and encourages competition among industry towards higher levels of environmental protection. From the very start

however, industry expressed misgivings about this principle. Singling out a percentage of products on the market, which correspond not only to a high level of environmental protection but, relatively speaking, to the highest, was not popular with producers for the simple reason that the initial effort required was off-putting and would not in any case guarantee getting the label. Moreover, industry adopted a principled stance against encouraging competition based on best environmental performance. Accusing the scheme of elitism not only undermined its credibility, but also hampered the application of its very *raison d'être*: namely, to award environmentally sustainable behaviour in the marketplace.

Poor stakeholder ownership   The final important principle relates to transparency, which is important not just because of the requirements of the 5th EAP. It was also included so that the important interest groups (or stakeholders) could be fully involved. It also aimed to deal with the international dimension in that importers into the EU were also permitted to apply for the award. It did not however make any reference to the GATT question. Transparency was to be provided by ensuring an open consultation process as constituted by the Consultation Forum, whose opinion on the draft criteria was included in the final dossier voted upon by the Regulatory Committee made up of Member States. While the forum was able to ensure open access to and provision of information, its operation has been hampered by a lack of clarity between the technical and political roles of the consultation process and the lack of cohesiveness between the stakeholders involved.

Poor coordination   With regard to the scheme's procedural guidelines, yet more problematic aspects existed. We have already discussed the difficulties concerning phase one of these guidelines which concern the problems attached to product group selection, and the difficulty of applying LCA which concerns phases two, three and four. We shall therefore now only discuss phases five and six, which concern setting the criteria and the presentation of the draft proposal for passing of the Commission Decision.

Phase five of the process directly relates to the decision making procedure engaged in by the Commission for setting criteria, and as with the preparation of any Commission Decision, 'DG XI engages internal Commission consultations and procedures with a view to presenting a draft decision to the Regulatory Committee'.[19] Many problems have been experienced during this phase due to policy differences and problems of effective coordination between the various Directorates General (depending on the product groups in question). The drafting of the criteria by the Commission has been very delayed in several cases due to difficulties in reaching agreement on the criteria among the DGs concerned: a situation which not only underlines the fact that the Commission is not a monolithic institution, but also epitomises the more traditionally regulatory nature of the EU ecolabelling decision making process. Such delays meant that on many occasions the presentation of the Draft Commission Decision to the Regulatory Committee was postponed. Decision making in the Regulatory Committee itself, was also very problematic. Voting is based on a weighted procedure as in the Council of Ministers[20] and therefore discussions (which were confidential) in this committee resembled both the political bargaining and the delays that are experienced in the Council itself. In this sense, the Ecolabel Scheme's procedures duplicated those very same problems that the voluntary approach is aimed at circumventing and which are found in more legislative examples of EU environmental regulation. Given the reliance on passing a Commission Decision, such problems were neither surprising nor insurmountable, but were heightened by two supplementary problems.

Bottom–up problems: the national dimension   First, some Member States sitting in the committee had not even set up their competent bodies.[21] For example, Ireland, Italy, Belgium and Luxembourg were represented in the committee's proceedings by civil servants from standardisation bodies or the Ministries of Environment who had no experience with ecolabelling, and little or no administrative support from their Member States. A rather uneven situation therefore developed whereby a core group of Member States effectively exerted more influence and authority in the adoption of the draft criteria. Germany, the UK, France and Denmark for example carried out virtually all of the studies, and set the pace for the remaining members of the committee. Second, when Austria, Sweden and Finland joined the EU in January 1995, and took up their seats in the committee, the situation became more complicated. Not only was it the case that three new governmental actors were fully admitted into the operational structure of the scheme, but more importantly, all three were actors with strong environmental policy strategies based on high levels of protection. More specifically, they all had their own ecolabel schemes, which in the case of the Nordic *White Swan*, were based on demanding ecological criteria. Therefore delays were usually exacerbated because these new members argued that the draft criteria were not at a high enough level of environmental protection. Such delays added to the pressure on the scheme, which in 1994 had already been severely criticised by the Environmental Council of October for not progressing fast enough.

In sum, problems during this decision making phase of the scheme were three-fold. First, coordination problems within the Commission services led to delays in the presentation of draft criteria to the Regulatory Committee; second, bargaining practices and disputes became more difficult after the 1995 enlargement; and, third an uneven situation developed in the sense that northern countries had much more influence than southern ones – a development, which undermined the credibility of the EU Ecolabel as a European-wide policy instrument.

Top–down centralisation   After the presentation of the draft Decision by the Regulatory Committee, phase six of the procedural guidelines concerns the formal adoption of the Commission Decision. Based on article 7(3) of the Regulation, 'the Commission engages the necessary internal procedures to establish a formal decision with a view to adopting the decision voted on by the Regulatory Committee'. While this final step was originally envisaged as being something of a formality, the contrary was in fact often the case. There have been many examples when draft Decisions presented to the College of Commissioners have been delayed or rejected by certain Commissioners and/or their cabinets. For example, Delors blocked the final approval of the criteria for toilet paper, paper kitchen towels and soil improvers in 1994 for six months; the adoption of the draft criteria for paints and varnishes were held up until December 1995 because of Swedish concern about permitted use of organic solvents; and, the dossier on single-ended light bulbs was postponed due to Danish concerns over mercury levels.

These delays directly contravened the Ecolabel Regulation, which clearly states in article 7(3) that 'the Commission shall adopt the measures envisaged if they are in accordance with the opinion of the committee', while 7(4) says that 'if the measures envisaged are not in accordance with the opinion of the committee... the Commission shall, without delay, submit to the Council a proposal relating to the measures to be taken'. In practice, this did not happen and the delays and uncertainty, which followed, severely undermined the credibility of the scheme.

In addition to the credibility problems, questions were increasingly asked about what the role of the Commission in the scheme was and should be. It seemed extremely incongruous that a bottom–up voluntary policy instrument designed to be flexible, was in reality being undermined by the problems it was supposed to circumvent in the first place: namely, complex, slow, costly and burdensome decision making procedures. The Commission's role was originally envisaged as being that of a broker and arbiter, as well as manager and supporter of the process. It was not envisaged that the Commission would have any say in defining the technical content of the criteria. However, such a scenario was in fact impossible given the complexity and incoherence of the procedural guidelines, and most importantly, the fact that since the ecolabel criteria were to be legally based on a Commission Decision, the usual problems associated with the legislative approach would develop.

Summary

When we consider the complexity, uncertainty and inconsistency of the scheme's objectives, principles and procedures, we can understand better why so many of the problems outlined above actually occurred and why the balance sheet of the EU Ecolabel Award Scheme over its first five year period cannot be measured in a positive light. Add the problematic nature of the rules governing the scheme to the fact that it has had to operate within the slow and complex environment of EU policy making, and we can see that not only is the EU Ecolabel a hybrid instrument but one that has suffered the disadvantages of the legislative approach without really enjoying the advantages of the voluntary approach to environmental regulation, which were outlined in section one. In addition, there have also been the problems usually associated with environmental policy in general: namely, a high level of technical and scientific complexity. However, the fact that so few ecolabels were available and they were invisible in the marketplace over the first five years of its life, was not only due to its legislative approach aspects. Its voluntary nature has also caused problems.

Despite the complexity of the scheme and the multiplicity of actors involved, the participation of industry was crucial to the scheme's success. Criticism has been levelled at the scheme because there has been a very low visibility of ecolabelled products. This visibility in turn depends on applications for awards from industry. However, industry's participation has on the whole been extremely lacklustre. At virtually all stages of the process, industry has refused to cooperate as a partner in the process. In nearly all instances, it has stated that it disagrees with the definition of a product group, that the approach being developed via LCA and Production Process Methods (PPM) is not scientifically based, that the ecological criteria are undermining the fitness of the product for use, and consequently, that it is going to boycott the scheme. In effect the scheme, because it is voluntary, has been held hostage to both the real and threatened veto from industry. This situation has been allowed to continue because of the failure to build adequate mechanisms to prevent industry from abusing its centrality to the scheme in this way.

We have noted the existence and permeation of the following problems. First, the fact that it is a market-based instrument, attempting to change the behaviour of a wide variety of market actors, has resulted in a certain level of complexity and a difficulty in application because it is not aimed at a clear or cohesive set of target groups given that it aims to establish quasi-sectoral agreements by using top–down mechanisms. Specifically, many problems have been experienced in the important area of building commitment and 'ownership' of the scheme: for example, the development of a 'stakeholder' approach operating 'shared responsibility' has been very problematic indeed. This aspect is of considerable importance as it relates centrally to one of the main advantages potentially associated with voluntary instruments. Second, the complexity of the procedural guidelines and the fact that over-centralised procedures have governed the operation of the scheme has led to problems resulting from what can be termed as burdensome and time consuming administrative rules which lack flexibility. Third, there have been problems due to a lack of consideration during the setting up of the scheme and the formulation of the Ecolabel Regulation, of existing ecolabel schemes and methodologies, as well as a lack of clarity about compatibility with international trade. Fourth, there has been the centrally important problem of reneging as exemplified by a lack of applications from industry for awards. This problem has persisted due to the absence of efficient ex-ante negotiation and the lack of potential in the procedural guidelines for ex-post re-negotiation.

Conclusion

This chapter has outlined the nature of the implementation deficit that is associated usually with what we have termed as the legislative approach to EU environmental regulation, and it has shown how an attempt has been made by the 5th EAP to overcome and circumvent this deficit by developing a strategy of regulatory reform which partially consists of applying a more flexible bottom–up voluntary approach to policy making. Regarding this attempt to deal with environmental policy implementation problems, we have drawn up a comparison of the relative strengths and weaknesses of both approaches and shown how in fact they are not dichotomous. Rather, they often and indeed inevitably overlap, given that they both stem from regulatory policy and are developed and applied within a regulatory context. In outlining and examining the nature of the EU Ecolabel Award Scheme and the implementation problems it has experienced during its first five or six years, I have shown how the EU Ecolabel is without doubt a hybrid policy instrument combining elements and features of both approaches, which has experienced so many problems because of its crucial failure to combine their advantages and strengths. Indeed, in many ways this voluntary policy instrument has actually resembled more of a legislative policy output. We shall now conclude by asking what does all this tell us about the implementation of voluntary environmental policy instruments?

First, we can see that without any doubt at all, they can never be completely voluntary. The case of the EU Ecolabel is possibly quite an extreme example of this, but nevertheless it shows that policy instruments, which aim to move away from more traditional legislative instruments in the attempt to develop more gradualistic and voluntaristic results, are always developed and applied within regulatory contexts, and also acquire many of the features of more traditionally regulatory instruments. Second, a voluntary approach, which relies so heavily on regulatory mechanisms, will face important dilemmas and problems that will be of detriment to its successful implementation. In particular, attempts to implement what can be called a 'framework' voluntary instrument from the top down, such as the EU Ecolabel Award Scheme, across the whole of the EU, in a variety of highly different markets and without any clear or cohesive target groups coordinated together in recognisable policy networks, do not enjoy the advantages of more explicitly voluntary policy instruments, which are more sectoral and less complex in nature. Third, while certain aspects of the legislative approach may be both unavoidable and indeed beneficial, they should not be allowed to outweigh the strengths of adopting a voluntary approach in the first place as happened with the EU Ecolabel. The best chance of implementing voluntary environmental policy instruments effectively in order to avoid the usual implementation problems would be to not only combine the strengths of both approaches but also to streamline the regulatory procedures that can strip voluntary instruments of their flexibility, dynamism and ability to adapt quickly to market demands and changes. In short, what is needed is the creation of an effective process of horizontal coordination that binds the relevant actors together in a framework of more self-regulatory networks. Fourth, while the problematic experience of the EU Ecolabel Award Scheme has not contributed to EU environmental policy's implementation deficit in so far as it has not required the same processes of transposal, implementation, enforcement and monitoring, which is required of EU Directives, it has still experienced the sort of problems associated with the legislative approach. Fifth, given all of the above, one has to question the capacity of policy instruments such as the EU Ecolabel to overcome and circumvent the traditional implementation gap. It seems that on the evidence presented it has a limited capacity in lessening the need for a continued reliance on the legislative approach. If it cannot develop the necessary conditions upon which voluntary instruments depend for their success (such as streamlined procedures), then perhaps the enthusiasm for applying them is exaggerated. In any case, the voluntary approach to EU environmental policy making still lives on the periphery in comparison to the legislative approach. Given this, we can only conclude therefore that the Commission's attempts to overcome the implementation problem would be better served by concentrating on improving the way in which EU environmental law is made.

This does not mean however that efforts cannot be made to also improve voluntary policy instruments, and this is exactly what the Commission has been attempting to do with its revision of the scheme which is at present under way. In accordance with article 18 of Council Regulation 880/92, which states that within five years of coming into force, the Ecolabel Scheme should be reviewed and if necessary amended in order to improve its operation, the European Commission began a review in 1996 and officially presented a Commission Proposal to that effect in December 1996.[22] The Commission has accepted the fact that the scheme's successful implementation has been burdened by a criteria-setting procedure which is administratively too centralised and slow, as outlined and discussed above. It recognises that decision making responsibilities have been confused and that immense difficulty has been experienced in coordinating the inputs from Member State competent bodies, relevant European interest groups and the various Commission services. However, it still views ecolabelling as having a role to play in directing market behaviour in a more sustainable direction. Therefore, it has proposed to modify and simplify the way in which the scheme operates in an attempt to improve its effectiveness as a policy instrument.

Quite simply, the Commission Proposal represents a political acceptance of the principle of ecolabelling; a realisation that despite the problems experienced so far, it must remain as a voluntary scheme; and, a determination to streamline its procedures, thereby reducing the regulatory baggage that has stunted its development. The main areas of proposed change are as follows.

First, to clarify what the underlying principles and purpose of the scheme are it set out more clearly what it is trying to achieve so that the confusion about what sort of policy instrument it is can be overcome. Second, the Commission hopes to increase the visibility and profile of the scheme in the market, by introducing a graded label which will replace the previous pass/fail system with a more flexible system which will invite more applications from industry as well as providing better information to the consumer. Third, it wants to streamline and clarify the procedural guidelines applied to operate the scheme. A central part of this relates to the proposed setting up of a new independent ecolabelling body, which will function along the same lines as the Committee for European Normalisation (CEN), under mandate by the Commission, and thereby avoid the need for the burdensome decision making procedures which the

Commission has had to try to coordinate. An attempt at decentralisation has therefore been made. Indeed, the Commission has been heavily criticised by Member States for 'disowning' the scheme rather than just attempting to decentralise it. It is also proposed that the consultation of interest groups should be changed. Fourth, the proposal also aims to ensure the compatibility between the EU Ecolabel and international trade agreements and standards.

These areas deal quite explicitly with attempting to solve the problems that have existed in the implementation of the scheme so far. Quite simply, it can be seen that they amount to an attempt to hold on to the voluntary nature of the scheme while at the same reducing the more traditionally regulatory aspects. A more efficient linkage between the two approaches is therefore being attempted. However, while the technical attempts to improve the efficiency of the scheme can be noted, the politics of the scheme's revision continue.

To date, the Commission's Proposal for revising the scheme has largely failed. First, the European Parliament voted a series of amendments to the proposal in May 1998, which called for its key elements to be substantially changed. The Commission had already attracted fundamental criticism from EU Member States in autumn 1997 for its idea that national labels should eventually be phased out for products. And the Parliament's Opinion went on to specifically state that any phaseout of national ecolabels should take place only if an independent study showed that the EU Ecolabel's criteria for a product were 'at least as strict as the best national ecolabel scheme'. Indeed, such a recommendation can be traced to the potential for conflict between EU and national environmental policy making contained in article 130r and 130t (Amsterdam articles 174 and 176).

The European Parliament also rejected the Commission's proposal to introduce a graded label containing up to three flowers for those products analysed as being less harmful to the environment. Of particular importance in terms of the operation of the scheme, it also opposed handing responsibility for criteria setting to a CEN-type body proposed as the European Ecolabel Organisation (EEO). Instead it proposed the setting up of a technical committee on ecolabelling which would be made up of national ecolabel officials under the guidance of the Commission. Whether or not this suggestion would really amount to much more than a change of name to the Regulatory Committee currently in operation is a moot point, however.

In June 1998, the EU Environment Council also voiced its unequivocal opposition to the main points of the Commission's Proposal. Following on from this, the Environment Commissioner Ritt Bjerregaard indicated that the Commission would comprehensively revise its original proposal in light of the Parliament and Council's rejection of its proposal to set up an EEO and phase out national labels. Hence in autumn 1998, DG XI held two workshops with Member State officials and stakeholders with the intention of coming through with new proposals. By December 1998 (two full years after the proposal had originally been published), DG XI officially decided to move away from its original proposal on the basis that it simply had no support and was therefore not going to take off or fly. Two main weak points were identified as being or particular importance in changing DG XI's mind. First, the attempt to achieve a gradual phase-out of national ecolabels in the end seemed too much like an enforced top–down approach from the Commission, which was cutting out the participation of those actors already running national schemes who had been actively involved in running the EU scheme right from the start. Second, it was felt that the Commission should not step away from the scheme. Streamlining the scheme's procedures was one thing but the Commission did not want to be seen as reneging from its commitment to its operation. In any case the idea of a CEN-type body operating the EU Ecolabel Award Scheme was never really seen as being appropriate, given the differences between standardisation and ecolabelling. The EU Environment Council in June 1999 is due to reach a common position on the Commission's minimalist revision of its original proposal. Meanwhile, a Green Paper on Integrated Product Policy (IPP) is also being prepared and is due for the end of 1999.

The fact that the Commission's attempt to revise the scheme itself has even been delayed and changed shows us that if the EU Ecolabel Scheme is both a legislative regulatory and a voluntary regulatory policy instrument. It is also still above all a political instrument, the reform of which is bound to attract political debates and conflicts and the resolution of which are still far from clear cut.

Notes

1 I would like to thank the editors of this book for their patience and direction of this work.

2 *Official Journal* C328/2, 7. 12. 87.
3 Council Regulation (EEC) No. 880/92 of 23 March 1992 on a Community Ecolabel Award Scheme, *Official Journal* L 99, 11. 4. 92.
4 Thirteenth Annual Report on Monitoring the Application of Community Law, 1995. *Official Journal* C 303, 14.10.96.
5 See Commission Communication entitled 'Implementing Community Environmental Law', COM (96) 500, 22.10.96.
6 The origin of transaction–cost analysis is generally traced to the work of Ronald Coase (1960) who analysed the importance of transaction costs in all forms of coordination and showed that a particular form of contracting will be chosen if its transaction costs are lower than another form. Williamson (1985) has identified the difference between ex-ante and ex-post transaction costs. Quite simply, the term itself can be defined as the costs involved with making policy and operating institutions (see Cheung, 1983).
7 The Commission Communication mentioned above, sets down a strategy for improving the implementation of EU environmental legislation.
8 The European Environmental Bureau (EEB) has presented results from a survey showing that environmental protection associations with 35 per cent are the most trusted by the public as a reliable information source on the state of the environment; scientists have 19 per cent; consumer associations have 16 per cent; and industry has 10 per cent; (EEB, Brussels).
9 It was also supported from the very start by the European industry interest group European Union of Employers Confederation (UNICE) for this reason. This aspect has also led the European Parliament to argue for the extension of the legal base of the Ecolabel Regulation (currently limited to article 130s) to article 100a (internal market and codecision making).
10 It is within this context that the development and application of a product-oriented approach in environmental policy making can be placed.
11 *Official Journal* C 75, 20. 3. 1991.
12 The European Consumers Organisation (BEUC) and the European Environmental Bureau (EEB) requested that they be made full members of any committee set up to advise the Commission on deciding which products would be included in the scheme, and how the criteria would be developed and awarded. They requested the right to object or even veto any Commission decision. While such powers were not in fact granted, these groups were permitted to provide their input to the scheme via the Consultation Forum which was established under article 6 of the Ecolabel Regulation (Agence Europe 5520, 26 June 1991).
13 Commissioner for the Environment, Yannis Paleokrassas, quoted in European Commission Newsletter on the EU Ecolabel, Issue No. 3.
14 *European Commission Information on Ecolabelling*, Issue No. 5.

15 See Smith and Potter (1996) who outline the ways in which this confusion has hampered the successful implementation of the scheme.
16 A stakeholder analysis of the Ecolabel Scheme refers to any actor or groups of actors who can affect the operation of the scheme and who are critical to its success. See Evan (1993) and Mitroff (1983).
17 'The pulp and paper industries of Canada, the US and Brazil have repeatedly requested an opportunity for a genuine exchange of technical information without any success whatsoever. It follows that whatever results from this process, will not reflect the best scientific information and knowledge required. The EU process should clearly be opened up to participation by non-EU interest groups', Brian McClay of the Canadian Pulp and Paper Association. Quoted in Silvia Calamandrei and Robert Wright, *The EU Ecolabel Award Scheme: Aspects and Implications for Third Countries*, publication for the Economic and Social Committee of the EC, 1994.
18 For a fuller discussion of the implications for trade of environmental measures such as ecolabelling see Kuilwijk and Wright (1996).
19 *European Commission Information on Ecolabelling*, Issue No. 5.
20 As laid down in article 148(2) of the Treaty.
21 Under the Ecolabel Regulation, Member States were legally obliged to constitute the competent bodies within six months of the Regulation coming into force.
22 COM 96 (603)

References

Berman, P. (1980) 'Thinking About Programmed and Adaptive Implementation: Matching Strategies to Implementation', in Ingram, H.M. and Mann, D.E. (eds), *Why Policies Succeed or Fail*. Beverly Hills: Sage, pp. 205–27.

Calamandrei, S. and Wright, R. (1994) *The EU Ecolabel Award Scheme: Aspects and Implications for Third Countries*. Publication for the Economic and Social Committee of the EC, Brussels.

Cheung, Steven N.S. (1983) 'The Contractural Nature of the Firm', *Journal of Law and Economics*, 26 (1), 1–21.

Coase, R.H. (1960) 'The Problem of Social Cost', *Journal of Law and Economics*, 3, 1–44.

European Commission (1992) *Towards Sustainability: A European Community Programme of Action in Relation to the Environment and Sustainable Development (Fifth Environmental Action Programme)*, COM (92) 23 final, 27 March, Volume II.

European Parliament (1992) 'Report of the Committee on Environment, Public Health and Consumer Protection on the implementation of Environmental Legislation', Doc. A3–0001/92, PE 152.144, 6 January, Rapporteur: Jacques Vernier.

Evan, W.M. (1993) *Organization Theory: Research and Design*. New York: Macmillan.

House of Lords Select Committee on the European Communities, Session 1991–92, (1992), 9th Report, *Implementation and Enforcement of Environmental Legislation*, March; Volume I: Report (HL 53–I); Volume II: Evidence (HL 53–II).

Kay, John and Vickers, John (1990) 'Regulatory Reform: An Appraisal', in G. Majone (ed.), *Deregulation of Reregulation? Regulatory Reform in Europe and the United States*. London: Pinter, pp. 223–51.

Kuilwijk, Kees-Jan and Wright, Robert (eds) (1996) *European Trade and Industry in the 21st Century: Future Directions in EU Law and Policy*. Beuningen: Nexed Editions Academic Publishers.

Macrory, Richard (1992) 'The Enforcement of Community Environmental Laws: Some Critical Issues', *Common Market Law Review*, 29, 347–69.

Majone, Giandomenico (ed.) (1996) *Regulating Europe*. London: Routledge.

Mazmanian, Daniel and Sabatier, Paul (1983) *Implementation and Public Policy*. Chicago: Scott Foresman and Co.

Mitroff, I.I. (1983) *Stakeholders of the Organizational Mind: Towards a New View of Organizational Policy Making*. San Francisco: Jossey-Bass.

O'Toole, L.J. (1993) 'Multiorganizational Policy Implementation: Some Limitations and Possibilities for Rational-Choice Contributions', in Scharpf, F.W. (ed.), *Games in Hierarchies and Networks: Analytical and Empirical Approaches to the Study of Governance Institutions*. Frankfurt am Main: Campus Verlag GmbH, pp. 27–64.

Pressman, Jeffrey and Wildavsky, Aaron (1973) *Implementation*. Berkeley: University of California Press.

Sabatier, Paul (1986) 'Top–Down and Bottom–Up Approaches to Implementation Research: A Critical Analysis and Suggested Synthesis', *Journal of Public Policy*, 6 (1), 21–48.

Scharpf, Fritz (1993) 'Co-ordination in Hierarchies and Networks', in Scharpf F.W. (ed.), *Games in Hierarchies and Networks: Analytical and Empirical Approaches to the Study of Governance Institutions*. Frankfurt am Main: Campus Verlag, pp. 125–65.

Smith, Mark and Potter, Stephen (1996) 'Ecolabelling and Environmental Policy: Policy Confusion Persists', *Policy Studies*, 17 (1), 72–80.

Von Weizsäcker, Ernst Ulrich (1990) 'Regulatory Reform and the Environment: The Cause for Environmental Taxes', in Majone G. (ed.), *Deregulation or Re-regulation? Regulatory Reform in Europe and the United States*. London: Pinter, pp. 198–200.

Williamson, Oliver E. (1985) *The Economic Institutions of Capitalism: Firms, Markets, Relational Contracting*. New York: Free Press.

Environmental management systems and audits as alternative environmental policy instruments?

Introduction

On the EU level as well as in the Member States it is increasingly recognised that 'command and control' regulatory instruments are not sufficient to ensure improvements in the environmental performance of business and private actors. Implementation failures in the past are one reason for the EU utilising 'new instruments' in its environmental policies. The Ecolabelling Scheme and the Information Directive discussed in other chapters reflect this trend. Here I will more closely examine the implementation and impact of the Environmental Management and Audit Scheme (EMAS).[1]

These policy instruments have in common that they stimulate an improvement of environmental performance on the basis of motives other than only compliance. Such motives are economic benefits or social responsibility. 'Communicative instruments', such as EMAS, stress the social responsibility of corporations; in addition they influence the economic calculus of firms by highlighting environmental costs as well as the cost minimisation potential. Generally, these instruments are no substitute for regulatory and economic ones, but complements, intended to help increase the effectiveness of these other instruments. I will attempt to illustrate the link between different policy instruments as well as show how the design of individual policy instruments affects this complementary dynamic.

Individual firms pose different problems for the environment and they have different potentials for minimising the negative effects and environmental costs for which they are responsible. Uniform 'command and control' measures are rarely capable to take into account case specific opportunities and constraints. This is the great advantage of the EMAS scheme, which allows for a great degree of self-regulation and adaptation. On the firm level, the challenge is not only to take into account the environmental context but also to integrate the scheme in already existing business practices. Because the environmental management systems should stimulate corporations to integrate the environmental factor into the regular management practices these should not remain as stand-alone systems. Rather, the design and implementation of EMAS should fit into existing organisational structures of corporations and be linked with their general management systems. These general management systems are company specific. For example, factors such as company size, type of production process and organisational culture highly influence the characteristics of general management systems.

Of particular relevance are management accounting systems as an integral part of the general management system. These are concerned with providing financial information to persons inside the organisation, especially managers. Typical decisions that require the use of management accounting are cost control, decisions on investments in new technologies (capital budgeting) and the design and marketing of products. Empirical evidence presented in this chapter shows that the link between environmental management systems and accounting systems is increasingly developed in corporations, however it is still weak and needs to be strengthened. Traditional management accounting systems often persist which fail to provide insights into the costs of environmental impacts (such as emissions to water, air and soil).

I argue that the development of environmental accounting systems is particularly important as they provide concrete information about the economic consequences of environmental management and hence increase the effectiveness of regulatory and especially economic environmental instruments. Environmental management systems can stimulate corporations to focus their accounting systems on environmental costs and benefits and suggest cost-optimising strategies. Some empirical findings are presented that explore the relationship between environmental management and management accounting in the Netherlands and in Germany.[2]

This chapter will proceed in the following way: in the next section I present a classification of policy instruments and focus upon EMAS as an example of communicative instruments. The potential as well as limitations in the implementation of these communicative instruments are described. Then I assess the promise of EMAS for the effectiveness of other policy instruments in general terms. Next, I show how an environmental management systems affects the integration of environmental aspects in regular decision making within corporations and pay special attention to the role of accounting systems. Based on these insights the potential effect of EMAS on the effectiveness of regulatory and economic policy instruments is mapped.

Policy instruments and environmental management systems

To achieve environmental policy objectives governments the EU uses a set of policy instruments to influence corporate behaviour. These policy instruments can be classified into three categories (Winsemius 1993):

1 *Regulatory instruments*: by means of direct regulation prescriptions are given to corporate behaviour.
2 *Economic instruments*: these instruments establish financial stimuli, for example subsidies, to influence corporate behaviour (indirect regulation).
3 *Communicative instruments*: through communication governmental authorities try to steer companies by means of self-regulation. The motivation for environmentally friendly behaviour is addressed and the corporate behaviour is expected to change on a voluntary basis.

Governments handle a mix of policy instruments. An exclusive focus on regulatory instruments is increasingly considered unfruitful. For example, in the Netherlands a discussion about self-regulation started in the mid-1980s. Evidence of continuing policy failure, reinforced by critical public opinion, the Queen's unusual intervention in her 1988 Christmas address and the innovative policy style of two subsequent ministers for the environment in the 1980s, triggered closer cooperation between government and business in order to improve environmental performance (Bressers 1997; Weale 1992). Among other things, the Dutch government supported self-regulatory measures such as environmental management systems (EMS) to become formalised in companies. Also in Germany, a country with an even stronger tradition in command-and-control legislation, we perceive a trend towards new environmental instruments. Here, public–private cooperation and leeway for self-regulatory means grow less out of the general rethinking of appropriate policy tools than out of a corporatist tradition now extended to the environmental field (Lenschow 1999; Weidner 1996). Despite initial resistance from government and business, environmental management schemes are spreading rapidly in the German industrial sector.

Turning to the special characteristics of EMS, it is a tool for environmental management and can be defined as: 'a coherent framework of organisational arrangements, containing [environmental] provisions on a personnel and administrative level' (Mantz-Thijssen 1992). These provisions refer to the structure of an organisation (the structure with regard to line and staff responsibilities and consultations) and procedures, instructions and orders for:

1 'good housekeeping' in existing business activities;
2 integrating environmental considerations in new activities;
3 measurement, inspection, registration and control activities;
4 administrative provisions supporting structure and procedures.
    (van der Woerd 1997)

The adoption of environmental management systems is stimulated by the EU through EMAS, a self-regulatory, market-based instrument which aims at improving the environmental performance of industrial sites and increasing the communication of environmental performance information between companies, governmental authorities and other stakeholders. For EU Member States the establishment of the administrative structure to support EMAS registrations is mandatory. Companies that verifiably meet the conditions of EMAS are registered and allowed to refer to this achievement in their communication to business partners and governmental authorities. However, the EMAS logo is not to be referred to on products or in product commercials. Table 6.1 presents the number of sites in the EU that have implemented EMAS.

Table 6.1 suggests that EU Member States are readily implementing the EMAS Regulation; even non-EU members such as Norway follow. Yet, no information is revealed regarding the practical implementation of the scheme and its actual impact for environmental performance of the relevant businesses. Let me briefly outline the hopes that were associated with the EMAS scheme as well as some of the conditions under which these hopes may be fulfilled.

To companies the potential benefits of EMAS are diverse. EMAS provides a scheme under which an EMS can be verified by interested parties. As a result, EMAS registration may result in an increase of

Table 6.1 *EMAS implementation by country*

Country	Number of sites
Austria	101
Belgium	3
Denmark	45
Finland	9
France	16
Germany	894
Greece	0
Ireland	4
Italy	3
Luxembourg	1
Netherlands	20
Norway	35
Portugal	0
Spain	8
Sweden	85
UK	48

Source: EMAS Help Desk, Brussels (March 1998).

sales because customers who care for the environmental quality of the production process are able to confirm the existence of an environmental management system. Also, EMAS stimulates a better structuring of environmental management at the respective sites. The initial environmental review of a site is a critical element of striving for EMAS registration. This review gives the management of the site the opportunity to see, for the first time, the complete environmental impact of the enterprise and adjust production accordingly. Related, EMAS implementation increases the environmental awareness amongst employees, especially those in management positions. Hillary (1997) describes that the raised awareness increases especially at four key stages of implementation: the adoption of the company's environmental policy; the involvement of staff in the initial environmental review stage; the execution of period audits and the compilation and publication of the environmental statement. Additionally, the ongoing training associated with the EMAS implementation raises awareness amongst employees and management. Such awareness is of great importance with respect to integrating the environment into the regular decision making at a firm, e.g. future investments, and thereby also the future environmental impacts. In this respect the relationship between the EMS and the capital budgeting process is crucial.

One characteristic of the EMAS Regulation, and many communicative instruments in general (though not of the Directive for Access of Environmental Information, discussed in chapter 8 by Clíona Kimber), is that it is built upon a voluntary basis, with firms deciding individually whether they want to 'sign up' (e.g. implement an environmental management system and conduct audits). Hence, the success of the EMAS Regulation depends on a receptive attitude on the part of industry, which is not always present. I suggest in this chapter that a positive reception may be enhanced, however, through the regulatory dynamic created by complementary regulatory, economic and communicative instruments. Financial or regulatory instruments often create costs for firms; a tool such as an environmental management system and particularly an environmental accounting system makes these costs visible to the firm's management and, more importantly, by clearly locating and measuring these, hints at management options to reduce these costs. In other words, it is likely to enable a management strategy allowing economically as well as environmentally favourable decisions.

I shall elaborate further on the dynamics implied in the mix of policy instruments in the following section. In section four I will turn to the relation between the extent to which the management of a firm is informed about the financial consequences of environmental impacts and the actual design and use of management accounting systems.

The influence of EMAS on the effectiveness of other policy instruments: some examples from The Netherlands

The EMAS scheme carries the potential to interact favourably with regulatory (command-and-control) as well as economic policy instruments in the environmental policy field. On the one hand, companies that want to be registered as an EMAS site are submitting themselves to a control of whether or not they are in compliance with existing direct environmental regulation. Hence, the scheme supports effective implementation of environmental legislation in general. In the context of economic policy instruments, EMAS helps provide the information and awareness needed for an effective response by companies to the incentives or disincentive implied in economic instruments.

Direct regulation

If a company or one of its locations want to become registered in EMAS they have to be in compliance with all existing applicable environmental regulation. Compliance is ensured by the following steps toward becoming registered as an EMAS site.

First, the implementation of an environmental management system starts with the identification of environmental impacts of this location and the relevant environmental legislation. When an audit takes place to certify an environmental management system it is checked if this information is available and documented. Second, before a location of a company becomes registered for EMAS, governmental agencies may prevent the registration if the company is not in compliance with existing environmental regulations. The Dutch Ministry of Housing, Physical Planning and the Environment (VROM), for instance, installed an institution that coordinates the verification and certification of environmental management systems. This institution ('The Foundation Coordination Certification Environmental Management System') informs the specific governmental agencies responsible for permitting and enforcement.

Given this compliance pressure one may ask why companies would want to become a registered site. Several inherent benefits of EMSs were already listed in the previous section. In addition, companies are attracted by the potential to escape rigid and uniformly applied top–down control of their compliance with environmental regulation in favour of more case-specific treatment. Such regulatory flexibility may serve not only industrial but also environmental interests by raising the rate of compliance and encouraging the integration of environmental considerations in regular business decisions.

For example, within the Netherlands there is a trend towards the development of further integration of the EMS in the process of permitting and enforcement. Already in 1989, the Dutch central government expected that local authorities would change their permitting and enforcement procedures. One main characteristic of the permitting arrangement will be that the permit will contain quantitative targets for a time period of about four years towards achieving strategic objectives. The EMS is an important tool for companies to reach these environmental objectives. For the governmental agencies, in turn, the external reporting implied in the EMAS scheme is crucial for monitoring progress. Van der Woerd (1997) describes how a new kind of interaction between companies and governmental agencies appears. Especially, well developed information channels are essential, both between a firm and government agencies and between agencies. The governmental agencies will rely on self-regulation only if the firms provide them with reliable information about environmental performance. Consequently, governmental agencies need not overload their permit requirements with detailed, and not necessarily appropriate, environmental conditions, while companies gain more flexibility in striving for strategic targets.

Financial instruments
Although the design of financial policy instruments is rarely directly influenced by the development of environmental management systems, these systems may highly influence the effectiveness of these policy instruments. Financial policy instruments are used by governments to internalise the negative externalities of environmental impacts. This is in accordance with the *polluter pays principle* that serves also as a guiding principle for EU environmental policy. Environmental impacts that used to be considered as priceless are through the use of financial policy instruments such as eco-taxes, effluent charges or liability systems (see Tsekouras, chapter 7, in this book) no longer without direct financial consequences.[3] Hence, it is expected that the use of financial policy instruments results in the prevention of environmental impacts that result in direct financial consequences for companies.

The threat of additional costs, implied in the use of financial environmental policy instruments, provides an incentive to reduce the environmental impact. EMAS can support this policy logic by providing informational feedback about how high the cost increase is likely to be, on the one hand, and about the best options to reduce environmental pollution and hence economic costs, on the other. For example, the internalisation of disposal costs through charging waste may result in redesigning products in a way that less charges are to be paid; if the management of a company is informed of these environmental costs such signals can steer the production process towards more environment-friendly directions. Braakhuis *et al.* (1995) provide a revealing example of a car manufacturer responding to financial (dis)incentive by reducing environmental costs. Due to environmental cost integration the manufacturer's cost price per product unit was likely to increase considerably, rather than decrease, as was forecast prior to cost integration. This cost information stimulated the management to put some effort into redesigning its cars.

The link between EMAS and financial instruments is an indirect one, especially because EMAS implies no obligation to install a cost accounting system to gain insight into the direct financial consequences of environmental impacts (Nederlands Normalisatie-Instituut, 1996). Nevertheless, an EMS increases awareness amongst those in a company that design and use management accounting systems. This is reflected in the responses of the companies participating in the survey to which I will now turn. The following part will show that the integration of environmental aspects in regular strategic decision making at companies influences the effectiveness of financial instruments.

The integration of environmental aspects in regular decision making processes[4]

There is increasing research interest in the potential implied in integrating environmental management at industrial sites through environmental management systems (see for example Le Blansch 1996; Bouma 1995; de Groene 1995). The data presented here result from an ongoing research project that is designed to find out how companies deal with management accounting in the context of environmental management. Management accounting is concerned with providing financial information to persons inside the organisation, especially managers. The information is used to fulfil organisational objectives by planning, evaluating and controlling the organisation's activities and assuring appropriate use of and accountability for its resources.

I will limit my elaboration to the part of the survey that was held in Germany (20 companies) and the Netherlands (11 companies). The survey is explorative and its scope is broad: a number of sectors (textile finishing, chemicals, printing, metal plating and treatment, electronics, utilities) and different size classes (5–50 employees, 50–250 employees, 250–500 employees and more than 500 employees) are involved. The environmental coordinator and the controller of the respective companies were interviewed. The results show that, in future, the role of management accounting in environmental management will increase.

The formal process of integrating environmental management

On the level of company environmental policy 32 per cent of the companies have integrated environmental objectives into the regular business-economic objectives. Table 6.2 presents the survey results with regard to the firms' general mission and strategy. Companies were asked if they document organisational objectives and, if so, which ones. The level of formalisation is taken as an indication of the centrality of the respective objective to overall company behaviour.

Table 6.2   *The extent of integration of environmental objectives in the formal company policy documents*

Level of integration	%
Firms that have formal environmental policy goals integrated into the business-economic policy goals	32
Firms that have formal environmental policy goals separated from the business-economic policy goals	19
Firms that only have formal business-economic policy goals	36
Firms that only have environmental policy goals	13

It may be surprising that 13 per cent of the companies have formal policy goals only with regard to the environment. In these cases the 'regular' business-economic goals are not documented and are consequently informal, though most probably no less dominating. In the context of EMAS, firms are urged to formulate environmental objectives as these environmental objectives are regarded as the starting points for further improvements in environmental performance. By contrast, with regard to general management systems the formal objectives are not per definition the starting point for improvements in the economic performance of a firm. From this experience, we may infer critically that an environmental management system is vulnerable to overestimating the positive effects of a formal management system.

Of the firms that have environmental management systems, 67 per cent have environmental departments involved in the management process that allocates the financial resources (the capital budgeting). As a consequence of the increase of environmental management issues that address core business-economic aspects, it can be expected that management accounting will increase in relevance. There seem to be linkages between environmental management and management accounting systems and techniques that have clear functions with regard to providing financial information in order to:

1 control costs;
2 decide on investments;
3 decide on the design and marketing of products;
4 report on environmental efforts to external stakeholders.

Although the general role of management accounting systems and techniques in environmental management remains less than considerable, some aspects of management accounting are increasing in significance. Table 6.3 provides insight in the usefulness of several accounting functions to environmental management (according to the opinion of the environmental specialist of the firms that were studied).

Table 6.3 *The usefulness of different functions of management accounting to environmental management*

Function of management accounting	Usefulness to environmental management		Number of firms that considers element of management accounting useful					
			Some		Considerable		Crucial	
	Now	*Future*	*Now*	*Future*	*Now*	*Future*	*Now*	*Future*
Bookkeeping system	16	8	4	8	3	4	23	20
Operational budgeting, budgeting setting	12	7	4	10	4	6	20	23
Budgeting control	12	4	5	13	4	6	21	23
Capital budgeting	5	3	12	12	10	12	27	27
Product costing	9	10	3	2	6	11	18	23
Performance measurement (financial)	6	5	5	8	5	6	16	19
Performance measurement (non-financial)	7	7	4	5	4	5	15	17

Table 6.3 shows that *capital budgeting*, particularly, is now and for the future perceived as useful to environmental management (87 per cent of the firms). Presently, the *bookkeeping system* is also regarded

as useful by most firms (74 per cent of the firms), with some decline anticipated for the future. By contrast, *cost control* (through budget setting and budget control) will increase in usefulness. This is also the case with *product costing*. Let me elaborate on these finding some more.

Capital budgeting

The relation between capital budgeting and environmental management is of great importance. This was to be expected as the outcome of the capital budgeting process determines the financial resources that are allocated to environmental care. The ECOMAC survey indicates that firms use a different set of financial indicators for the investment project justification. The survey indicates that hurdle rates (threshold for approval) for environmental projects are in 29 per cent of the firms lower than those for non-environmental projects. This means that in only 29 per cent of the firms that were studied may the economic return of environmental investments be lower than for regular, non-environmental investments. Hence in 71 per cent of the firms the economic return of an environmental investment is at least as important as for other investments. For these firms an EMS that stimulates an accounting system to reflect the financial benefits of environmental investments becomes crucial for achieving environmental objectives.

In 41 per cent of the firms the hurdle rates are the same for both environmental and non-environmental projects. Hence, even firms employing an environmental management system (80 per cent of the firms of the survey) do not necessarily apply lower hurdle rates for environmental projects. Of the firms that have environmental policy goals (41 per cent of the firms), 46 per cent have lower hurdle rates for environmental projects, however. Integrating environmental concerns in the capital budgeting process within firms can occur in at least two ways.

1 The identification of all costs and benefits of environmental projects.
2 The involvement of an environmental specialist in the capital budgeting process. Such involvement would result in putting a higher weight on other evaluation criteria than the hurdle rates. Moreover, it can result in the identification of alternative investment plans that have lower environmental impacts.

With regard to the identification of costs and benefits it should be noticed that there are different degrees of detail in calculating these. In the capital budgeting process the future costs and benefits to the firm are calculated. This contrasts with the bookkeeping system which primarily focuses on recording ex post data with regard to costs and benefits.

Bookkeeping system

Independent of the reactive or proactive character of the environmental strategy, the management may need to acquire an insight into the resources that are allocated to environmental measures. The costs of environmental measures can be used as an indicator of their efforts. Of the companies that have written environmental policy goals, 84 per cent had taken concrete steps to have more detailed information on environmental costs. Of the companies that noticed a need for more detailed information on environmental costs, 68 per cent had taken concrete steps and 8 per cent have plans for concrete steps. Often these steps imply that the bookkeeping system has to deliver cost information. Additionally, the effort to establish consensus about the definition of environmental costs is mentioned.

The bookkeeping system often has to be improved to provide an insight into the proportion of environmental costs in cost prices for reasons of cost control and price setting. With regard to price setting, management accounting techniques can be of crucial importance to environmental management. However, this can be a stimulus to environmental management (when environment-friendly products have lower cost prices) as well as an impediment (when environment-friendly products have higher cost prices).

As mentioned before, bookkeeping systems will in future decrease in significance for environmental management. This can be explained by a shift of attention on the part of management from current environmental impacts to future impacts and hence, future costs and benefits. However, the role of the bookkeeping system will remain an important one.

Allocation of environmental costs

For both operational control and price setting the allocation of environmental products to products and/or processes is crucial. Although the necessity for accurate allocation of environmental costs is recognised, in theory in business practice this is often not reflected.

Table 6.4 indicates the extent to which firms allocate environmental costs. Only if environmental costs are clearly allocated to the relevant products and steps in the production process can we expect that cost

Table 6.4 *Extent to which environmental costs are allocated*

Cost item	Number of firms where initial assignment is always or usually to overhead	Number of firms where cost item is always or usually assigned to product/process	Number of firms where cost item is first assigned to overhead and then allocated
On-site air/wastewater/ hazardous waste testing/monitoring	21	6	1
On-site air emission controls	13	10	1
On-site wastewater pre-treatment/treatment/ disposal	13	7	1
On-site hazardous waste pre-treatment/treatment/ disposal	18	8	1
On-site hazardous waste handling (e.g. storage, labelling)	22	3	1
Manifesting for off-site hazardous waste trans- port	21	6	1
Off-site hazardous waste transport	20	7	0
Off-site wastewater/ hazardous waste pre-treatment/ treatment	17	5	1
Energy costs	18	11	1
Water costs	18	10	1
Licensing/permitting	22	3	1
Reporting to government agencies	22	2	1
Environmental penalties/ fines	16	1	0
Staff training for legal compliance	21	3	1
Environmental staff labour time	24	1	1
Legal staff labour time	15	2	1
Insurance costs	20	5	2

accounting to have an impact on future management decisions intended to reduce the environmental cost, e.g. future product design, investments in production or distribution processes.

The small number of firms that allocate cost items mentioned in table 6.4 can be explained by the fact that only 25 per cent of the companies use cost accounting systems that were recently updated to provide an insight into environmental costs. Most accounting systems were implemented at a time when environmental costs were not large enough to be of any relevance to the management. As a consequence of the implementation of environmental management systems there is an increase in awareness of the need to integrate environmental aspects in a more systematic way in regular decision making (for example capital budgeting and product pricing). This awareness is reflected in a more adequate allocation of environmental costs. This allocation results in a costs transparency where the direct financial consequences of environmental policy instruments become visible to the management of corporations. When this financial information is provided to the management the effectiveness of these policy instruments increases. The management is stimulated to undertake activities to reduce environmental costs by minimising environmental impacts. Increasingly, empirical data confirm that environmental management is stimulated by its potential to reduce costs (Gege 1997).

Some of the implementation problems with environmental issues of EMAS can be solved by stressing the abilities of environmental management systems and audits to reduce the burden of direct regulation and economic instruments at a company level. As long as companies do not identify the benefits of EMAS they will not voluntarily implement environmental management. These benefits can become apparent when companies have accounting systems that show them the impact of direct regulation and economic instruments that governments put into force to internalise the negative external effects of environmental impacts. Both at a European level and national levels the relationship between environmental management and accounting at the micro level should be further explored. Clearly, firms do already use accounting systems to generate cost information. These systems should be designed to generate information on internalised environmental costs. Accounting systems at the macro level (European Union and national level) should be linked to accounting systems at the micro level in order to generate information on environmental costs. Insight into the effects of EMAS and other policy instruments on environmental costs could be used in the further development of a proper mix of policy instruments to achieve environmental objectives.

Conclusions

In this chapter I argue that the environmental management system and its audits are good complements but no substitutes for direct and indirect regulation. An EMS is an instrument that is a crucial element of self-regulation. The improvements in environmental performance that are initially stimulated by direct and indirect regulation is in a number of companies further supported by the existence of an EMS. Especially, as a consequence of the interface of an EMS with the management accounting systems the effectiveness of both regulatory and economic policy instruments increases.

The reduction of negative environmental impacts on the part of firms using an EMS cannot completely be assigned to this management tool. Direct and indirect regulations often provide the initial motive for more environmental-friendly behaviour. As the integration of environmental aspects and costs is a prime goal of EMS, management accounting is expected to be of more importance for environmental management. This is underpinned by the results of a survey performed in Germany and the Netherlands. Some aspects of management accounting are particularly crucial for the further development of environmental management. This holds for the capital budgeting (identification of costs and benefits of environmental projects); the bookkeeping system (defining and accounting environmental costs) and the allocation of environmental costs to products and processes.

Further development of integrating environmental management into regular management systems will greatly influence the effectiveness, particularly, of indirect (financial) regulation. This chapter argues that as a consequence of integrating environmental matters into regular decision making, management accounting systems can be used to make the financial consequences of environmental impacts more visible to the management of a company. Only when this information is available can it be expected that management becomes aware of financial stimuli to reduce environmental impacts.

Additionally, EMAS may result in a change of the way governments use direct regulation (by means of environmental permitting and enforcement) to achieve environmental objectives. Again, an EMS will not serve as a substitute for policy instruments, but it promises to facilitate corporate compliance with governmental environmental objectives and to ease the task of top–down control. The EMAS is a capacity and awareness enhancing tool that may contribute to the effective implementation of regulatory and economic policy instruments by targeting these bottlenecks which have already been identified in chapter 2 of this book.

Notes

1 The Community Environmental Management and Audit Scheme (EMAS), Council Regulation (EEC) No. 1836/93 of June 1993.
2 The empirical data are drawn from a collaborative research project Eco-Management Accounting as a tool of environmental management (ECOMAC) supported by the Environment and Climate Programme of the European Commission.
3 Also, direct legislation may enhance the internalisation of external effects. For example, permit requirements may stimulate onsite waste management as management is confronted with the cost of these environmental activities that used to be external to business decisions.
4 The major content of this section was presented and discussed at the ECOMAC workshop, Greening of Industry Network Conference, Heidelberg, 26 November 1996.

References

Blansch, C.G. Le (1996), *Environmental protection in companies: governmental steering in perspective of the internalization principle*, Thesis, Athrocyte University, Athrocyte.

Bouma, J.J. (1995), *Environmental care in the Dutch Air Force and industry: a study of the integration of environmental aspects in strategic decision making processes*, Thesis, Erasmus University, Rotterdam.

Braakhuis, F.L.M., M. Gijtenbeek and W.A. Hafkamp (1995), *Milieumanagement: van kosten naar baten*, Samsom, Alphen aan den Rijn.

Bressers, Hans (1997), 'The Netherlands'. In H. Weidner, ed., *Performance and Characteristics of German Environmental Policy: Overview and Expert Commentaries from 14 Countries*. WZB Schriftenreihe FII 97(301), Berlin, 55–7.

Gege, Maximilian (1997), *Kosten senken durch Umweltmanagement: 1000 Erfolgsbeispiele aus 100 Unternehmen*, Vahlen Verlag, München.

Groene, J. de (1995), *Beheersen of beïnvloeden: de respons van bedrijven op milieuproblemen*, Thesis, Tilburg University, Fanoy, Middelburg.

Hillary, Ruth (1997), 'Environmental management standards: what do SMEs think?', in Christopher Sheldon, ed., *ISO 14001 and beyond: Environmental Management Systems in the Real World*, Sheffield, Greenleaf Publishing, 333–58.

Lenschow, Andrea (1999), 'Transformation in European environmental governance'. In B. Kohler-Koch and R. Eising, eds, *Transformation of Governance in the European Union*, London, Routledge, ECPR Series, 39–60.

Mantz-Thijssen, E.L. (1992), 'Begrippenkader voor bedrijfsinterne milieuzorg' in *Handboek Integrale Milieuzorg*, Deventer, Kluwer Bedrijfswetenschappen.

Nederlands Normalisatie-Instituut (1996), *Environmental Management Systems, Specification with Guidance for Use*, Delft.

Weale, Albert (1992), *The New Politics of Pollution*, Manchester: Manchester University Press.

Weidner, Helmut (1996), *Umweltkooperation und alternative Konfliktregelungsverfahren in Deutschland. Zur Entstehung eines neuen Politiknetzwerkes*, WZB Schriftenreihe FII 96(302), Berlin.

Winsemius, P. (1990), *Gast in eigen huis: Beschouwingen over milieumanagement*, Samson, Alphen aan den Rijn.

Woerd, F. van der (1997), *Self-regulation in corporate environmental management: changing interactions between companies and authorities*, Thesis, Free University, Amsterdam.

7 Konstantinos Tsekouras[1]

Exploiting the implementation potential of alternative instruments: design options for environmental liability funds

Introduction

Environmental policy in Europe was undergoing a transformation process during the 1990s characterised by a shift away from traditional concepts of hierarchical 'command and control' approaches. There is a broad consensus that – besides the general political climate of deregulation and subsidiarity – the implementation deficits associated with traditional approaches were major forces driving this development. The failure to achieve an optimal level of environmental protection led to the recognition that command and control policy must be at least coupled with a regulatory model which would relieve the national state and the European Union from bearing the entire burden of designing and enforcing environmental policy.

As mentioned in part one of this book, the new approach in EU environmental policy is expected to achieve these objectives by explicitly seeking the support of the implementing actors and relevant interests. Strong emphasis is placed on the participation of economic and other societal actors in the process of policy formulation and implementation, the cooperation and communication between public and private actors, as well as the provision of more flexible and more widely acceptable solutions (e.g. the creation of economic incentive structures rather than strict regulatory standards) in order to motivate risk generators to adopt and develop an environmentally more friendly attitude. At least in theory, this less rigid, less hierarchical and more cooperative regulatory model promises to produce more desirable results in the field of environmental protection than was the case with traditional regulatory approaches.

However, as Knill and Lenschow demonstrate in chapter 2, the theoretical relationship between 'new approach' and 'policy effectiveness' is much less straightforward than one might expect from the above considerations. As revealed by their analysis, the implementation success of the new approach is not to be taken for granted. To actually achieve the expected improvements in terms of implementation effectiveness, the attribute 'new' is not a sufficient condition. Rather, the success of new concepts is contingent upon additional *design requirements*: to effectively motivate and stimulate a favourable context for domestic compliance, new (as well as old) approaches have to take account of institutional conditions and existing interest constellations at the national level. Apart from avoiding excessive changes in existing institutional arrangements, European policies should indicate clear and sufficiently strong incentives for stimulating the support of domestic actor coalitions. In other words, the complete exploitation of the implementation potential of new instruments requires careful consideration in terms of policy design, taking account of given political and institutional limits and capacities at the domestic level.

Against this backdrop, it is the objective here to discuss potential benefits and difficulties of various design options for the specific case of civil liability for environmental damage[2] as an instrument, which can serve the goals of the new regulatory philosophy. I will argue that the most promising option in order to fulfil the above design conditions has to be seen in a liability funds model financed by risk creators according to the level of risk each of them creates. The operation of the model would be determined to a high degree by polluters themselves, while it would be guaranteed that non-state actors advocating environmental and possibly other social interests are represented in the decision making process regarding compensation claims. Moreover, causation requirements for compensation awards from the fund would be more relaxed than current liability rules in order to allow compensation for those types of environmental damages, which today remain uncompensated.

To pursue this argument, I shall examine at the outset the relationship, if any, among civil liability and the protection of natural resources. Afterwards, I shall present in sum the criteria according to which the success of a civil liability system for environmental damage must be measured, and explain why current liability systems fail to fulfil these criteria. Problems of performance are both functional and institutional in nature. Next, I shall examine the main directions that are implicit in recent reform proposals made in both Europe and the US[3] and show why a liability funds model is preferable to other options. In the final section I will elaborate the main principles which must condition the function of a liability funds model in order to satisfy the political and institutional implementation capacities at the domestic level.

The perspective taken in this chapter is by necessity a normative one, as a European liability system for environmental damages does not exist yet. Therefore, there is no experience to draw upon as regards the impact of such a regime on the design and the implementation of European environmental policy. Taking this for granted, the chapter examines how a liability regime could in theory fit within the deregulation process in European environmental policy and under which conditions it could operate successfully as an alternative instrument in the same policy area. Moreover, the chapter adopts in principle a legal perspective. However, the argument is rooted in political-institutional analysis.

Liability in the context of new instruments

One may consider the Community's efforts to 'harmonise' the civil liability laws of the Member States with regard to environmental damage as integral part of the above mentioned tendency to move towards a new approach in EU environmental policy.[4] To do so, it must be shown however that civil liability for environmental damage is valuable as an instrument for the design and the implementation of a more flexible and cooperative regulatory approach.

If one follows the traditional view on liability rules, the relationship among liability and environmental policy would appear to be attenuated. According to this view, liability rules are concerned in the first place with compensating individuals for damages they have suffered by the illegal acts of other individuals. In this sense, they aim merely at doing justice in the specific dispute between the individual litigants and are irrelevant to public policy targets (for a recent vindication of this concept see Weinrib 1995, 211–14). Accordingly, if liability serves environmental targets, this is only an incidental result, alien to the goals of liability. Liability, as such, is structurally irrelevant to the protection of natural resources.

However, it is probably the most significant merit of the economic analysis of law (see Calabresi 1970; Posner 1992) to have demonstrated that liability rules should not be merely understood as a closed set shedding light exclusively on the individual features of the particular litigation. On the contrary, liability can and should be approached in a functionalist way, and thus used as a valuable tool for attaining public goals, like environmental protection (Brüggemeier 1988, 514). As regards the improvement of the level of environmental protection in particular, scholars agree that this can be an indirect result, a 'side effect' of the application of liability rules (Medicus 1986). By bearing the costs for harms incurred by individuals because of operations hazardous to the environment, market actors will be given incentives to reduce the risk they create. In this way they are made responsible for carrying out adequate risk controls themselves by taking precautionary steps and/or by lowering their activity level. Furthermore, polluters may in some cases be motivated to cooperate with each other, to pool information on risks and to engage in a self-standardisation process to confront jointly the threat of liability. In this way, liability can obtain a significant role for the attainment of environmental goals in the context of a policy model based on cooperation and flexibility.

General features of a successful liability system for environmental damage

What are the criteria a liability system for environmental damage must fulfil in order to work effectively?[5] First, as already mentioned above, it must be instrumental to the protection of natural resources to give proper incentives to polluters to control the risk they create to the environment. However, activities hazardous to the environment do not harm only environmental goods. On the contrary, they often create at the same time risks and dangers for human health, for property rights and for other economic interests. A liability system should consequently develop a deterrence effect also with regard to damage to these goods and interests.

Second, liability systems must balance the opposing interests at stake in an equitable way. A fair balance of interests would demand in the first place that innocent victims get compensation for the harm they suffered.[6] As victims cannot control the conditions which give rise to the occurrence of the damage, it does not seem fair to leave them to bear the entire losses on their own. This is especially so in the case of environmental risks, which potential victims cannot avoid being exposed to.

Considerations of fairness demand, furthermore, that compensation is paid by risk creators. This corresponds to the basic principle that those who create extraordinary risks should bear the losses arising out of these risks. Regarding damage to natural resources in particular, this way of allocating costs conforms to the 'polluter pays' principle, nowadays enshrined in art. 130r of the EU Treaty. Moreover, it is in conformity with the normative premise that those who profit from an activity should also bear the costs incurred by it. Last, shifting costs to risk creators does not place an excessive burden on them, as they can easily spread costs by increasing the price of their products or services.

On the other hand, a just interest balance should take into account that operations dangerous to the environment may benefit the whole of society in many ways. Such operations create, for instance, the goods necessary in a modern economy and modern life as well as working places. Last, society has an interest in limiting the financial burden placed on economic operators, so that they are able to offer their products or services at a low price and thus make them accessible to wide population groups. As society as a whole and potential victims as members of that society also profit from potentially hazardous operations, they could reasonably be asked to bear a part of the external costs created by those operations. In other words, it is not just to impose full liability on operators, but to balance the gravity of a specific injury with the social benefits of risky operations in order to define liability thresholds. Moreover, from the premise that harm should be compensated for by those who caused them it follows that each individual operator should be held responsible only for the damage he or she creates him- or herself and not for harm arising from operations carried out by third persons.

Third, liability systems should be measured as to whether and how they can work in practice in a specific legal and social system and perform the function attributed to them. Their success at the implementation level depends on the degree of administrative efficiency and on the degree of legitimacy and support they enjoy in the system in which they operate. Administrative efficiency means that a dispute resolution does not entail high administrative costs, that it takes place according to simple procedures and within a short time period. With particular respect to environmental liability, administrative efficiency should also include the system's capacity to clarify as much as possible complex scientific issues relating to the harmful potential of pollution sources and to the conditions giving rise to the occurrence of damages.

The legitimacy and support of liability schemes is crucially affected by the extent to which they correspond with existing regulatory traditions and philosophies at the domestic level. In view of different state, legal and administrative traditions, there is a high variety of institutional arrangements with respect to the regulation of public problems across countries. Depending on which mechanisms a society gives preference to, the judiciary, public administration, social groups or the private insurance market might play a more or less important role in the regulation of environmental risks and damages. Leaving extensive regulation tasks to institutions which society views with distrust or reluctance might prove to be counter-effective. To be more concrete, this might result in institutional conflicts, which in turn will adversely affect the outcome of regulation.

To conclude, a successful civil liability scheme for environmental damage must give correct incentives to risk creators in order to minimise the risk they create to environment, health and other individual goods. In addition, it must ensure that risk creators compensate for any harm according to liability rules which assess the victims' and the operators' interests in a reasonable way. Moreover, its administration must be simple and effective and operate in an institutional form whose legitimacy to regulate environmental damages will not be seriously disputed.

The failure of current liability systems

In view of the wide variety of legal and administrative traditions across Member States, the development of general statements applicable on all current tort systems is a rather complex exercise. Tort systems contain different rules as regards issues like the relationship between liability for environmental damage and fault, the scope of application of non-fault liability, the conditions for compensation for ecological damages (on this last issue see, for instance, the comparative study of Seibt 1994). Nevertheless, traditional tort systems share some common elements, which justify speaking of a failure of tort systems in general in the area of compensation for environmental damage.[7]

To begin with, tort systems include causation rules, which are in general inspired by the same notion of causation. This causation concept refers to individual hazardous conduct and individual damage as exclusive elements of a clear-cut relationship, whose existence can only be either confirmed or denied in an absolute sense according to a logical process derived from common experience. On the basis of this concept, causation rules demand that a specific causal link be proved between an individual act and a specific harm. Moreover, the existence of this causal link should be established in continental Europe with a very high degree of probability, almost reaching the level of certainty.[8] Meeting this requirement is very burdensome, however. Substances released from different sources produce synergetic effects, so that attributing a specific damage to a specific risk source is almost impossible. Furthermore, other causes, like natural phenomena, concur frequently with environmental pollution as possible causes of a harm. In addition, the harmful potential of many substances cannot be fully explored, so that one cannot tell with certainty whether a substance is involved in the occurrence of a kind of harm or not. Under these circumstances, tort rules do not give proper incentives to risk creators to control the risk they cause and they cannot serve the legitimate interests of individual victims to get compensation.

Moreover, current liability systems function on the basis of individual court litigation which is problematic in optimally managing issues regarding liability for environmental damage. Disputes on environmental damages frequently involve complex technical matters, whose clarification is dependent upon the employment of scientific expertise and scientific data. Such expertise and data are not always available to judges, and even when they are available they are used by the parties to manipulate the outcome of the process. As judges are not experts, they will face big difficulties in correctly evaluating such data (Elliott 1985, 1374–5; Viscusi 1989, 75). Under these conditions, they will normally decide the case in a rather deliberate way and thus give false incentives to operators for risk control. A further disadvantage of individual court litigation is that it provokes high administrative costs (for an overview, see Sugarman 1985, 596ff). Finally, the restriction of the binding effect of judicial decisions only to the specific case may result in a differential treatment of similar cases, adjudicated by different courts.

Consequently, causation rules of the traditional tort system hardly guarantee that costs will be shifted to risk creators nor can they ensure compensation to victims. Moreover, even if causation rules did not pose great obstacles, the lack of expertise on the part of the judges, high administrative costs and the danger of contradictory judicial decisions on similar issues undermine the capacity of the traditional adjudication system to regulate adequately the issue of environmental damages.

Why liability funds?

In the light of these deficits, one can conceive of basically two ways to improve compensation for environmental damages. More precisely, it may be enough to introduce amendments of a substantive and/or procedural nature to the judicial system. In the alternative, a proper solution could be found outside the judicial system, in mechanisms like insurance or administrative compensation schemes. In this section I will first examine proposals which explore possible solutions within tort law and then draw attention to proposals which show a preference for non-judicial institutions.

Proposals within the boundaries of the judicial system
Two ways have been proposed for ensuring that the allocation of costs of environmental damages via tort law will be optimal. The first way would be to impose liability for exposure to a risk according to the defendants' risk share. The second option is also based on the assumption that the introduction of a proportional liability rule is necessary, but it contends that litigation should be carried out in the form of class actions.

Individualised tort system with proportional liability rule
According to the first option, it is sufficient to improve the victims' position by changing causation rules, without performing any institutional change. The new causation rules should be drafted in such a way that liability will be imposed for risk generation and its amount will be proportional to the extent of risk creation (Robinson 1985). Claimants must prove exposure to a risk, and will then get awards according to the probability that they will suffer harm in the future because of exposure to this risk. Recovery costs will be borne then by the risk generators according to the proportion to which they have contributed to the creation of the risk at large. To assess this

proportion, it suffices to rely on purely statistical evidence. This new cause of action will, however, not replace traditional liability for actual losses, so that potential victims will be eligible to choose between either claiming probable future losses before damage manifestation or claiming actual losses after harms have been manifested. In case, however, victims were granted benefits for risk exposure and the amount of actual future damages finally exceeded the amount of these benefits, they will not have the right to claim amounts equal to the difference between actual losses and received awards (Robinson 1985, 788).

Due to the minimal requirements with regard to institution building, this model seems promising for successful implementation. In functional terms, the proposal is particularly interesting to the extent that it puts the accent on risk generation and, consequently, on a purely probabilistic notion of causation (Robinson 1985, 785). In this sense, it lowers liability standards and, especially, standards related to the evidence victims will need to produce, to be granted compensation. Moreover, it excludes the possibility of defendants avoiding liability by establishing that they could not have caused liability in the specific case. Finally, by enabling potential victims to take legal action at the time of risk exposure, it offers them considerable protection against the risk of insolvency or non-identifiability of risk creators at the time of the manifestation of harms.

However, this model demonstrates many weaknesses as well, in particular with respect to claimants' compensation and to its capacity to operate properly. As regards claimants' compensation, claimants who are exposed to the same level of risk get the same awards, if they claim compensation ex ante, despite the fact that some of them will suffer at the end greater and others smaller losses. In this way, some claimants will be unreasonably undercompensated, while others will gain windfalls.

Regarding how this proposal will function in practice, one can state that it will work only in the case that the plaintiff has been exposed to substances released by a few sources. However, if the number of potential contributors to the risk is high, then it would be difficult for the plaintiff to identify and to join all of them in the action to get full compensation. In addition, regulation of environmental damages, according to this proposal, continues to take place through the individual litigation system. In this sense, the proposal does not address the limited capacity of this system to perform its regulatory task successfully.

Last, it is highly questionable to what extent the liability model presented here can be successfully implemented within the given institutional capacities for domestic adaptation. The limitations are less rooted in demands for institution building (see above) but rather focus on the application of institutional rules and legal norms. To be precise, notions of justice in European legal systems are still very strongly linked to the protection of individual autonomy. This, some fear, might be disregarded, if a purely probabilistic notion of causation replaces the traditional concept of causation based on particularistic evidence and requiring a high level of probabilities (Diederichsen 1986, L 89, L 94). Even if we assume that proportional liability will be introduced by a legislative act whose authority European judges will follow (Legrand 1997, 55), this deeply rooted idea of justice might lead to a very strict interpretation of the rule.

Class actions The employment of class actions aims at eliminating or at least mitigating the operational deficits of individual litigation (Rosenberg 1984, 905ff). More concretely, class action significantly reduces administrative costs. Additionally, it gives the adjudicator the opportunity to have an overview of the entire issue and thus to come to solutions better serving the general interest. Moreover, it offers more guarantees as regards equal treatment of the individual members of each group. Furthermore, because in a class action the total amount of liability costs is assessed at a time when an at least considerable part of damages has already been manifested, its calculation will be possibly more accurate than if it had taken place previously. Last, class action strengthens the plaintiffs' position in the sense that it makes judges more receptive to victims' arguments and it gives incentives to people who would otherwise not dare to fill an individual claim to join the plaintiffs' class. This last advantage is mainly due to sociological factors related to the function of class actions, like the publicity they acquire and the psychological impact this has on both participants and public opinion.

However, it is very doubtful whether class action is the best mechanism to resort to, for tackling the issue of compensation for environmental damages. First, the circumstances giving rise to the opening of a class action procedure reveal that not all types of harm can be compensated through class actions. A class action will be normally put in motion, only if the number of potential victims is big enough or if the whole issue finds a sufficient echo in public opinion. In the rest of cases, a class action will most probably not take place. Moreover, the final cost allocation might be different in different class actions, because of fundamental differences not in the factual and legal matters underlying each litigation, but in the contrasting ideologies and attitudes of the judges handling each of them. Furthermore, class actions are litigated a long time after risk creation, so that victims have to face the risk of non-identifiability, insolvency or the going out of business of a bigger or smaller number of operators, which will by the same token reduce the amount of compensation they will be awarded.[9]

Finally, against class actions are considerations of legal traditions and culture related to the role of judges in most European countries. To be more precise, empirical evidence suggests that judges in class actions do not act as mere adjudicators, but they play, in fact, a rather 'managerial' role. Their function is similar to that of a political mediator, who uses legal sanctions to make the disputing parties join a negotiation process and agree on a commonly acceptable and practical solution (Schuck 1987, 258–60). European societies are, however, rather reluctant to assign such an enhanced role to courts (Fleming 1994, 519 and 528). European civil law judges are not trained to deal with such highly politicised cases (Cappelletti 1989, 294). Recent developments in European legal practice and in legal theory suggest, furthermore, that, to find alternatives to state regulation, it would be preferable, instead of enhancing the role of judges, to strengthen either the role of individual citizens (Habermas 1996, 410–14) or the power of social groups, organised in corporal entities (Ewald 1985, 52–9; see also the Agreement on Social Policy of the Treaty of Maastricht). Against this background, it is certainly doubtful whether there is a place for class actions in European legal systems. Taking into consideration that even in the legal system of the US, where it has been mainly applied, class action is used very cautiously (Fleming 1994, 517), its generalised use in European legal systems would appear to be even more problematic.

Non-judicial solutions

There are three options to secure compensation for environmental damage outside the judicial system. First, it could be secured that the entire population can cover losses through a first party insurance.

Second, one might resort to social security models. The last solution would consist in creating liability funds.

First party insurance and social security schemes   I have decided to examine first party insurance and social security schemes in the same section, as both models show close similarities as to their merits and shortcomings. This is due to the fact that the operation of both models is based on the same core concept, namely risk insurance by risk spreading. The main advantage of first party insurance and social security systems is that they lead to equitable results, as losses are spread among a large number of actors, so that they do not place an excessive burden on any individual (Abraham 1987, 900). Second, first party insurance and social security demonstrate operational advantages. Third, compensation claims are decided more quickly and in a simpler procedure than would be the case by means of a judicial process and the administrative costs required for their function are kept at a much lower level than in judicial litigation. Finally, first insurance and social security models do not expose parties to the rivalries of the adversary litigation system, thus preserving solidarity links among society members (Ewald 1985, 55; Barta 1995, 21).

However, the main problem with first party insurance and social security systems is that they cannot shift costs to the operators of risky activities.[10] In first party insurance, for instance, losses are borne by the entire group of potential victims; social security expenses are covered by the state, the insured persons themselves and their employers. Even in sectors of the social security system, which in some countries are financed absolutely by employers and cover a big part of personal injuries due to environmental risks, like workers' compensation for workplace accidents and occupational diseases, employers' payments are not proportional to the level of environmental risks each of them generates, but are mainly calculated on the basis of the risk level, to which their employees are expected to be exposed (for more details see Bley 1986, 193–8 on German law; Dupeyroux 1997, 90–1 on French law). Both first party insurance and social security systems are, accordingly, deficient with regard to damages' prevention and the achievement of a reasonable interest balance.

Liability funds   The third remaining solution is the foundation of
liability funds. The core idea underlying the concept of liability funds
is that victims obtain compensation directly from an administrative
fund, which is financed by risk generators according to the level
of risk each one creates. The financial contribution of individual
operators is paid to the fund at the time of risk creation and
compensation to victims is awarded at the time of the injury's
manifestation. Liability funds constitute a satisfactory solution. By
requiring payment from individual polluters at the time risks are generated they minimise the risks of operators' insolvency or going out
of business and by remedying for damages after they have occurred
they avoid the problem of mismatching awards with actual damages.
Thus, they can guarantee victims' compensation, loss spreading
among the contributors to the fund and give to risk generators
proper incentives for optimal risk generation. Moreover, they have
the operational advantages of administrative solutions. In particular,
they can employ part of their administration to collect and evaluate
information on potential risks and their effects and thus ensure that
a compensation system based on them will operate properly.

Summary
Our analysis has shown that no approach trying to tackle the issue
of liability for environmental damage within the boundaries of the
adjudication system seems to be promising in a European context. I
have reviewed their functional deficiencies as well as the institutional challenges they would imply. Neither individual nor collective
litigation models seem to be effective tools for the regulation of mass
cases in a satisfactory way. Moreover, a collective litigation scheme
assimilating to class action would necessitate conferring extensive
powers to courts, which in turn would provoke legitimacy problems.
Among non-judicial models social security schemes and first party
insurance have the disadvantage of not shifting costs to the operators of hazardous activities. Thus, the only non-judicial mechanism
that can pay due attention to the need of risk prevention and a reasonable interest balance is liability funds.

Implementing liability funds: the effectiveness of various design options

Despite the above mentioned advantages, the practical implementation of the liability funds model poses a series of important issues, including the relationship between individual and collective liability, the organisation of liability funds, their administration, the requirements for compensation awards, contribution among different funds, as well as the funds' financial resources. With respect to all of these aspects, special attention has to be paid to two factors affecting effective implementation. First, potential policy options must indicate clear and sufficiently strong signals in order to motivate and stimulate the support of the involved actors. Second, and closely related to this feature, the (limited) capacity for institutional adjustment of legal and administrative arrangements has to be taken into account; i.e., to avoid policy options that are in contradiction with well-established institutional core principles.

The relationship between individual and collective liability: getting the incentives right

There are two main ways to organise the relationship between individual and collective liability. On the one hand, liability funds may function only as complementary to individual liability systems. In this sense, they will offer compensation only in those cases in which victims' compensation through the individual liability system is not or might not be feasible. On the other hand, compensation may be awarded exclusively through collective liability funds. Notwithstanding whether funds should replace the individual litigation system or supplement its function, we have to deal further with the question of whether and, if so, under which conditions the funds should be entitled to claim reimbursement of compensation costs from individual tortfeasors.

The majority of scholars, especially in Germany, prefer liability funds to perform a subsidiary function to the individual liability system (Knebel 1988, 278; Ganten and Lemke 1989, 8–9; Salje 1991, 327ff.; see also Lambrichts 1990, 102), arguing that collectivisation of liability is necessary only to the extent that losses are not covered by the individual liability system.

However, a parallel existence of both systems will result in the unequal treatment of victims by the legal system. Indeed, victims whose cases are more obscure will get compensation from the fund quickly and with very low administrative costs. The rest, who should normally be in a better position, because they can prove the causal link between a concrete source and their particular harm, will have to bear the excessive costs of a judicial process and get recovery with delay. They will, consequently, be unreasonably disadvantaged. It follows from this that all victims should, for reasons of fairness, be entitled to compensation directly from the liability funds.

Moreover, for a dual compensation system to work properly, the boundaries between the courts' jurisdiction and the funds' competence must be drawn in a clear way. In some cases it is difficult, however, to predict whether victims will be able to obtain a court decision awarding them compensation. This happens in cases to which the application of legal rules or legal principles aiming at helping victims to overcome the difficulties with regard to causation and causation evidence is ambiguous. How should victims proceed in such cases to receive compensatory awards? To avoid such coordination problems between judicial litigation and the funds' compensation system we could simply allow all victims to claim compensation directly from liability funds. Issues of equitable treatment of victims as well as administrative coordination therefore, point toward the collective liability system as the preferred policy design.

With respect to the treatment of harm creators, reimbursement claims of the funds against individual operators who can be identified to have actually contributed to the occurrence of a specific harm have the advantage of enhancing individual responsibility. Moreover, a part of the funds' expenses is directly allocated to the actual tortfeasors and this, in turn, simplifies the task of calculating the amount of individual contributions to the funds' budget.

However, from the perspective of creating clear incentives for risk creators there are strong arguments against collective liability funds. First, inherent in the allocation of costs to risk generators through reimbursement claims are the general weaknesses of the judicial allocation of losses. There are no guarantees that similar cases will be judged in the same way, so that generators of identical types and levels of risk may be called to pay different awards. Second, risk creators will not be given the incentive to reduce risk levels, but, rather, to organise their operations so as to produce harmful effects which cannot be linked directly to them (Ladeur 1993, 263). Third, it is not likely that funds will in practice engage in costly and long lasting processes to get payments reimbursed. On the one hand, they will always have enough financial resources available to ensure compensatory payments to all victims. On the other, they possess other, less expensive means, like calculation of contributions to the fund through a bonus–molus system, to attach consequences to the fact that some concrete contributors to a specific damage have been identified. A norm entitling liability funds to claim reimbursement from identified potential or actual tortfeasors would be accordingly rather superfluous. The only case in which such a provision would make sense is when accidents bearing extraordinarily grave consequences have occurred.[11] This exemption is justified by the fact that the amount of harm will be too high to be covered only by means of a bonus–molus system.

The organisation of liability funds: exploiting the capacity of existing institutions

There are two ways to apply funds' solutions in practice. The first one would be to create only one fund, responsible for the compensation of every type of environmental damages. The second solution would be to create more liability funds, each one competent for compensating some specific kinds of environmental damage.

The idea of creating only one fund does not appear to be very attractive for administrative reasons. It will be extremely burdensome for a fund to calculate the costs of all different types of environmental damage, to determine the causes of each particular damage category and then to estimate the risk share created by each individual operation. It thus seems reasonable to create more liability funds, each with restricted responsibilities (Knebel 1988, 279; Hohloch 1994, 207; Ladeur 1993, 264). Liability funds could then be organised to award compensation either for damage incurred in a particular geographical area (regional funds) or for harm arising out of particular kinds of activities (branch or sectoral funds).

It would be reasonable to pay attention in this regard to German scholars who have expressed a clear preference for branch funds. These scholars have pointed to the German experience with the 'Berufsgenossenschaften' (Wagner 1990), which are collective bodies organised according to economic branches and are competent to compensate for damages occurring due to workplace accidents and occupational diseases. The experience with the 'Berufsgenossenschaften' model has been generally positive as regards not only compensation, but also regulation and deterrence of workplace risks (Wagner 1990, 102). It would make sense, under these conditions, at least to take inspiration from the 'Berufsgenossenschaften' model to regulate harm arising from environmental risks as well (Kinkel 1989,

298; see also Barta 1995, 42, with regard to medical malpractice liability; contra Rehbinder 1989, 151, arguing that private corporations are not better suited than state administration to control modern, complex risks).

This conclusion may also apply more generally, given that in almost all European countries there already exists an institutional framework based on cooperation and interaction among operators belonging to the same sector. This framework could be expanded to accommodate cooperation related to the task of regulating environmental damages and risks. Such cooperation may consist in producing, processing, and assessing information on hazardous activities by engaging in common scientific research and experimentation. Furthermore, cooperation may take the form of collective self-control with the aim of setting common standards or avoiding moral hazard effects. On the other hand, it is not obvious that such cooperation networks do always exist at a regional level, so that the participation of all regional actors in a collective entity will be more difficult to achieve.

Branch funds should moreover take up the task of compensating for damages inflicted by people who do not belong to an economic branch. This happens for example with damage from acid rain, to whose creation car drivers and users of heating systems contribute. In such an instance, trying to create cooperation among car drivers or users of heating systems for the purpose of risk control by means of a separate fund seems to be unrealistic (see Kinkel 1989, 296). If, in the alternative, compensation is granted by the branch funds of producers, importers or retailers of the substances whose release creates the respective risks (see Wagner 1990, 230), better results as regards risk deterrence are possible to achieve, because of the feasibility of cooperation among the branch's members and because the branch members are better placed to produce or collect information on the harmful effects of the substances they are dealing with.

From the assertion that funds with restricted responsibilities are more likely to work effectively it follows, moreover, that sectoral funds should not be set up at a Community level. On the contrary, each fund should operate only within the boundaries of a Member State. This will also enable Member States to organise sectoral funds as they deem opportune, by taking into consideration the specific social, economic and environmental conditions prevailing in them. The creation of funds operating at a national level will, however, render necessary the establishment of a contribution system among funds of neighbouring countries as a means of avoiding externalities arising from pollution export.

It follows from the previous arguments that the organisational requirements for the effective implementation of liability funds must not be in contradiction with institutional traditions at the domestic level. Not only is it possible to exploit the capacity of existing – and successful – institutional models, but doing so will also significantly increase the opportunities for effective compliance.

Administering the funds: avoiding interference with domestic arrangements

This section will deal with the question who should take responsibility for the tasks attributed to the fund. Choices range among leaving the entire administration of the fund to the state, relying exclusively on the respective branch of economic activity, opting for a mixed system, according to which both the state and the respective corporation would be involved in fund management, and a more 'open' model, foreseeing additional participation of non-governmental environmental organisations and other non-governmental public interest groups, like trade unions. As indicated by different experience from related areas, a mixed model implying shared responsibilities of public and private actors reflects the most promising choice in order to secure the desired policy outcomes. Apart from this basic framework suggestion, however, the definition of the concrete organisational arrangements should be left to the Member States in order to benefit from the specific political and institutional capacities at the domestic level. In other words, Member States should comply with some, rather broad, basic requirements, but have considerable discretion with respect to the specification of these requirements in the light of domestic conditions.

The model of state-managed funds is based on the idea that the state is the protector of the general interest[12] and of individual rights. However, there are strong arguments against leaving the funds' management solely to the state. First, the overwhelming influence of economic interest groups on the design and the implementation of state policy may lead to the fund adopting a restrictive approach towards victims' compensation (see Lambrichts 1990, 101, regarding the function of the Dutch Air Pollution Fund). Second, experiences with the state-managed social welfare system point to its administrative inefficiency, mainly as a result of the formation of a rigid bureaucratic apparatus (Ladeur 1995, 53–8) and its consequent incapacity to prevent potential abuses by citizens claiming compensation without being entitled to it (Ladeur 1995, 24). For these reasons rendering funds' administration an exclusively state responsibility will probably create a weak deterrence effect on hazardous operations. It might moreover fail to achieve a fair balance of interest.

Leaving fund management in the hands of the respective economic sector has advantages that cannot be overlooked. Apart from avoiding the shortcomings of state administrative systems, these advantages lie in the fact that corporate bodies are better placed to facilitate cooperation among their individual members. Nevertheless, trusting fund administration exclusively to corporate bodies runs the risk that economic interests will prevail over environmental and victims' interests. Therefore, while guaranteeing the involvement of enterprise branches in the funds' management seems to be opportune mainly from the point of view of deterrence, some other procedural elements are needed to enhance the weight of environmental and victims' interests.

A balance of the conflicting interests at stake can be ensured if non-state social groups or organisations share responsibilities for issues affecting the public interest, as, for instance, decisions on individual compensation claims, the calculation of what costs risky operations will incur in total, and the design of risk detection policy (see Hager 1995, 407; for a more differentiated opinion see Wagner 1990, 199). On the other hand, internal sectoral issues, mainly those of cost distribution among the sector's individual members, could be resolved only by the sectors themselves.

As regards which social actors should defend the society's interest in achieving a high level of environmental quality and compensation for environmental damage, I suggest that the issue should be arranged in each country according to the prevailing social, political and legal circumstances. However, we should indicate that a model that is open to the participation of as many actors as possible is better placed to achieve a proper balance of interests. In this regard, involvement in carrying out the respective responsibilities of the funds may be awarded, for example, to representatives of the central government, environmental groups, consumer associations, municipal or regional authorities, or trade unions.

In view of the experience and the expertise judges have with issues like causation and damages' assessment, the possibility of judges' participation in the panels which decide on compensation claims must be considered seriously. Another good idea in this regard would be to create, following the example of some forms of alternative dispute resolution (see Cappelletti and Garth 1978, 90ff and 109ff), legal advisory services within each fund, which will have the task, among others, of informing panel members and individual citizens on legal aspects of compensation for environmental damage.

Requirements for compensation awards
Stating that liability funds seem to be the most adequate solution reveals nothing yet about the conditions under which individuals should be entitled to receive awards from liability funds. Problems refer to the question of whether negligence or strict liability should be the liability standard, which kinds of damages should be recoverable by the funds and, most importantly, to the issue of causation and of causation proof.

The liability standard   In the context of liability for environmental damage and consequently of funds' liability, fault liability should be substituted for strict liability. I will not deal with this issue extensively here but just mention that introducing no-fault liability will certainly not break new ground. The attempts to harmonise the law of liability for environmental damage at international and Community level provide the best evidence for this,[13] and render easier the reception of no-fault liability in a fund scheme.

Recoverable damages   One of the most cumbersome tasks is to define the types and extent of damages for which funds will grant compensation. The problem is that a variety of different types of damages are at stake, such as harm due to health or body injury, damage due to encroachment of property rights, pecuniary loss, pain and suffering, and ecological damages. Compensation for each of these types performs a different function and it is therefore subject to different conditions. Moreover, each national legal order treats the same type of damages differently. Because of the complexity of the issue it is not feasible to examine it in detail here. I will therefore limit this section to some general remarks.

As a basic principle, funds' rules on compensation should not in general be less favourable to applicants than tort law rules. The existence of the funds is necessary to overcome the causation problems which impede compensation for environmental damages. From this it follows that liability funds should compensate for the same types of damages as tort law. Compensation should be consequently given for damages arising out of injury to body or to health and for damages to property, while compensation for pain and suffering should be awarded at least under the same conditions as the general rules of tort law. Compensation for purely economic loss is a more complex issue, at least in cases in which the exercise of an economic activity is inevitably dependent upon a clean environment.[14] Moreover, the funds' rules should not restrict compensation by means of top ceilings or by limiting compensation up to a percentage of the losses. In many instances such a rule would place an unreasonably heavy burden on victims, especially when the amount of losses is high, and will give less incentives to operators to strive for deterrence.

Nevertheless, the need to achieve a fair interest balance by taking into account that hazardous operations may have also social benefits and reasons of procedural simplicity may both justify some deviation from general tort law rules. One should not exclude the possibility, for instance, of qualifying a damage as recoverable, only if its amount exceeds a minimal ceiling (Hohloch 1994, 216; Ganten and Lemke 1989, 11).[15] In addition, one could think of fixing lump sums for pain and suffering at the same level for all similar cases, as this would simplify the decision making process (see Abraham 1987, 895–6).

Another important issue refers to 'ecological damages'. Present rules very often leave a big part of these damages, especially damages to common goods, uncompensated,[16] thus neither creating a sufficient deterrent effect nor serving the society's interest by paying the costs for harms caused by specific operations. However, whether the issue of ecological damages should be tackled in the framework of the funds discussed here or whether its regulation should be left to funds or other institutions dealing exclusively with this problem (see Hohloch 1994, 266, arguing that each fund's responsibilities should be as restricted as possible), is a debate that goes beyond the aim of this chapter.

Overcoming the obstacles posed to compensation by the traditional causation requirements   A bold step towards overcoming the inability to establish a clear-cut causal relationship between harmful conduct, for which a fund is responsible, and a specific harm, as traditional rules require, would be to adopt the substantial factor test ('wesentliche Bedingung'), applied to causation issues in the German social security law (Hager 1986; Wagner 1990, 131ff; Barta 1995, 35).[17] In continental Europe the application of the substantial factor test could, furthermore, be combined with a reduction of the evidence standards (Hager 1986, 1968). In the following lines we will first describe the substantial factor test, examine its utility in the area of funds' liability for environmental damage, pinpoint its limits and finally consider possible solutions to cover the short-comings of the substantial factor test in the area of liability for environmental damage. I will leave aside, however, the problem of how the substantial factor test should operate in the case of contrib-utory negligence.[18]

According to the substantial factor test, the claimant is entitled to full compensation, if he or she can prove that a particular type of activity has 'substantially' contributed to his or her harm. Which contribution should be qualified as substantial, is not decided according to rigidly fixed criteria, but on a case-by-case basis, thus leaving space to consider the particular circumstances of each single case (Bley 1986, 239; Deutsch and von Bar 1979, 539–40). The sub-stantial factor test is not solely based on the examination of whether a factor has contributed more than a fixed percentage to the occur-rence of a damage. Other circumstances are taken into account as well. In the context of liability for environmental damage such cir-cumstances could, for example, be whether a particular type of operation was the sole cause of the entire damage, whether it con-tributed to a specific harm in a linear way or jointly with other causes or to which degree natural risks were also involved in its occurrence.

The most important merit of the substantial factor test is that it allows compensation for categories of damage which under tradi-tional causation rules are not compensated and thus it gives more incentives to polluters to take precautionary steps and enhances environmental and victims' interests *vis-à-vis* economic interests. To be more precise, the adoption of the substantial factor test enables victims to get compensation, when they cannot identify the individual operator who caused their damage, but they can, never-theless, link their damage to a particular type of operation. In addi-tion, it guarantees compensation even when it cannot be proved that a type of operation was the sole cause of a particular damage, even though it can be established that it contributed significantly to its occurrence.

The substantial factor test has two further features, which contribute to the attainment of a reasonable balance of interests. On the one side, it can be applied in a flexible way. Given the fact that many environmental liability cases have a complex factual and normative background, it is useful to leave a degree of flexibility to the decision making body, so that it can come to a solution doing justice to the particular circumstances of the case. On the other side, the substantial factor test performs a restrictive function (see Diederichsen 1986, L 90), as it limits the funds from which the victim can claim compensation. Hence, it protects sectors with a small contribution share to the occurrence of a type of damage against the risk of paying amounts disproportionate to the risks they create. A system foreseeing contribution among funds will of course guarantee that mismatches between the amount of paid awards and the level of risk creation will be corrected. As this system is applied, however, only at the end of a fixed time period, the substantial factor test is still useful as a means to restrict the funds' risk of becoming disproportionately liable.

Further advantages with regard to deterrence and fairness will result from the relaxation of the standard of evidence in continental Europe. This will ensure compensation in those instances, in which there is considerable evidence that a type of operation was a substantial factor in the occurrence of a harm, even though this cannot be established with absolute certainty. As to how much the standard of evidence should be relaxed, we are not going to give a definite answer in this place. Our suggestion is, however, that the standard of evidence leaves enough leeway to decision makers to consider the particular features of each case, as happens with the substantial factor test.

To evaluate each individual case, the responsible fund panel should, rather, make use of and combine both evidence of a more general nature and evidence relating to the particular circumstances of a specific case. As an example, to establish a causal relationship between a particular activity and the damages suffered by the specific claimant, the fund may be initially based on purely statistical, probabilistic evidence. However, for the final decision on each case to be taken, particularistic evidence concerning, for instance, the time of exposure to the hazardous activity, information on the general medical status of the specific claimant and other possible causes of the harm in the particular case might be taken into consideration. This combination of probabilistic and empirical evidence will result in the differentiation among different groups of cases, each of which will include individual cases that share similar features and therefore must in principle be decided in the same manner (see Hohloch 1994, 278; on the dangers of categorisation see Nesson 1986, 534–5).

Despite these advantages, the substantial factor test has still some weaknesses. First, it does not shift costs to branches according to the risk each one generates. To be more precise, liability funds responsible for operations that are a substantial factor in the occurrence of a type of harm will bear a liability share higher than their risk share. In reverse, liability funds responsible for operations that contribute in the occurrence of the same damages, but cannot be considered to be substantial factors will pay less money than would correspond to their risk share. In this sense, some branches will have to pay for costs they did not create, while others can ride free. In addition, polluters are given distorted incentives to avoid damages. We will see in the next section how this drawback can be corrected.

Second, the application of the substantial factor test leaves uncovered harms for which no single type of operations can be said to constitute a substantial factor. This applies to situations in which several operations contribute only a small proportion each to the occurrence of a harm. A good example of such a situation is damage caused to forests due to acid rain (a phenomenon known in German as *Waldsterben*). Acid rain is caused by emissions from certain industrial installations, cars and heating systems. These three kinds of activities contribute almost equally to the creation of the acid rain effect, so that none of them can be said to be a 'substantial factor'.

The problem of compensation for environmental damage in such cases could be resolved in two ways: on the one hand, the particular liability funds, whose members contributed jointly to the occurrence of a particular kind of damage, could participate in the creation of a separate fund, responsible for granting compensation for those harms. On the other hand, each liability fund could restrict its compensation payments up to an amount corresponding to the overall risk it created, and compensate victims fully with this amount according to the temporal priority principle, that is, pay full awards to those claimants who claimed compensation first. Later claims should be referred to the other funds.

Contribution among funds

It was said before that subjecting funds' payments to the substantial factor test does not match funds' liability shares with their risk share. It is suggested therefore that a system of contribution among funds be established. The function of this system would entail a closed collaboration among the various funds both at a regional and centralised level to monitor common risks jointly and to agree on the distribution of the final costs among them over a fixed time period (Wagner 1990, 211). By giving correct incentives to the funds' members and by promoting information exchange and common scientific research among economic branches such contribution among funds can lead to better risk control. In addition, it will safeguard a fair distribution of costs among economic branches.

The funds' financial resources

We have already mentioned that shifting costs to the operators of risky activities underlies the concept of liability funds. More precisely, every risk creating company should pay sums proportional to the overall risk it generated (Ladeur 1993, 263). In this section I will deal with issues relating to the calculation of the amount of charges which individual operators should pay to the fund. In the first place I will try to answer the question of whether the estimation of each operator's risk share should be based on generic evidence or on particular circumstances. I will then draw attention to the issue of how charges should be calculated. Last, I will tackle the problem of scientific uncertainty.

It has already been said that identifying every single harm to which a specific operation has contributed and the degree of this contribution is not feasible. In these conditions, statistical evidence is indispensable for the calculation of the risk each operator generates. This does not mean that particular features relating to each individual operation, like breaches against administrative standards, should not also be taken into account. The combination of both abstract and specific evidence enables us to infer with proximity the risk level each operator most probably produces and to correct these inferences every time there are serious indications that they do not correspond to the actual circumstances. Combining statistical with particular evidence is consequently the best available way to estimate the risk of each individual operator and is a necessary condition for a determination of charges which will promote risk control and result in a reasonable allocation of costs.

There are two ways to calculate the amount of charges to individual polluters. On the one hand, it can be estimated on the basis of the costs of damages that need to be currently compensated. On the other hand, the calculation might occur by reference to the total costs that are expected to be incurred by operations in the present and the future.[19]

The first method has the advantage of being simple, while calculating the overall risk level of present activities entails big difficulties, as scientific data on the potential harmful effects of many operations will often be lacking, controversial or vague. However, calculating charges on the basis of damages occurred in the present does not establish any relationship between the harmful effect of current operations and the financial burden placed on those who undertake them. Consequently, it does not give proper incentives for risk control. Moreover, this method distorts the proportional distribution of costs among past and current operators. As an example, let us suppose that damage that occurred today through past activities is higher than damage expected to occur in the future due to current operations. Under these circumstances, it would be unfair for current operators to pay the costs for old sins. As a conclusion, calculation of charges on individual operators should be made for both deterrence and fairness reasons on the basis of the total losses which could be expected to arise out of current activities.

Opting for a calculation of fees on the basis of future damage creates an additional problem, namely how to react in the case of scientific uncertainty. In this context, we have to answer whether individual operators should also be charged for risks that are not sufficiently detected yet by scientific research, and, if this is to be answered in the affirmative, how the amount of such charges should be determined.

It is opportune from the deterrence point of view to impose charges on individual operators for risks whose harmful potential is not sufficiently known yet, as it will motivate risk creators to invest in further scientific research to determine whether a specific risk exists, how serious it is, and how it can be reduced. Charges for not sufficiently determined risks are also necessary to serve the victims' interest in compensation for harm potentially arising out of such risks. At the same time, however, an interest balance suggests that individual operators should not be charged for risks if in the end they prove to be non-existent or less serious than was initially suspected. Both deterrence and a reasonable interest balance in the above mentioned sense can be achieved through the establishment of a deposit-refund system (Costanza and Cornwell 1992, 17 and 19). According to this, operators will be obliged to pay sums to the fund for risks not fully detected. These sums will be deposited in the fund until scientific data permit a more precise and reliable risk assessment. If scientists come to the conclusion that there is no causal link between specific operations and the harm they were suspected of inflicting, these sums will be returned to the individual operators. If, on the contrary, scientific research succeeds in establishing a causal relationship, then they will definitely stay within the fund.

To determine the amount of such charges, the same authors have adopted the 'worst case scenario' approach (Costanza and Cornwell 1992, 17). This approach is based on the premise that the deposited sums should cover the costs that would arise if the worst scientific prediction on the harmful potential of the operation at stake were fulfilled. The worst case scenario approach has the advantage that it gives serious incentives to polluters to engage in intensive scientific research in order to prove that the worst case scenario cannot be realised or in order to reduce the respective risks. Furthermore, it provides for guarantees that risk creators will compensate victims even in the worst case. However, this approach might overburden economic operators, particularly in those cases in which scientific research is still at an early stage. For instance, assuming that some suspicion exists that a substance may cause, but with a rather low probability, some specific type of harm. Assuming, in addition, that, because of the extended use of the substance or of the gravity of damages that might result from it, the substance would, in the worst case, inflict huge damages. In this instance, requiring individual operators to pay this huge amount in advance might be very burdensome to them, especially in view of the small degree of probabilities that the substance will actually cause the harm. To take into due consideration the interests of both victims and polluters, we should, rather, weigh the chance of the worst case scenario occurring against the probability that other scenarios will take place. This method might not offer such strong incentives for risk control as the worst case scenario approach, but it still offers considerable incentive for the reduction of the risk level and, as already said, it balances better the opposing interests at stake. Furthermore, the calculation of expected losses should be revised every time new relevant scientific data are discovered.

Summary

The ideas advanced in this section suggest the development of a liability funds model, to replace the courts' jurisdiction in the area of liability for environmental damages. The design of the model takes into account both the functional objectives of a liability system as well as the framing interest constellation and institutional factors for ensuring effective implementation.

The model proposed is based on the creation and operation of various funds according to sectors of economic activity. The respective branches take the decisions on funds' affairs, unless those decisions affect general interests. In this case, representatives of the state and other social groups have a co-determination power. Compensation is granted for damage for whose occurrence the operations carried out by the members of the respective branch were most probably a substantial factor. To decide whether a type of operation was a substantial factor in the occurrence of a harm, funds would consider both statistical evidence and the particular circumstances of the case. In certain instances, in which no operation can be said to be a substantial factor, victims would get full compensation, but each fund would limit its total liability to the degree to which the operations for which it bears responsibility contributed to the occurrence of the damages at stake. Apart from medical expenses and income loss, damages to property and damages for pain and suffering should be compensated as well. A system of contributions among funds will supplement the whole compensation system to balance possible discrepancies among the sums funds have paid and the risks their individual members have probably generated. The funds' funding comes from the contributions of the individual members of the respective sector. The amount of these contributions corresponds to the overall risk that each member creates, and is not calculated by reference to the amount of damage manifested currently. A deposit–refund model resolves problems arising in the case of scientific uncertainty.

Conclusion

The substitution and combination of classical command and control policies with so-called new approaches is generally viewed as a promising means of to improving the implementation effectiveness of EU environmental policy. However, it would be misleading to assume that new concepts are *per se* sufficient to achieve this objective. As pointed out in the introduction to this volume, new instruments can make things even worse, if they are designed in an inappropriate way. To exploit the potential of new instruments in terms of improved implementation performance, it is necessary to carefully consider various design options in terms of their compatibility with specific institutional and political configurations at the domestic level. The successful design of alternative instruments is a complex task which requires a systematic assessment of the advantages and disadvantages of the different options with respect to these criteria.

It was the objective of this chapter to discuss various design options and their impact on implementation effectiveness for the specific case of liability systems as an alternative instrument of EU environmental policy. For this purpose, several suggestions were developed in order to exploit fully the potential of liability funds in improving the performance of EU environmental policy. If properly designed, liability funds may not merely cover the loopholes of current liability systems with regard to protection of individual rights. They can, in addition, effectively serve the ideas of self-control of economic actors and of social cooperation for the regulation of environmental hazards. Moreover, they will relax the overstrained social security system of the European countries. It remains to be seen whether and to which degree a liability funds approach, which has already been partially proposed by the EU Commission in its 1993 Green Paper, will be finally chosen as the basis of a common European civil liability system for environmental damage.

Notes

1 I am indebted to Prof. Karl-Heinz Ladeur, University of Hamburg and EUI, Florence, for the motivation and the insights he gave me regarding the structure of this chapter. My thanks go furthermore to Christoph Knill and Andrea Lenschow for helping me to give my research project an interdisciplinary dimension and particularly to link

the legal debate on civil liability for environmental damage to the ongoing political scientists' debate on the use of alternative instruments in European environmental policy. I profited furthermore from fruitful discussions with Mercedes Fernandez Armenteros and Patricia Bailey, both researchers at the EUI.

2 Environmental damage does not mean only damage to natural resources. The term is used in a wider sense and includes all damages resulting from a human conduct affecting the environment. A substance release affects for instance the environment, but at the same time it may affect human health or property rights. The term has a similar meaning in article 22 of the German Water Management Act. Damages to natural resources are indicated in the chapter by the term 'ecological damage'.

3 I pay attention to proposals stemming from the US, because the US has instituted many innovative proposals and practices, which might be transferable in the European context.

4 See the Commission's original proposal for a Council Directive on civil liability for damage caused by waste, OJ 89/C 251/3; see also the Commission's amended proposal on the same issue, OJ 91/C 192/6. Neither of these two proposals has been adopted, as the Commission considered it better to elaborate a proposal dealing with environmental damage in general, and not only with damage caused by waste. Some general thoughts on the issue were published in the Green Paper on Remedying Environmental Damage, COM (93) 47. According to information published in *Europe Environment*, No. 493, 11 February 1997, pp. 1–2, the Commission intends to publish a White Paper on the issue, in which its thoughts will be clearer. A draft White Paper was published in April 1998.

5 By 'liability systems' we mean both the substantive rules and evidence rules which regulate liability and the institutional arrangements, in which these rules are applied.

6 The term 'victims' should normally include boh persons who suffer individual harm and society as a whole, whose interests in the preservation of a health and sound environment are infringed upon, whenever natural resources are damaged. However, the term here refers only to individual victims, as a result of the fact that the chapter is mainly oriented towards regulation of damages to individuals.

7 The presentation of traditional tort systems is admittedly simplified here. As regards causation, for instance, doctrines like joint and several liability for alternative causation, 'market share' liability or reversal of the burden of proof were employed to mitigate the hard results of causation rules. Nevertheless, such doctrines have had only limited use and in any case they are merely exceptions to the basic premise that liability is imposed only if a causal link between a specific conduct and a spe-

cific harm is clearly established.

8   In common law countries the evidence standard is more relaxed, as it has to be shown that it is more likely than not that a particular conduct caused the specific harm. Nevertheless, this does not mean that the causation problems discussed here do not appear also in common law countries.

9   The proposal by Rosenberg 1984, 919–24, that this drawback can be corrected, if class actions take place already at the stage of risk creation and before any damages show up and judges order the creation of an insurance fund for future probable losses, does not adequately address the question of whether judges are able to find sufficient scientific evidence to make accurate predictions at this early stage.

10 Another problem of social security systems is that they provide for coverage only for medical expenses and income loss, thus leaving property damages uncompensated.

11 Such an accident bearing 'extraordinarily grave consequences' was, for example, the Sandoz accident, which took place in 1986 and affected the regions along the river Rhine. This accident occurred in 1986, when a fire broke out in the factory of the pharmaceutical company Sandoz, which is situated near the Swiss city of Basel. As a consequence of the efforts to put out the fire, 30 tonnes of farming chemicals and hundreds of kilograms of mercury and other types of chemicals entered the river Rhine. This resulted in irreparable damage to the fauna and flora of the Rhine amounting to an ecological disaster, not only in Switzerland, but also in the regions of Germany which the river flows through. The Sandoz accident is very important from a legal policy point of view, as it induced the legal establishment in Germany to shift its attention to the potential of civil liability as a viable alternative to the regulation of environmental and health externalities.

12 In the case examined here the general interest consists in resolving the tension between environmental protection and economic development.

13 See the 1993 'Convention of the Council of Europe on Damage Resulting from Activities Dangerous to the Environment', art. 6(1) and 7(1); no-fault liability is also foreseen by the two Commission proposals for a Directive on civil liability for damage caused by waste, see art. 3 of the first proposal and art. 3(1) of the amended proposal.

14 To give an example, the fishing industry should get compensation for loss due to water pollution, because a necessary condition for its activity is that waters are clean.

15 See also the analysis in section three which stresses the necessity to put some limits to liability.

16 See the limited scope of article 16(1) of the German Environmental Liability Act (Umwelthaftungsgesetz).

17 We should recall that not only is the substantial factor test familiar to common law systems, but some court decisions and scholars have also pointed to its utility in the area of toxic torts see Marchant and Baram 1990, 118–19.

18 The tort law approach that contributory negligence should be considered is contrasted by an insurance law concept, according to which contributory negligence is not taken into account once the substantial factor test has been established. See Wagner 1990, 178 (German law) and Sugarman 1985, 619–20 (American law). On the issue of whether compensation for toxic torts should be based on tort or non-tort principles in general see Schuck 1987, 255–97.

19 As Abraham (1987, 893) indicates, this issue is connected to the retroactive effect of funds' liability. In this chapter I will not be concerned with this issue.

References

Abraham, Kenneth S. (1987): 'Individual Action and Collective Responsibility: The Dilemma of Mass Tort Reform', *Virginia Law Review*, 73, 845–907.

Barta, Heinz (1995): 'Kann das historische Modell der gesetzlichen Unfallversicherung einer modernen Arzthaftung als Vorbild dienen? Eine historisch-aktuelle Ideenskizze', in M. Heinze and J. Schmitt (eds), *Festschrift für Wolfgang Gitter zum 65. Geburtstag*. Wiesbaden: Chmielorz, 9–52.

Bley, Helmar (1986): *Sozialrecht*, 5. Aufl., Frankfurt am Main: Metzner.

Brüggemeier, Gert (1988). 'Produkthaftung und Produktsicherheit', *Zeitschrift für das gesamte Handelsrecht und Wirtschaftsrecht*, 52, 511–36.

Calabresi, Guido (1970): *The Costs of Accidents: A Legal and Economic Analysis*, New Haven: Yale University Press.

Cappelletti, Mauro (1989): *The Judicial Process in Comparative Perspective*, ed. with the collaboration of P.J. Collmer and J.M. Olson, Oxford: Clarendon.

Cappelletti, Mauro and Garth, Bryant (1978): 'Access to Justice: The Worldwide Movement to Make Rights Effective. A General Report', in M. Cappelletti (gen. ed.), *Access to Justice*, Vol. I: *A World Survey*, M. Cappelletti and B. Garth (eds), Book I, Milan: Giuffrè and Alphenaandenrijn: Sijthoff, 3–124.

Costanza, Robert and Cornwell, Laura (1992): 'The 4P Approach to Dealing with Scientific Uncertainty', *Environment*, 34 (9), 12–21.

Deutsch, Erwin and Bar, Christian von (1979): 'Schutzbereich und wesentliche Bedingung im Versicherungs- und Haftungsrecht', *Monatsschrift für Deutsches Recht*, 33 (7), 536–41.

Diederichsen, Uwe (1986): 'Referat zum Thema: Ausbau des Individualschutzes gegen Umweltbelastungen als Aufgabe des bürgerlichen und des öffentlichen Rechts', in *Verhandlungen des 56. DJT*, Berlin 1986, hrsg. von der Ständigen Deputation des Deutschen Juristentages, Bd. II (Sitzungsberichte), München, L 48–L 106.

Dupeyroux, Jean-Jacques (1997): *Droit de la sécurité sociale*, 8th edn, by Xavier Prétot, Paris: Dalloz.

Elliott, E. Donald (1985): 'Goal Analysis versus Institutional Analysis of Toxic Compensation Systems', *Georgetown Law Journal*, 73, 1357–76.

Ewald, François (1985): 'A Concept of Social Law', in G. Teubner (ed.), *Dilemmas of Law in the Welfare State*, Berlin; New York: de Gruyter, 40–75.

Fleming, John G. (1994): 'Mass Torts', *American Journal of Comparative Law*, 42 (3), 507–29.

Ganten, Reinhard H. and Lemke, Michael (1989): 'Haftungsprobleme im Umweltbereich', *Umwelt- und Planungsrecht*, 9 (1), 1–14.

Habermas, Jürgen (1996): *Between Facts and Norms: Contribution to a Discourse Theory of Law and Democracy*, tr. W. Rehg, Cambridge, MA: MIT Press.

Hager, Günter (1986): 'Umweltschäden: Ein Prüfstein für die Wandlungs- und Leistungsfähigkeit des Deliktrechts', *Neue Juristische Wochenschrift*, 39 (32), 1961–71.

Hager, Günter (1995): 'Ökologisierung des Verbraucherschutzrechtes', *Umwelt- und Planungsrecht*, 14 (11–12), 401–7.

Hohloch, Gerhard (1994): 'Entschädigungsfonds auf dem Gebiet des Umwelthaftungsrechts: Rechtsvergleichende Untersuchung zur Frage der Einsatzfähigkeit einer "Fondslösung"', *Berichte Umweltbundesamt 1/94*, Berlin: Schmidt.

Kinkel, Klaus (1989): 'Möglichkeiten und Grenzen der Bewältigung von umwelttypischen Distanz- und Summationsschäden: Bestandsaufnahme und rechtspolitischer Ausblick', *Zeitschrift für Rechtspolitik*, 22 (8), 293–8.

Knebel, Jürgen (1988): 'Überlegungen zur Fortentwicklung des Umwelthaftungsrechts', in R. Breuer, M. Kloepfer, P. Marburger and M. Schröder (eds), *Jahrbuch des Umwelt- und Technikrechts 1988, Band 5*, Düsseldorf: Werner, 261–80.

Ladeur, Karl-Heinz (1993): 'Der Umwelthaftungsfonds: ein Irrweg der Flexibilisierung des Umweltrechts?', *Versicherungsrecht*, 44 (7), 257–65.

Ladeur, Karl-Heinz (1995): *Social Risks, Welfare Rights and the Paradigm of Proceduralisation: The Combining of the institutions of the liberal Constitutional State and the Social State*, Florence: European University Institute, Working Paper in Law 95/2.

Lambrichts, Roger (1990): 'Der niederländische Luftverschmutzungs-Fonds', *Natur und Recht*, 12 (3), 97–102.

Legrand, Pierre (1997): 'Against a European Civil Code', *Modern Law Review*, 60, 44–63.

Marchant, Gary E. and Baram, Michael S. (1990): 'The Use of Risk Assessment Evidence to Prove Increased Risk and Alternative Causation in Toxic Tort Litigation', *Federation of Insurance and Corporate Counsel Quarterly*, 41, 95–126.

Medicus, Dieter (1986): 'Zivilrecht und Umweltschutz', *Juristen-Zeitung*, 4 (17), 778–85.

Nesson, Charles (1986): 'Agent Orange Meets the Blue Bus: Factfinding at the Frontier of Knowledge', *Boston University Law Review*, 66, 521–39.

Nicklisch, Fritz (1995): 'Risikosteuerung durch Haftung im deutschen und europäischen Technologie- und Umweltrecht', in F. Graf von Westphalen and O. Sandrock (eds), *Lebendiges Recht: von den Sumerern bis zur Gegenwart, Festschrift für Reinhold Trinkner zum 65. Geburtstag*, Heidelberg: Recht und Wirtschaft, 617–31.

Posner, Richard (1992): *Economic Analysis of Law*, 4th edn, Boston, Toronto: Little, Brown.

Rehbinder, Eckard (1989): 'Fortentwicklung des Umwelthaftungsrechts in der Bundesrepublik Deutschland', *Natur und Recht*, 11 (4), 149–63.

Robinson, Glen O. (1985): 'Probabilistic Causation and Compensation for Tortious Risk', *Journal of Legal Studies*, 14, 779–98.

Rosenberg, David (1984): 'The Causal Connection in Mass Exposure Cases: A "Public Law" Vision of the Tort System', *Harvard Law Review*, 97, 849–929.

Salje, Peter (1991): 'Risikovorsorge durch Errichtung eines Umwelthaftungsfonds am Beispiel des "Hamburger Entwurfs"', *Kritische Vierteljahresschrift für Gesetzgebung und Rechtswissenschaft*, 74 (314), 324–43.

Schuck, Peter (1987): *Agent Orange on Trial: Mass Toxic Disasters in the Courts*, enlarged edn, Cambridge, MA, and London: Harvard University Press.

Seibt, Christoph (1994): *Zivilrechtlicher Ausgleich ökologischer Schäden – Eine rechtsvergleichende Untersuchung zum repressiven Schutz kollektiver Rechtspositionen an Naturgütern und zum Ausgleich von Beeinträchtigungen des Naturhaushalts im Zivilrecht*, Tübingen: Mohr.

Sugarman, Stephen D. (1985): 'Doing Away with Tort Law', *California Law Review*, 73, 555–664.

Viscusi, W. Kip (1989): 'Toward a Diminished Role for Tort Liability: Social Insurance, Government Regulation, and Contemporary Risks to Health and Safety', *Yale Journal on Regulation*, 6, 65–107.

Wagner, Gerhard (1990): *Kollektives Umwelthaftungsrecht auf genossenschaftlicher Grundlage*, Berlin: Duncker und Humblot.

Weinrib, Ernest J. (1995): *The Idea of Private Law*, Cambridge, MA, and London: Harvard University Press.

8 *Clíona Kimber*[1]

Implementing European environmental policy and the Directive on Access to Environmental Information

Introduction

It is increasingly recognised that implementation and enforcement of environmental legislation is not effective in the European Union and that this is a serious shortcoming of EC environmental law (Krämer 1996). Although much environmental legislation has been adopted by the Community, this has not yet achieved the desired or expected results of improvement in the condition of natural resources and environmental quality. In fact, a report on the state of the environment indicated in 1992 a slow but relentless deterioration in the general state of the environment of the Community, notwithstanding the measures adopted over the past two decades to halt this decline (Commission 1992).

In view of these developments, the Commission emphasised that the implementation and enforcement of EU environmental policy needs to be improved and that this has to be done through an increased emphasis on shared responsibility for the environment, through review and simplification of existing legislation where required, and through broadening the range and mix of instruments of environmental policy (Commission 1995, 1996). In this context, the availability of environmental information is an important component in the process of improving the implementation and enforcement of Community environmental policy. This has been recognised in some of the most important Community documents in this area (Commission 1995, 1996, 1996a) as well as the Fifth Environmental Action Programme, which was adopted in 1992.[2]

To date the most important European Community policy instrument which provides for availability of environmental information is the 1990 Directive on Freedom of Access to Information on the Environment.[3] The objective of the Directive is to provide a right of access to information on the environment. This is designed to act as an aid to enforcement by individuals of environmental measures and as a means of devolving power from public authorities to citizens and public interest groups. Indeed, recital 4 of the Directive confidently asserts that 'access to information on the environment held by public authorities will improve environmental protection'.

This chapter will examine the extent to which the substantive text of the Directive and its subsequent implementation and enforcement allow for the achievement of these objectives.[4] Following a critical analysis of the implementation problems that arise directly from the legal text and design of the instrument, the essay will focus on the implementation and enforcement of the Directive in four Member States, namely the UK, Germany, Ireland and Spain. Identification of weaknesses, problems or defects in the current legal regime are necessary to review and amend the system and to improve its effectiveness. It is important to emphasise at the outset that this chapter does not attempt to explain or account for the differences found in the countries examined with respect to the effectiveness of the implementation of the Directive in each country. Rather, its objective is to investigate the implementation of the Directive in light of its strengths and weaknesses in different administrative contexts, all of which are hoped to respond positively to the Directive. On the basis of this comparative analysis, the chapter will suggest some reforms of the system of access to environmental information as a whole, in addition, in line with the arguments developed in the introductory chapters to this book, it will use the Information Directive as a case study to highlight the institutional challenges for the effective implementation of Community law.

Directive 90/313: strengths and weaknesses

The political background against which the Directive was proposed in 1988 was that of secrecy in the working of public administrations. Of the then twelve Member States, only Denmark, France and the Netherlands had legislation granting a general entitlement to have access to environmental information. New legislation was required in all of the remaining Member States to open up their administrations and to provide a broad right of access to information. The Directive represents, therefore, a break with the tradition of official secrecy in the administration of most Member States.

The main achievement of the Directive is that it establishes a positive right to have access to information held by any public authority of the Member States, for any natural or legal person, without having to demonstrate an interest. A response to a request for information must be given within two months, and information must be supplied at a reasonable cost. The right established by the Directive is also justiciable, in that there must be a possibility of judicial or administrative review of a decision to refuse to provide information. This is a considerable advance on the pre-existing situation, and has the potential, if implemented fully, to make a significant contribution to facilitating and supporting the effectiveness of Community environmental policy.

However, the Directive is flawed in many important respects, both in terms of its substantive provisions and in terms of its drafting. These flaws place obstacles in the way of its implementation and enforcement and limit the amount of information, which reaches the ordinary citizen. Thus, the potential of freedom of access to environmental information for making Community environmental policy more effective, is not realised. The most important deficiencies are the following.

First, information can only be requested from public authorities of the Member States. Excluded, therefore, are both Community institutions and private bodies. This limitation has caused difficulties for NGOs seeking to hold Community institutions accountable for their environmental decisions. For example, WWF sought access to Commission documents relating to a decision to grant structural funds for a project in Mullaghmore in Ireland. Access to these documents was refused on grounds of protection of the public interest and of the Commission interest in the confidentiality of its own proceedings.[5] Although there is a Code of Conduct on public access to Commission and Council documents which must be read with subsequent decisions of the Council and Commission,[6] it is not legally binding and it is less generous in its right of access than Directive 90/313.

The inclusion of a right to request information from private bodies would have been controversial and radical, particularly in light of business fears regarding commercial confidentiality. However, an earlier draft of the Directive did include under the definition of information which could be requested, information on public *or private* projects, and the European Parliament suggested that information held by private bodies as well as public authorities be included in the right of access. Certainly a case could be made for the extension of the right to have access to information, to private entities which release significant amounts of damaging substances into the environment or whose activities would have significant effects on the environment. Certain information on the activities of private bodies is made available in the United States, for example, by the toxic release inventory (Percival *et al.* 1996), and in the UK, more recently, by the chemical releases inventory, modelled on the US approach (Bell 1997).

Second, the inclusion of a large number of broadly drafted exceptions to the obligation to disclose information is a significant shortcoming of the Directive. Quite clearly, a right of access to information cannot be absolute, as certain basic privacy rights including the privacy rights of companies and of private individuals, mandate a certain number of exceptions to the right of access to information. However, the view is taken by many commentators that the nature and extent of the exceptions in the Directive are so broad in themselves and capable of such a wide interpretation, that they threaten to destroy the very right itself (Bakkenist 1994; House of Lords 1996).

The addition of a so-called 'harm test', that is, a presumption that information would be released unless its disclosure was likely to cause significant harm to the interests protected by the exception, would restrict the scope of the exceptions and, it is suggested, create a better balance between the interests of privacy and the interests of openness. It is significant to note that the European Parliament was in favour of a harm test, to limit the effect of any exceptions, arguing that 'these exceptions should be formulated in such a way that it would only be possible to keep environmental information secret if it can be shown that publication would cause excessive damage to important interests' (European Parliament 1989, 232). Moreover, a harm test is widely supported by many bodies, including, in the UK, the House of Lords (House of Lords 1996, para. 61), and in Ireland by the Office of the Ombudsman.

Third, the drafting of the legislation is weak, with considerable ambiguity in the definition of key concepts. There is no clear definition for example, of what is meant by information on the environment, for example, or of what constitutes 'a reasonable cost' for supplying information. In particular, the provisions setting out who is under a duty to supply information are labyrinthine in their complexity. The Directive states in article 1 that its objective is to ensure freedom of access to information held by public authorities. It then goes on to define public authorities in article 2(a) as 'any public administration at national, regional or local level with responsibilities, and possessing information, relating to the environment with the exception of bodies acting in a judicial or legislative capacity'. The Directive later on, in article 6 extends the obligation to provide information to 'bodies with public responsibilities for the environment and under the control of public authorities is made available … either via the competent public authority or directly by the body itself'. In practice, as will be discussed in the next section, many problems of practical application have arisen. The application of the Directive to certain bodies which have environmental responsibilities but are on the fringes of the public administrators, or which are private bodies such as the privatised utilities in the UK, has led to considerable tension and disagreement.

Fourth, the practical arrangements by which information could most effectively be made available have not been established. By contrast, freedom of information legislation in the United States, Canada, Australia and New Zealand provides, amongst other things, for the keeping of catalogues or databases of information, for information officers, for inventories of places where information can be found and provides for more regulation of the day to day methods of making information available (Birkenshaw 1996). It is interesting to note that the 1997 Irish Freedom of Information Act requires public bodies to keep reference books describing their structure and organisation, their functions, powers, duties and services, and all classes of record under athat body's control (Meehan 1997b).

It may be argued that these are not matters that are appropriate for Community law to regulate. The Preamble to the Treaty of Rome requires, in line with the subsidiarity principle, that decisions should be taken as closely as possible to the citizen. Indeed commentators have noted a move away from detailed and Community law that is directly applicable, towards looser measures which allow Member States to draft and formulate the details, and in particular to decide what the specific obligations of administrative bodies will be in complying with Community law (Weatherill and Beaumont 1995, 12–15). At the same time there is a recognition in a 1996 Commission communication that measures to improve the implementation of Community environmental law must include a new, broader approach encompassing the whole regulatory chain. The regulatory chain is defined as the whole process through which legislation is designed, conceived, drafted, adopted, implemented and enforced until its efficiency is assessed (Commission 1996, Annex I).

Thus a better legal model might be one where the way in which the entire administrative organisation is likely to work and of the interaction between agencies, industries and the general public is taken into account in drafting Directives (Moe 1993). Such an approach would require much more detailed and, from the point of view of the Member States, more intrusive, provisions in environmental Directives. Finally, it may have been preferable for the Directive to adopt an active policy of dissemination of environmental information, in addition to simply granting a passive right to have access to information. Research has shown that the general public is often not aware of its right to information and for a variety of reasons, does not actively go to public authorities and consult databases of information. Research by Rowan-Robinson shows that the use of registers of information in the United Kingdom by the general public has been low (Rowan-Robinson *et al.* 1996). Research by the author, which is discussed below, supports these conclusions.

In the light of the Directive's strengths and weaknesses, it is questionable whether the Directive completely realises its potential in terms of supporting and facilitating an improvement of the effectiveness of Community policy. Whether or not its potential is realised depends on the effectiveness of its own implementation and enforcement which. These will be examined in the next section.

Access to environmental information in four Member States: enforcement and implementation of Directive 90/313

This section of the chapter will examine the implementation and enforcement of Directive 90/313 in four Member States of the EU, namely, the UK, Germany, Ireland and Spain. These countries were chosen because they represent a cross-section of the different types of Member States, northern and southern, more and less industrialised, federal and unitary and those having a strongly and a weakly developed environmental consciousness. In order to obtain information about the practical experience of access to environmental information in the Member States, a survey of experience of users (requesters) was undertaken. A framework was developed in order to ensure that a representative sample of types of users and comparable results was obtained in each country.[7]

From an analysis of the questionnaires and from interviews, the conclusion was that the experience in practice with the operation of the Directive and the implementing legislation can only be described as mixed, with some successes and some failures. Within the countries examined, the legislative system has resulted in a noticeable step forward in terms of the availability of information on the environment. Yet requesters still encounter many difficulties. That the traditional culture of secrecy, which pertained to a greater or lesser degree in the countries studied, continues to exert an influence on the accessibility of information, was a fact noted by different groups in all the countries studied. As one Irish environmental alliance group stated: 'We feel that the present system is hampered by a culture of secrecy – civil servants seem instinctively to react negatively to sharing any information they hold with the public' (interview, January 1997). The success of requests for information on the environment can vary considerably from requester to requester and from public body to public body. In the words of one Spanish NGO 'the experience is very varied, from enormous facilities for obtaining the information to real obscurantism' (interview, March 1996). In general, subject to the problems set out below, information has become more easily accessible, but it is still not as accessible as requesters would like, nor as accessible as intended under Community legislation.

If lessons are to be drawn from this practical experience, it is necessary to isolate more specific factors which condition the success of requests for information and which identify specific problems encountered in practice. Three areas of particular interest and significance will be discussed, namely, the implementing legislation, the conditioning factors on which availability of information is dependent, and the interpretation and application of the implementing legislation.

The implementing legislation

The countries examined in this study had historically experienced, to varying degrees, a public administration that tended towards secrecy rather than openness. Government in the United Kingdom operated in a culture of secrecy and confidentiality, a circumstance which was supported by legislation prohibiting unauthorised dissemination of official information (Birkenshaw 1996, chapter 3). At the time of the adoption of the Directive, the United Kingdom stood apart from most other common law countries, in that it had not enacted legislation providing for a general right of access to information held by public authorities. Some efforts had been made in the UK to introduce more openness in specific sectors. In particular, a system of registers, including water registers and planning registers, made certain information on the environment available to the public (Rowan-Robinson *et al.* 1996). Official information, however, was protected by official secrets legislation. In contrast, freedom of information legislation has existed in the USA since 1966, and in Canada, Australia and New Zealand since 1982. In Ireland, although public participation and access to public information had been a feature of the planning process since 1963, mainly through the public notification process and the use of planning registers, Irish government regarded the introduction of a broad right to freedom of information with some trepidation. In legislation similar to that in force in the UK, official information was protected, inter alia, by the Official Secrets Act, 1963 (Meehan 1997b).[8] Spain had only a limited right to access to information in its constitution (Kimber and de la Torre 1997). In Germany, the lingering 'Prussian' tradition of secrecy in the public service, made its administration perhaps the most secretive of the four countries examined. (Kimber and Eckardt forthcoming)

Implementing Community law providing for freedom of environmental information required, therefore, a considerable change of tradition in these countries. Thus it is not surprising that the adoption of legislation in Germany and Spain to implement the Directive was significantly late and that the legislation was in fact deficient in many respects when adopted. Spain revised its initial legislation following a letter of formal notice from the Commission. Implementation of the Directive was finally effected by Act 38/1995, which came into force in December 1995 – three years late.[9] Germany adopted implementing legislation eighteen months after the deadline for implementation had passed.[10] Ireland and the UK, where the gap between national practices and the EU Directive was less extreme, brought in implementing legislation within the correct time.[11]

Furthermore, it is likely that the German implementing legislation will be found by the ECJ to be deficient in a number of respects.

The Commission took the view that the German implementing legislation was not in compliance with the Directive and began infringement proceedings against Germany for its failure to transpose the Directive correctly.[12] The matter is currently being heard before the Court of Justice and judgment is awaited. In the opinion of Advocate General Fennelly, Germany has failed to correctly transpose the Directive with regard to the following matters: (1) failure to include in its implementing legislation any provision specifically requiring public authorities to supply information in part where it is possible to separate out information on items which it is permissible to withhold under article 3(2) of the Directive, (2) failure to restrict the derogation allowed by paragraph 7(1)(2) of the UIG, the German implementing legislation, to administrative procedures which immediately precede a contentious or quasi-contentious procedure, (3) failure to ensure that the costs with respect to supply of information are not excessive, and (4) by allowing public authorities to impose a charge where a request is refused.[13] It remains to be seen whether the ECJ will follow the reasoning of the Advocate General.

Apart from areas of non-compliance, the implementing legislation in the countries examined simply replicated the provisions of the Directive with some adaptations, and by and large retained a similar structure. In other words, Member States implementing the Directive enacted legislation that achieved, at best, the minimum necessary for compliance. In the case of Germany, the implementing legislation even fell below that which was required for compliance with the Directive.

There were nevertheless some examples of good practice as regards the implementation of the Directive in the Member States studied. The Spanish legislation requires public authorities to gather and publish information relating to *requests* for access to environmental information received by them. This is a welcome innovation on the part of the Spanish system, especially as the statistics published could be a valuable instrument in evaluating the functioning of the system. Ultimately it could also be employed as an instrument of accountability.

The Irish ENFO[14] centre, a drop-in information centre which provides a wide range of information to the general public and which gives assistance with accessing more specialised information, is a model to be recommended. The centre is housed in a two-storey building in the centre of Dublin, has a specialist library and adequate resources and is attended by specialised staff. Empirical work by the author in Ireland, as well as a visit to the centre, found that there is general satisfaction on the part of the public and NGOs with facilities and service provided by the centre.

Nevertheless, the overwhelmingly minimalist approach to the implementation of the Directive leads to a failure of implementation in an important respect. As has been discussed above, the very nature of a directive is that it specifies the objective to be achieved, and leaves the Member States to decide the means of achieving that objective. In other words, Member States are required to make the general norms agreed at Community level more concrete and to flesh out the general provisions contained in a particular directive. This has not been done in the implementing legislation for the Information Directive in the Member States examined. The most important matter, which Member States were required to make provision for in their national legal systems, namely, setting out the terms and conditions on which information should be made available, establishment of the practical arrangements whereby information is effectively made available, such as designation and preparation of places and methods where information might be obtained, hours of opening of public authorities to the public, adoption of codes and policies for administrators in making decisions as to the release of information, has not been attended to. National implementing legislation in the Member States studied fails to set out any practical arrangements whatsoever for making information available, leaving it instead to individual public bodies to decide on their own arrangements. In practice this often only took place following the first request for information and procedures varied considerably from body to body, leaving the courts to fill in the gaps created by ambiguities in the legislative provisions. For example, the entitlement (or not) of requesters to stipulate the form in which information should be made available to them is a matter which one would expect to be dealt with in legislation which sets out practical arrangements by which information is to be made available. Yet, from among the Member States examined, only the Spanish legislation gives requesters the option to choose the media in which they would like the information to be made available to them. In a significant decision, the Federal Administrative Court in Germany achieved a similar result, by holding that where a requester expressly demands that information be made available to him or her in a particular form, this information can only be made available in a different form when important justifiable reasons exist.[15]

Considering the tendency to enact a minimalist transposition at the domestic level, there are lessons to be learned from this experience for the drafting of future Community legislation, especially if the recognition that measures to improve the implementation of Community law must include a new broad approach encompassing the whole regulatory chain and all relevant actors, is to be taken seriously. Legislation ought to be drafted so that it places a stronger and clearer obligation on Member States to address the practical implementation of Community legislation and to specify and notify the Commission of concretising measures. In addition, the preparation of recommendatory annexes to directives, which could contain guidance, suggestions and recommendations as well as examples of good practice from other jurisdictions, could assist legislators and administrators who may not have the time or expertise to give consideration to the details of practical implementation for each new piece of Community legislation that is adopted.

The conditioning factors on which availability of information is dependent

One of the strengths of the Directive is that it establishes that any person has a right to obtain information without that person having to demonstrate an interest. Nevertheless, the research undertaken revealed that success in obtaining information depended on several factors, namely the nature of the group, its working methods and its likely use of the information, the nature of the information requested, the nature of the institution or authority from which the information was requested.

Clearly the legislative scheme established by the Directive and the implementing legislation, does not permit access to information to be conditioned by these factors. These are factors, however, which one would instinctively expect to be taken into account by a reluctant or hesitant administration faced with a request for information. They demonstrate the significant influence which an underlying political and administrative culture can exert on the operation of legislation in practice (see Knill and Lenschow in chapter 2 of this book).

Nature of group, working methods and purpose of information   The survey conducted revealed that significant factors in obtaining information were: the type of group, the nature of their work, their working methods and their objectives. As might be expected, public bodies were much more reluctant to give information to requesters which were involved in protesting or campaigning publicly against the state on environmental issues. The research revealed, in all countries, a marked difference between the ease with which NGOs which worked with the state obtained information compared with experiences of requesters who were politically active in a more controversial manner. It seems that authorities are less reluctant to provide information to professional groups who have good relations with the state than to groups who wish to use it to campaign on sensitive political issues. In Spain, in particular, the creation of the Environmental Assessment Council, a consultative body examining proposed legislation and making reports which includes various types of environmental groups, has helped these groups to have access to certain information held by public authorities which they would not otherwise have obtained so easily. In Ireland, the Conservation Volunteers stressed the importance of building up good relations with public bodies, saying that when such a relationship was built up, it was much easier to get information.

Nature of the information   Another important factor in obtaining information was the kind of information requested. As could be expected, there were few difficulties in obtaining access to information already in the public domain. Difficulties increased, however, as the information became more controversial or concerned an issue on which public bodies were sensitive, especially if public authorities took the view, mistakenly or otherwise, that information might be used out of context to manipulate or inflame public opinion. Greenpeace (Spain) pointed out, that it is with regard to issues on which it is campaigning that it experiences greatest difficulties in obtaining information. It noted particular difficulties, for example, with regard to getting information about the generation of nuclear energy in Spain, and in obtaining information concerning fisheries and discharges of pollution to the environment. Similar experiences were related by other Spanish, Irish and British environmental NGOs.

In addition, it was found that it was easier to access data which was technical, or factual or which was 'raw' as opposed to obtaining information on decisions taken or policy information. It was particularly difficult to get information on policy and proposed or prospective measures. As regards decisions already taken, NGOs felt that they had no insight into the basis for decisions made by public bodies.

The experience might be summed up by the comment of Friends of the Earth, (UK), that it was extremely difficult or almost impossible to get 'the last five per cent of information' (interview, October, 1996) i.e. that information which is politically controversial or sensitive. If, the general public or NGOs wish to take action to hold bodies accountable or to take action to achieve environmental justice, this last 5 per cent of information could be the most important.

Institution or authority addressed   It was also apparent that the ease with which information could be obtained from a public body varied considerably from body to body. Some government departments or local authorities of public bodies are well organised, function efficiently and are willing to give information. Others are reluctant to give information or do so only after considerable delay. In certain circumstances this was due to lack of organisation of the public body or an ongoing shortage of resources. One Irish environmental group explained that its attempts to obtain information were hampered by the fact that some public authorities did not have sufficient staff resources to catalogue and organise information held. At other times the staff of a body, particularly more junior staff or desk clerks, were not aware of their obligations to provide access to information. In the UK there was a contrast between local authorities, which were more willing to disclose information, and central government departments, which were less willing to do so. This is perhaps due to the fact that local authorities have been required since 1988 by the Local Government (Access to Information) Act 1988 to open meetings to the public and provide access to a range of local authority documents (Birkenshaw 1996, 190–9). Hence, besides issues of political and administrative culture, we need to consider administrative capacities as a potentially limiting factor for effective implementation.[16]

The interpretation and application of the legislation
The research undertaken also indicated that there were difficulties

with the interpretation and application of the national implementing legislation by bodies to which requests for information were addressed. It was found that the legislation was often interpreted incorrectly, or extremely restrictively, particularly where there was a reluctance to provide access to information for the reasons described in the previous section. A restrictive and obstructive interpretation is facilitated, in certain cases, by the ambiguities in the Directive and the national implementing legislation. Consequently, the relative openness in the formulation of the Directive, intended to allow for more flexible adaptation on the national level, did in fact prove counterproductive in several cases. Although the research found that there were problems in relation to the interpretation or application of a wide number of provisions of the legislation, there were particular difficulties with regard to the following features.

Narrow interpretation of the definition of 'information on the environment'   In many cases the term 'information on the environment' was interpreted narrowly in order to exclude from its ambit much information which would commonly be considered 'information on the environment'. In the UK, for example, the Campaign for Freedom of Information related that information on traffic flows, which had relevance in challenging the necessity for a by-pass around the town of Salisbury, was excluded from the definition of information related to the environment (House of Lords 1996). In another instance, a government department refused to supply the inspector conducting a public inquiry into a controversial proposed road by-pass scheme, with a copy of a commercial agreement between the government department and the road building consortium, on the ground, inter alia, that this was not information on the environment. A request by a local environmental alliance for the same information was also refused. The case went to judicial review where the court emphasised that the term 'information on the environment' should be given a wide definition. It held that a concession agreement between a government department and a road building consortium was capable of containing information on the environment despite the fact that it was a commercial agreement.[17] In Spain, Greenpeace challenged in the high court in Spain an exclusion by an authority of information on fisheries from the definition of information on the environment, and obtained judgement in their favour. In a similar case in Germany, a request for information on the para-

meters and methods of gauging levels of noise, was initially excluded
from the definition of information on the environment. On appeal,
however, the Schleswig Administrative Court held that the basis for
making forecasts as to the future state of the environment, such as
information on how noise levels are calculated, although not itself
information on the environment, is an essential prerequisite for the
making of such forecasts and thus should be included in the definition of environmental information.[18]

In an interesting decision, the Higher Administrative Court in
Schleswig referred a number of questions to the ECJ for a preliminary ruling, inter alia, the question of whether a statement of views
given by a countryside protection authority in development consent
proceedings is information on the environment.[19] The ECJ found
that such a statement did constitute information relating to the environment if that statement was capable of influencing the outcome of
the development consent proceedings.[20] In coming to this decision,
the court stated quite forcefully that the wording of article 2(a) of
the Directive makes it clear that the Community legislature intended
to make the concept of access to information a broad one, embracing both information on the state of the environment and information on activities which may affect the environment.[21] This
clarification in such direct terms by the ECJ that the definition of
information on the environment should be a wide one, will be of
great benefit in making more information available to requesters,
and will help to create a more effective system of access to information.

The bodies under a duty to provide information   Another weakness
in the Directive and national legislation, to which attention has been
drawn above, is the lack of clarity with regard to the definition of
bodies, which are under a duty to provide information. There is considerable ambiguity in the legislation in this regard, and this vague-
ness has been exploited by many bodies in order to argue that they
are not subject to the requirement to provide access to information.
In Spain, for example, there are difficulties with autonomous bodies,
such as the Nuclear Security Council, which are detached from the
state. There are also problems with semi-public bodies. These have a
highly complex structure and are both users and producers of information, but have argued that they are not 'holders' as such in accordance with the Directive. These bodies may fund their activities from

different sources, sometimes undertaking work for private clients (Kimber and de la Torre 1997). In Germany, too, there have been conflicting judicial decisions in this area. In one case, an authority with responsibility for overseeing the safety and economic efficiency of energy installations was held not to be a body with responsibility for the protection of the environment.[22] In another, authorities with responsibility for the building of roads, because of their duties with regard to prevention of noise pollution, were classified as authorities with responsibility for the environment.[23]

In the UK, problems have arisen because of the privatisation of many formerly public functions. This has been of particular difficulty with privatised utilities. The claim by water services companies and British Nuclear Fuels not to be within the scope of the Directive is currently the subject of a formal complaint to the Commission, which has been pursuing the matter with the UK government. British Coal also refused a request to provide information, on the ground, inter alia, that as a private company it was not subject to the regulations.[24] The refusal of the request was challenged by way of judicial review. It is interesting to note that although the court failed to find in favour of the requester, the issue of whether or not the Directive applied to British Coal was not subject to discussion (Charlesworth 1995). In Ireland, An Bord Pleanála, the planning appeals board, maintained that it was not a body with a duty to disclose information as it operated in a judicial capacity in relation to planning appeals (Wates 1996). Some companies or institutions, while denying that they are under any legal obligation to provide information, are seeking to introduce a more open policy that will improve their credibility and public face. The UK Water Services Association has, for example, introduced a code of practice for their members on the provision of information to public.

Grounds for exempting information from disclosure   A narrow and restrictive interpretation of the grounds for exempting information from disclosure has also been apparent in all the Member States examined. Such a narrow approach to the interpretation of legislation is perhaps used to avoid the disclosure of information and to discourage requests. It is feared that bodies that are reluctant to disclose information go through the list of exceptions to find one which they feel is most suitable for their use.

There is a particular difficulty with the exemption relating to commercial and industrial confidentiality. An example from Ireland illustrates some of the difficulties in this regard. Mayo County Council, in the west of Ireland, refused to comply with a request for information on effluent discharges from an industrial plant in the locality on the grounds that release of the data would seriously conflict with the confidentiality associated with the industrial, technological and commercial know-how of the company. Following an inquiry from the Ombudsman, the Council admitted that the decision had been made mainly because of the company's desire to maintain confidentiality of its trade secrets, which the County Council wished to respect. The Council stated that it was also concerned about the use to which the requester might put the information. The data, when examined by the Ombudsman, revealed that the company was operating well within the conditions contained in its effluent discharge licence. In addition, the information was already in the public domain in a local newspaper report. The Ombudsman took the view that there was no evidence to suggest that this data was commercially confidential and criticised the Council for accepting the opinions of the company without satisfying itself that the information was within the scope of the commercially confidential exception. The Council was also criticised for 'picking and choosing between requesters' and for the considerable delay in handling the request. The information requested was finally made available 16 months after the date of the original request (Ombudsman Annual Report 1995). The UK case of *R v. Secretary of State for Environment, Transport and the Regions and Midland Expressway Ltd, ex parte Alliance against the Birmingham Northern Relief Road,* is another example of this problem. It will be recalled that this case concerned the refusal by a government department to disclose a concession agreement it had concluded with a road building consortium on the ground that it was not information on the environment. The department also argued that the agreement was commercially confidential. This refusal was challenged by way of judicial review. In deciding the case, Sullivan J. stated quite firmly that it is not enough to simply state that information is commercially confidential and to cite that the information comes within a particular legislative provision. Rather, there is a formal obligation to give specific reasons why information is to be considered confidential. He went on to hold that it is for the courts to decide as a jurisdictional fact, based on these specific arguments, whether information is capable of being treated as confidential. This approach is to be welcomed as it should help to ensure, in the UK at least, that public bodies will not be able to undermine the effect of the Directive by giving a wide interpretation to what is confidential.

The correct interpretation of one particular exception in the German implementing legislation was referred by the Higher Administrative Court in Schleswig to the ECJ for a preliminary ruling. German law provides that information on the environment will not be made available if it is the subject not only of preliminary investigative procedures but also if it is the subject of an administrative procedure. The question referred by the administrative court was whether the administrative procedure of an authority is a preliminary investigation procedure within the meaning of the permitted exemption in article 3.2 of the Directive.[25] The ECJ held (*Mecklenberg*, paragraph 29), that the term preliminary investigation proceedings as referred to in the Directive must be linked to the activities which precede contentious or quasi-contentious proceedings and which arise from the need to obtain proof or to investigate a matter before the procedural phase so called has even begun. This decision is to be welcomed as the exclusion of matters that are the subject of administrative proceedings from the right of access to information would mean that information that is important for participation in the relevant administrative proceeding, would be denied to the requester right at the moment of its greatest interest and greatest relevance.

These examples reveal the difficulties associated with superimposing a regime of openness on a public administration, which is reluctant to release information and which regards requesters for information with suspicion. Legislation alone cannot achieve change. The hope that procedural law, such as the Information Directive, will have a considerable impact on public attitudes and behaviour, seems exaggerated. Effective implementation of Community legislation will often, therefore, require the training and education of those who are obliged to apply it.

Reasonable costs   Finally, it has been difficult to decide what exactly a 'reasonable cost' for the supply of information means. Although legislation only allows reasonable costs to be charged for supplying information, 'reasonable costs' is not defined. The result in practice is that costs for providing information have often been quite high.

Charging high costs for the supply of information seems to be used in some cases as a method of discouraging requests. There have been certain problems with costs in the UK and Ireland,[26] but it is in Germany that the problem is greatest. Two of the most important environmental NGOs in Germany, namely the ÖKO-Institut and the BUND, were of the opinion that the charging of high costs was a serious problem in Germany (Kimber and Eckardt forthcoming). Requesters for information have been asked to pay for costs of making public officials familiar with the German legislation or to pay for other expenses of officials. One particular example from Germany illustrates this concern. In Rotenburg (Lower Saxony) a request for information on water contamination from the local authority was granted on condition that inspection of the relevant files could only take place if the requester was accompanied by an engineer from a private firm who had helped to prepare the files, in order to prevent the requester drawing unwarranted conclusions from the files. The requester would be obliged to pay the travelling costs and expenses of the engineer even though the engineer lived some distance away. The Federal Administrative Court subsequently limited the rights of authorities to act in this way.[27] As mentioned above, the European Court is currently considering whether the German UIG is in fact compatible with the Directive, on a number of matters, including costs. It is to be hoped that the Court will follow the opinion of the Advocate General in this case, and find that the German UIG is contrary to the Directive with regard to costs.

Conclusions

The purpose of this chapter was to examine whether the implementation and enforcement of the Community Directive on Access to Environmental Information was effective, to identify any weaknesses or problems with its implementation and enforcement and to discuss review and amendment of the Directive and the system of access to environmental information which it establishes. The general conclusion to be drawn from the research undertaken is that there is much that is positive to report. Information is more readily available and there have been many positive developments in the countries examined. In particular there has been a significant cultural shift occurring in the UK and Ireland towards greater transparency and increased public access to official information, illustrated by the adoption of freedom of information legislation in both countries. Ireland enacted, in 1997, a freedom of information act which gives the public a general right to have access to information in the possession of public bodies. It also provides for an information commissioner with strong powers to oversee the working of the Act. The UK plans to enact a similar freedom of information act and provide for an Information Commissioner (DoE 1997). It is important to note, though, that these changes are not directly related to the EU Directive. However, by reducing the adaptation challenge and supporting the development of a climate of opinion in the public service, which is more favourable towards the ready provision of information on the environment, it is likely that the change will contribute to a more effective operation of the Directive in these countries.

Despite these positive developments, considerable problems remain with the implementation, practical application and enforcement of the Directive. These difficulties make it less effective than it might otherwise be. Very many bodies simply do not release information, do not release information within the required two months period or release only partial, incomplete or inaccurate information. As discussed above, the extent of the failure to provide information is partly due to flaws and limitations in the drafting of the 'parent' legislation, namely Directive 90/313 itself, partly to problems with the implementing legislation in the Member States and partly to the fact that public bodies and bodies with public responsibilities for the environment simply do not comply with the legislation as it stands. Too often the legislation is interpreted incorrectly, or extremely restrictively, in compliance with the letter of the law rather than with its spirit. Such domestic resistance is linked to adverse political and administrative capacities. Furthermore, the Directive has had only limited success in changing administrative attitudes or in producing a greater level of public mobilisation.

From the perspective of policy design, are there any improvements possible in the context of the Directive 90/313? Drawing on the results of the research undertaken, I will now consider review and amendment of the Directive and the system for providing access to information, which it establishes. This consideration will take place at three points on the regulatory chain, namely at the stage of the drafting of legislation, at the stage of its application in the Member States, and at the enforcement stage.

Redrafting of legislation

First of all, it is suggested that the parent legislation, namely the Directive, needs to be amended and redrafted. The weaknesses of the Directive and the implementing legislation, both in terms of drafting and in terms of substance, have been discussed above, and various suggestions put forward. It is appropriate, therefore, simply to summarise these suggestions here.

To begin with, the drafting of the legislation needs to be improved, and a more precise definition of the key concepts is required. In terms of substantive changes to the legislation, the following are suggested:

1 an extension of the duty to give information to Community institutions and in certain circumstances to private bodies.
2 a narrowing of the scope of the exceptions to the duty to give information, the redrafting of the exceptions to avoid any ambiguity in their interpretation and the addition of a harm test.
3 the placement of a stronger and clearer obligations on Member States to take practical implementing measures, together with guidance in an annex or guidance document, or from appropriate Community institutions, as to how this might be done.

Application of the legislation

Establishing fora where relationships of trust could be built up between public bodies and environmental NGOs or members of the public who request information, would assist greatly in dispelling the climate of fear and suspicion which makes public bodies reluctant to disclose information. The research undertaken by the author found that availability of information was dependent on a number of conditioning factors, in particular the nature of the group, its working methods, and the nature of the institution or authority addressed. It was seen, as part of these findings, that the relationship between the requester of information and the body providing the information was of central importance as regards ease of obtaining information. Of particular significance was the finding that when groups established a working 'trusting' relationship with public bodies, it was much easier to get information.

For this reason the establishment of new consultative fora involving the general public, NGOs and public bodies, and the extension of the composition and scope of existing fora of this kind, would be of great value in creating relationships of trust between these respective groups. The research undertaken has shown that where groups have been involved in consultative fora in Ireland, Spain and the UK, there have been positive benefits. NGOs are regarded with less suspicion by public bodies and there is often a greater acceptance of the decisions of public bodies where NGOs and the public have participated in the decision making process (Kimber 1998). In the longer run, such institutional interface may be of assistance to trigger the desired attitudinal and behavioural changes among the implementing actors.

The realisation that the availability of information was also highly dependent on the authority addressed, is also of great significance. The finding that public bodies were often unaware of their obligations under the legislation, were uncertain how to fulfil these obligations, were sometimes disorganised, and often adopted procedures for supplying information only when the first request was received, reveals a great degree of ignorance and uncertainty on the part of public bodies with regard to their legal obligations. This realisation reveals the need for education and training of administrators and those applying the legislation, and the need for both education as to their obligations under the legislation and also guidance as to best practice and good procedures in fulfilling these obligations.

Establishment of non-judicial complaint investigation procedures
Our research revealed that in many instances there is an outright failure to comply with legislation, either by failing to supply the information requested or by supplying information only after considerable delay. This finding illustrates the need for a new approach at the stage of enforcement, i.e., the application of not only 'carrots' (see above) but also more effective 'sticks'. At present, in the Member States examined, enforcement of the legislation at national level can only take place by way of judicial review. In the UK and Ireland, resort can be had to the Ombudsman, but decisions of the Ombudsman are not legally binding. Neither the Directive nor the national implementing legislation in the countries examined provided for the establishment of new enforcement or appeal mechanisms. In Spain the new legislation in fact removes one tier of review by providing that the decision of a public authority exhausts the administrative remedies (Kimber and de la Torre 1997).

This in effect leaves judicial review as the only remedy.

Yet judicial review is not entirely satisfactory as a review mechanism, in particular because it is too expensive and too slow. For example, an action for judicial review brought by Greenpeace in Spain took three years to conclude.[28] The Commission has recognised the deficits of relying exclusively on court action to enforce Community environmental law and proposed a non-judicial complaint investigation procedure which could provide a quick and low-cost settlement of an issue in a manner that is more accessible to the citizen and where the citizen has no need for legal assistance (Commission 1996, para. 31). It put forward two main models for such a procedure; the institution of an independent Ombudsman and a system for review of a decision within administrative structures.

In two of the Member States, namely Ireland and the UK, the institution of the Ombudsman or as it is called in the UK, the Parliamentary Commissioner for Administration, is already in place. In the UK and Ireland, some organisations have made use of the possibility of appealing to the Ombudsman. In Ireland, the Office of the Ombudsman has been prepared to take a proactive role in investigation complaints of refusal to disclose information. The Irish Freedom of Information Act, 1977, discussed above, provides for an Information Commissioner with the power to review public body decisions on foot of an application from an individual and with the power to make decisions. The Commissioner is given strong powers to pursue investigations. The legislation also makes it a criminal offence to hinder or obstruct the work of the Commissioner. There is a power of appeal to the high court from a decision of the Commissioner (Meehan 1997a). In the UK, the Parliamentary Commissioner for Administration (PCA) is less active and the jurisdiction of this office is more limited. The PCA is precluded from investigating a complaint unless he or she is satisfied that, in the circumstances, it would not be reasonable to expect the applicant to use any legal remedy (Parliamentary Commissioner Act 1967, section 5(2)). The proposed UK freedom of information legislation has recognised the limitation of this office and provides for an Information Commissioner with additional powers. There is to be no appeal to a court of law, however, from the decision of the Information Commissioner. Spain did have a procedure of review within the administrative procedure, but, as noted above, this was removed by the Spanish legislation implementing the Directive.

It is suggested in contrast with the UK freedom of information legislative proposals that an effective enforcement mechanism needs to incorporate a non-judicial enforcement mechanism into an overall enforcement process, which does in fact culminate in a judicial enforcement procedure. A quick, cheap and easy enforcement mechanism is clearly necessary to deal with most complaints and to exert some pressure on public bodies to comply with legislation. Certainly, in Ireland, the Office of the Ombudsman has proved effective in resolving many complaints regarding requests for information on the environment. Nevertheless, the possibility of an appeal from the decision of such a tribunal to the courts is a useful and necessary ultimate sanction. The threat of litigation is a powerful tool to induce potentially liable decision makers to comply with legislation. This is recognised by the Commission (Commission 1996, para. 40). Thus the UK legislative proposals are deficient in this regard.

In short, the research findings and recommendations presented above, support the general approach to resolving problems of implementation and enforcement of Community environmental law advocated by the Commission, namely, the recognition that the approach to addressing implementation problems must take implementation and enforcement across the regulatory chain at the successive stages of implementation into account. In this context, public access to environmental information, as promoted by Directive 90/313, should be seen as key piece in the jigsaw of improving the implementation and enforcement of Community environmental policy. However, as demonstrated above, this Directive suffers from its own problems of implementation and enforcement. Similar to traditional regulatory instruments it imposes a considerable challenge for administrative adaptation without effectively inducing public authorities to rethink old practices. Its potential to assist with improving the implementation and enforcement of Community environmental law is thereby diminished.

To overcome current deficits associated with the Community's recent approach, research by the author indicates that some changes are needed. These would include improving of the quality of Community legislation, improving the education and training of those applying and complying with Community environmental law, and the introduction of a simple and cheap non-judicial complaints facility *in addition* to enforcement through court action at national level.

The extent to which the Member States are willing to support such strategic changes is a crucial factor affecting the extent to which reform might be achieved in the near future. The prospect of realising political support for such changes in the short or medium term does not seem hopeful, however. Member States reveal instead a marked reluctance to make great changes towards increasing access to environmental information and increasing public participation in environmental decision making, as is indicated by the restrictive stance that was taken by the Member States at the negotiating sessions for the recently adopted Aarhus Convention (9th Session of the Working Group for the Convention on Access to Environmental Information, Public Participation in Environmental Decision Making and Access to Justice in Environmental Matters, 12–16 January 1998). Political support for the changes to Directive 90/313, which I have put forward in this chapter, is, therefore, unlikely to be forthcoming at the present time.

Notes

1 The research described in this chapter is part of a wider research project which was undertaken by Clíona Kimber, Maria de la Torre and Meropi Voyatzi at the Aberdeen University Centre for Environmental Law and Policy. It was funded by the ESRC. The funding and support of the ESRC is gratefully acknowledged.

2 Community policy in this regard is in line with international understanding of the role of the availability of environmental information in assisting the success of environmental policy. Successive international fora, such as the Declaration of the United Nations Conference on the Environment held in Rio de Janeiro in 1992 and more recently, the Convention on Access to Environmental Information, Public Participation in Environmental Decision Making and Access to Justice in Environmental Matters adopted in Aarhus in 1998, have emphasised the assistance access to information can give in implementing environmental policy in the realm of citizen action and citizen participation in environmental decision making.

3 Directive 90/313/EEC of 7 June 1990, OJ No. L 158, 23.6.90.

4 The exact nature of the causal link between making information available and achieving an improvement in the implementation of Community environmental law has been examined elsewhere, and will not be discussed here (Kimber 1997). The EC is now also party to the UNECE Convention on Access to Information, Public Participation in Decision

Making and Access to Justice in Environmental Matters. Aarhus, 25 June 1998.

5 *World Wildlife Fund* v. *Commission of European Communities*, Case T-105/95.

6 See Council Decision 93/731/EC of 20 December 1993 on Public Access to Council Documents, OJ L. 340, 31.12.93; Declaration 93/730/EC on a Code of Conduct Concerning Public Access to Council and Commission Documents; Commission Decision 94/90 ECSC, EC, Euratom of 8 February 1994 on Public Access to Commission Documents, OJ No. 146, 18.2.94.

7 The sampling scheme was developed to allow the identification and selection of comparable subjects in each country, including research institutes, environmental organisations, as well as business and professional associations. The survey groups were consulted by means of questionnaires or interviews. In total an average of 60 questionnaires was sent to groups of different nature and size in each country. In addition other entities were consulted in order to obtain information whose experience was of specific relevance, for example the Office of the Ombudsman in Ireland and the House of Lords Select Committee in the UK.

8 Ireland has since adopted a Freedom of Information Act, 1997 (No. 13 of 1997).

9 Ley 38/1995, de 12 diciembre, sobre el derecho de accesso a la información en materia de medio ambiente. (Spain).

10 Gesetz zur Umsetzung der Richtlinie 90/313/EWG des Rates vom 7.6.1990 über den freien Zugang zu Information über die Umwelt vom 8 Juli 1994, BGBl I 1994, p1490, (Germany).

11 The principal pieces of implementing legislation in the UK and Ireland are: Environmental Information Regulations 1992, (SI 1992/3240) (UK), Access to Information on the Environment Regulations, 1993, (SI 1993/133) replaced by the Access to Information on the Environment Regulations, 1996, (SI 1996/185) (Ireland).

12 Case C-217/97 *Commission of the European Communities* v. *Germany*.

13 Opinion of Advocate General Fennelly delivered on 28 January 1999.

14 ENFO is an acronym for 'environmental information'.

15 Entscheidungen des BVerwG, Bd. 102, 1996, AZ. 7C 64.94 (Anspruch auf schriftliche Mitteilung von Umweltinformationen).

16 Compare Caddy, chapter 10, and Knill and Lenschow, chapter 11, in this book for similar conclusions with respect to the special case of Central European countries.

17 R v. *Secretary of State for Environment, Transport and the Regions and Midland Expressway Ltd, ex parte Alliance against the Birmingham*

Northern Relief Road, Judgment of Sullivan J., Queens Bench Division, 29 July 1998.

18 Judgment of the Administrative Court of Schleswig of 30.7.1995.

19 Judgment of 10.7.1996.

20 Case C-321/96 *Mecklenberg* v. *Kreis Pinneberg - Der Landrat* [1999] ECR. I - 3809 at para. 22.

21 Mecklenberg, at para. 19.

22 Higher Administrative Court Schleswig, Judgment of 13.12.1994.

23 Administrative Court Schleswig, Judgment of 30.7.1995.

24 *R* v. *British Coal Corporation ex parte Ibstock Building Products Limited* (October 1994).

25 Judgment of 10.7.96.

26 This problem should be solved in Ireland following the introduction of the Freedom of Information Act 1997. Regulations made under this Act prescribe the costs of obtaining copies of records of information as: 3 pence per sheet per photocopy, 40 pence per computer diskette, and £8 per CD-ROM. Freedom of Information Act, 1997 (Section 47(3)) Regulations, 1998, SI No. 139 of 1998.

27 Entscheidungen des BVerwG, Bd. 102, 1996, Az. 7C 64. 94 (Anspruch auf schriftliche Mitteilung von Umweltinformationen).

28 An action brought on 11 of March, 1991, was resolved by judgment of the High Court on the 30 of June 1993 (Sentencia num. 106/91 de la Audiencia Nacional de 30 de junio de 1993).

References

Alexander, D. (1990). 'Freedom of Access to Information on the Environment'. *New Law Journal*, 25 (4) 1315–16.

Annual Report of the Ombudsman (1995). Dublin, Government Publications.

Bakkenist, G. (1994). *Environmental Information: Law, Policy and Experience*. London, Cameron May.

Bell, S. (1997). *Ball and Bell on Environmental Law*. London, Blackstone Press.

Birkenshaw, P. (1996). *Freedom of Information: the Law, the Practice and the Ideal*. 2nd edn, London, Butterworths.

Charlesworth, A. (1995). 'Examining the Applicability of the Environmental Information Regulations 1992: A Strange Case'. *Journal of Environmental Law*. 7(2), 297–303.

Commission (1992). *Report on the State of the Environment*, prepared in conjunction with the Community Fifth Action Programme on the Environment. COM (92) 23 final – Vol. III.

Commission (1995). Progress Report from the Commission on the Implementation of the European Community Programme of Policy and Action in Relation to the Environment and Sustainable Development 'Towards Sustainability'. COM (95) 624 final, 10.1.96.

Commission (1996). *Implementing Community Environmental Law*. Communication from the Commission, COM (96) 500 final, 22.10.96.

Commission (1996a). Communication from the Commission to the Council and the European Parliament on Environmental Agreements (1996) COM (96) 561 final, 27.11.96.

Department of the Environment (DoE) (1997). *Your Right to Know: the Government's Proposals for a Freedom of Information Act*, Cm 3818, London, HMSO.

European Parliament (1989). *Opinion of the European Parliament on the proposal from the Commission to the Council for a Directive on the freedom of access to information on the environment*. OJ C120/231, 16.5.89.

Hallo, R. (ed) (1996). *Access to Environmental Information in Europe: the Implementation and Implications of Directive 90/313/EEC*. London, Kluwer.

House of Lords (1996). *Freedom of Access to Information on the Environment*. Select Committee on the European Communities, 1st Report, Session 1996–97 (HL Paper 9), London, HMSO.

Kimber, C. (1997). 'Access to Justice and Access to Environmental Information'. *European Business Law Review*, 8(5), 157–64.

Kimber, C. (1998). 'Understanding Access to Environmental Information'. In Jowell, T. and Steel, J. (eds), *Environmental Decision Making*. Oxford, Oxford University Press, 39–160.

Kimber, C. and de la Torre, M. (1997). 'Access to Information on the Environment in Spain'. *European Environmental Law Review*, 6, 53–62.

Kimber, C. and Eckardt, F. (forthcoming). 'Umweltinformation in Deutschland und Großbritannien'. *Natur und Recht*.

Krämer, L. (1992). *Focus on European Environmental Law*. London, Sweet & Maxwell.

Krämer, L. (1996). 'Public Interest Litigation in Environmental Matters Before European Courts'. *Journal of Environmental Law*. 8(1), 1–18.

Meehan, D. (1997a). 'The Freedom of Information Act', 1997, Public and Private Rights of Access to Records held by Public Bodies'. *Irish Law Times*, 15(9), 178–83.

Meehan, D. (1997b). Freedom of Information Act in Context'. *Irish Law Times*, 15(12), 231–5.

Moe, M. (1993). 'Implementation and Enforcement in a Federal System'. *Ecology Law Quarterly*, 20, 151–64.

Percival, R., Miller, A., Schroder, C. and Leape, J. (1996). *Environmental Regulation: Law, Science and Policy*. Boston, Little, Brown & Company.

Rowan-Robinson, J., Ross, A., Walton, W and Rothnie, J. (1996). 'Public Access to Environmental Information: A Means to What End?', *Journal* of *Environmental Law*, 8(1), 19–42.

Wates, J. (1996). 'Ireland'. In Hallo, R. (ed). *Access to Environmental Information in Europe*. London, Kluwer.

Weatherill, S. and Beaumont, P. (1995). *EC Law*. 2nd edn, London, Penguin.

9 *Joanne Caddy*[1]

Implementation of EU environmental policy in Central European applicant states: the case of EIA

Introduction

As one of the main preconditions for accession, the acceptance of the *acquis communautaire* requires Central and Eastern European applicant countries to achieve legislative approximation to the EU in all policy fields, including that of the environment.[2] Such efforts have been underway in the three Central European countries (CECs) examined here since 1991, when the Europe Agreements were signed with Hungary and what was then Czechoslovakia.

A review of CECs approximation to the 300 or so items of EU environmental law currently in force is beyond the scope of this chapter (Commission of the European Communities 1997b). Rather, the objective here is to illustrate the principal obstacles to the implementation of EU-origin environmental legislation faced by Central European (CE) applicant countries through the comparative review of a single environmental measure.

The EU legislation of reference in this case is Directive 85/337/EEC of 27 June 1985 on the assessment of the effects of certain public and private projects on the environment, in short EIA Directive. This piece of legislation applies to, 'the assessment of the environmental effects of those public and private projects which are likely to have significant effects on the environment' (art. 1) and requires Member States to ensure that information relating to an environmental impact assessment (EIA) is made available to the public and that, 'the public concerned is given the opportunity to express an opinion before the project is initiated' (art. 6) (European Council 1985).

With this procedural emphasis focusing on cross-media integration and transparency, the EIA Directive shares elements with other so-called 'new instruments' examined in this book. Especially, considering the deficits in terms of substantive environmental standards in the CECs, one may expect that these new instruments impose relatively lesser implementation challenges and have a positive consciousness-raising effect. I will investigate this hypothesis critically in the following sections.

This chapter sets out an approach to the comparative assessment of implementation of newly transposed European Union (EU) environmental legislation by Central European countries, using the example of environmental impact assessment by way of illustration. First, the degree of approximation of national EIA legislation of the Czech Republic, Hungary and Slovakia to the 1985 EIA Directive is briefly reviewed. It will be shown that approximation tables are of limited utility in assessing the actual progress made in CECs towards raising their environmental standards. To move further in that direction, a comparative overview of the formal and informal institutional capacities for implementation in these three applicant countries is introduced. The chapter concludes by underlining the importance of ensuring attention to both outcomes and processes in the evaluation of environmental policy implementation in CECs and calls for further research into the dynamics of implementation processes in applicant countries as they progress towards future EU membership.

EIA approximation by Central European states

The source of much present-day domestic environmental legislation in the Central European region is to be found in the EU's environmental *acquis,* which has been incorporated through legislative approximation. This is particularly evident in the case of EIA where all CECs have passed laws or regulations on the subject since 1990 and compatibility with the 1985 EIA Directive (337/85/EEC) has been explicitly sought in each case. The EIA laws in the three CE applicant countries of the Czech Republic, Hungary and Slovakia reflect such a concern with the future compliance with the EU *acquis* with their inclusion of: lists of activities subject to mandatory EIA, clarification of the links with other permitting procedures, details of the EIA procedure (either within the main act itself or in subsequent regulations), provisions for access to information and public participation (comments periods and/or public hearings) (Bellinger *et al.* 1997; Czech National Council 1992; EBRD 1994;

Joanne Caddy   199

Government of Hungary 1995a and 1995b; REC 1996; Slovak
National Council 1994):

- In the *Czech Republic*, EIA provisions are covered by the 1992
  Act on Environmental Impact Assessment of the National Council (Act no. 244/1992 S.B.) which is based in large part upon the
  EU Directive (George *et al.* 1997). A Decree of the Ministry of
  the Environment (Decree no. 499/1992 S.B.) sets out the operational guidelines with which to apply the EIA Act, while the
  general framework of national environmental legislation is provided by the Act on the Environment (Act no. 17/1992 S.B.);
- The 1994 Act on Environmental Impact Assessment of *Slovakia*
  (Act no. 127/1994) sets out a list of activities to be covered
  by EIAs, which covers all those in Annex I of the EU Directive
  and most of those in Annex II, while provisions are made for
  public participation by means of both written comments and
  public hearings. In drafting the 1994 Act, the experience of
  other countries was drawn upon and the, 'final legislation was
  designed to be fully compatible with EC Directive 85/337'
  (George 1997, 168);
- In the case of *Hungary*, provisions for EIAs are to be found both
  within the 1995 national environmental framework law (Act
  LIII on 'General Rules of Environmental Protection', articles
  67–71) and in Government Decree no. 152 of 12 December
  1995. While the framework law sets out the general requirements for EIA procedures, the decree provides detailed rules
  concerning related administrative procedures and makes several
  provisions for both public participation and access to information. The approach to EIA is similar to that of the EU Directive,
  although the Hungarian EIA process is divided into two parts: a
  preliminary EIA phase (screening) and a detailed EIA phase
  (Fülöp 1995).

An evaluation of the degree of approximation achieved by the CECs
may be obtained by applying the 'table of convergence' set out in
Annex 3 of the European Commission's August 1997 'Guide to the
Approximation of European Union Environmental Legislation'
(Commission of the European Communities 1997b). Following the
methodology presented therein, each article of the EU legislation of
reference (here, EU Directive 85/337/EEC) is compared with the
corresponding legislative text of the applicant country in question

(the respective national EIA laws) and assigned a score for compliance along the scale shown in table 9.1.

Table 9.1   *Scoring approximation to EU legislation*

Score	Interpretation
–	Direct conflict
0	No legislation
–/+	National requirements are inconsistent with EU requirement or partially conform
+	Full transposition

Source: Commission of the European Communities 1997b.

It is of note that the EIA Directive serves as a vivid illustration of the 'moving target' problem, one which plagues the approximation programmes of CE applicant countries on all fronts. The recent amendment of the original 1985 Directive (by the EIA Amendment Directive 97/11/EC of 3 March 1997) introduces a number of new elements. Among these are: limitations on the exemption article in those cases where transboundary impacts may be expected and the transfer of certain categories of projects from Annex II (optional EIA) to Annex I (obligatory EIA) (European Council 1997; Sheate 1997). As a result, the three CECs considered here are now faced with the unappealing prospect of having to update national legislation to conform with the provisions of the new 1997 amendments, having only just harmonised their EIA legislation to the 1985 Directive in the period 1992 to 1995.

Given that the amended Directive is only to be brought into force in Member States by 14 March 1999 and that during the interim period the 1985 Directive will continue to apply, the prospect of future legislative changes does not affect the comparative analysis of current implementation processes. For the purposes of this chapter then, the 1985 EIA Directive represents a common legislative background against which to examine the specific characteristics of domestic implementation in the three CECs under examination. The results of this chapter's assessment of the level of approximation of the Czech, Slovak and Hungarian legislation with the EU Directive are provided in table 9.2 (see Caddy 1996).

Table 9.2 *Approximation to EU Directive 85/337/EEC on EIA by the Czech Republic, Slovakia and Hungary*

	EU Directive 85/337/EEC of 27 June 1985	Czech Republic Act no. 244/1992	Slovakia Act no. 127/1994	Hungary Act LIII and Decree no. 152
Article	Obligation		Level of approximation	
art. 1	Scope of application; definitions; exemption of national defence projects	+	−/+	−/+
art. 2	Requirement of EIA prior to consent; exemptions and consequent obligation to provide information by authorities	−/+	−/+	−/+
art. 3	Factors to be assessed in EIA	+	+	−/+
art. 4	Reference to Annex I (obligatory EIA projects) and Annex II (optional EIA projects); delegation to Member States to set criteria/thresholds for Annex II projects	−/+	−/+	−/+
art. 5	Reference to Annex III (information to be included in EIA); minimal information to be provided (incl. non-technical summary)	+	+	+
art. 6	Consultation of authorities, access to information for public; consultation of public	+	+	+
art. 7	Obligation to provide information in case of transboundary impacts	−/+	+	0
art. 8	Obligation to consider information collected in arts 5–7 in issue of consent	+	+	+
art. 9	Obligation to inform public of decision taken and any conditions attached	−/+	+	−/+
art. 10	Deference to national regulations on industrial/commercial secrecy	+	+	+
art. 11	Obligation to inform Commission of thresholds set (art. 4); 5 year report	0	0	0
art. 12	Compliance within 3 years; inform Commission of national laws adopted	0	0	0
art. 13	Member States may establish stricter rules	0	0	0
art. 14	Directive addressed to Member States	0	0	0

Source: Czech National Council 1992; European Council 1985; Government of Hungary 1995a and 1995b; Slovak National Council 1994.

From table 9.2 it appears that the EIA legislation of the Czech Republic, Slovakia and Hungary are all substantially in line with the EU Directive and correspond closely with regard to the key provisions for public participation set out in Directive 85/337/EEC, namely:

- *requirement of a non-technical summary* (article 5): the EIA legislation of all CECs require the inclusion of a non-technical summary in the environmental impact statement (EIS), while the Hungarian 1995 Decree even goes as far as to specify in detail the information it must contain;
- *access to information* (article 6): all CECs uphold the principle of access to information and contain detailed procedural requirements regarding the manner by which members of the public may view the EIS;
- *consultation of the public* (article 6): provisions for public participation in the form of comment and notice periods and/or public hearings are contained in the EIA legislation of all CECs and constitute one of the foremost instances of public participation in environmental decision making in all such countries;
- *obligation to consider information collected under articles 5 and 6* (article 8): given that public consultation runs the risk of becoming merely a formal exercise in the absence of legal requirements that the public's views be effectively taken into account, the incorporation of this provision into the EIA legislation of all CECs represents an important step in establishing the accountability of public administration officials.

By considering a given EIA law solely in terms of congruence with the EU Directive the limits of such an exercise in approximation evaluation soon become clear. For how are we to assess a provision in, say, the Czech 1992 EIA Act (Act no. 244/1992 of 15 April 1992), which introduces an element of strategic environmental assessment (SEA) in its requirement of an environmental impact assessment for national level policy 'concepts' (art. 14) in such fields as energy, transport, agriculture policy? Such a provision is not captured in the tables of convergence by which the mechanical article-by-article comparison of EU and prospective Member States is to be carried out (see table 9.2). Equally, how should outright non-approximation be considered when, for example, the EU Directive (art. 2) allows Member States ('in exceptional cases') to exempt projects from the obligation of an EIA whereas, say, the Slovak 1994 EIA Act (Act no.127/1994 of 29 April 1994) makes no such allowance. In this case, the Slovak EIA law is not fully approximated to that of the EU, but in substantive terms this is only to its merit, as the fewer provisions for exceptions there are in an EIA law, the better. Having briefly described the framework of legislative approximation, the discussion now turns to the issue of the potential success of CECs in implementing EU environmental legislation.

EIA implementation in Central European states

Although the factors which may potentially influence policy implementation are numerous and varied, they can be grouped as follows (Mazmanian and Sabatier 1981):

- the nature of the policy problem itself;
- formal institutional capacities for implementation – both legislative and non-legislative;
- the impact of informal institutions.

Although the analysis of implementation presented below follows the lines of classic 'top–down' implementation studies in its progression from policy problems to solutions to outcomes, it also includes some elements characteristic of the 'bottom–up' approach with its attention to informal institutional actors and their effective participation in implementation processes – thereby achieving a degree of synthesis (Hanf 1982; Sabatier 1986).

Nature of the policy problem
Environmental impact assessment (EIA) constitutes an important challenge for all countries where it is adopted, incorporating as it does:

- *the principle of preventive action* with respect to activities with a potential impact on the environment, rather than that of remedial action for damage done;
- *the principle of shared responsibility* for, and transparency in, environmental decision making which makes implementation an eminently public affair rather than the exclusive preserve of public authorities and investors;

- *specific procedural provisions* which must be followed for all projects subject to EIA.

Among their most significant impacts on traditional models of environmental protection and control, EIA procedures generally:

- *introduce new requirements with respect to long-established administrative practices* in the sphere of land use planning and other sector-specific permitting procedures;
- *provide guarantees for access to information* and result in higher levels of visibility in administrative decision making processes and outcomes;
- *explicitly require public consultation* as part of the decision making process and due consideration of subsequent contributions when formulating final decisions.

It is worth noting that ever since the adoption of the EIA Directive in June 1985, problems with practical implementation have been registered in all Member States, which testify to the inherent difficulties raised by the policy problem itself. Among the deficiencies in the practice of EIA highlighted by the European Commission's 1993 review of the 1985 Directive's implementation were: omissions of projects from EIA, incomplete scoping, poor quality of the environmental impact statements produced, unsatisfactory consultative practices, limited use of EIA outputs in effective decision making and a lack of post-project monitoring (Lee 1995, 80). More recently, the 1996 communication from the Commission on 'Implementing Community Environmental Law' noted that the EIA Directive, 'constitutes one of the most frequent legal bases for complaints, petitions, parliamentary questions and infringement procedures' (Commission of the European Communities 1996, 30).

The comparative overview of EIA legislation presented in the previous section reveals the high degree of success in approximation obtained to date by each of the three CE applicant countries considered. Yet, if the implementation of EIA procedures poses a challenge for current Member States, on balance it would appear to represent an even greater one for CECs once they move from formal compliance with the legal requirements set out in the Directive to the stage of practical implementation. The core policy problem is identical in both country groupings – that of mitigating the impact of proposed projects on the environment – as do many of the features of the policy solutions devised in CECs, modelled as they are upon the common template of the EU Directive. What differs radically is the overall setting in which such a policy is to be implemented.

With reference to the basic provisions enshrined in EIA legislation, the following problems currently faced by CECs may be expected to seriously impinge upon their practical implementation efforts:[3]

- the movement from a reactive environmental policy developed under the logic of the centrally planned economy (which imposed few remedial actions upon state-owned enterprises (SOEs) and largely consisted of a system of fines collected from the state by the state itself) to one based upon prevention and sustainability (Vári 1995);
- the replacement of centralised state control of all spheres of public life with the drastic curtailment of public authority and the development of proactive links with an emerging array of autonomous social, economic, institutional and political actors (Bozóki *et al.* 1992);
- the elimination of arbitrary and secretive administrative decision making and its substitution with transparent and accountable administrative process guaranteed by the rule of law (Stec 1993).

The innovative potential of EIA procedures for CE environmental policy as a whole has been recognised by several commentators in the region, including the Minister for the Environment of Slovakia, Jozef Zlocha, who in 1995 stated: 'We are convinced that [the] development of the EIA process ... will represent a new quality and will become a significant element [in the] realization of environmental policy of different governments in countries within our region' (Slovak Ministry of the Environment and Comenius University 1995, 3). Nevertheless, legal and administrative traditions are likely to restrain the conversion of this innovative potential into tangible changes.

Formal institutional capacities for implementation:
legislative and non-legislative
The formal institutional capacity to respond to a given policy problem may be specified in terms of legislative and non-legislative elements, the former including statutory *specificity* and *enforceability*,

the latter including *tangible* and *intangible resources* for action (Rosenbaum 1981).

Legislative: specificity and enforceability   It has long been recognised that many of the difficulties that arise in the course of policy implementation may be ascribed to defects in the original legislation which establishes the policy itself. The importance of due attention to statutory provisions has been highlighted by many authorities (including the OECD's Public Management Service, PUMA: see PUMA 1993) and such scholars as Nelson Rosenbaum who, whilst acknowledging that legislative clarity is not in itself a *sufficient condition* for successful implementation, asserts the importance of 'legislative craftsmanship as a *necessary condition* in many instances' (Rosenbaum 1981, 63, emphasis added; see also Kimber, chapter 8, in this book, for a similar perspective). Two measures of statutory structure which greatly influence the subsequent phase of implementation may be identified, namely, *specificity* and *enforceability*, each of which may be assessed in terms of a specific set of variables.

The degree of legislative definition is reflected in the extent to which a given law or regulation sets out the objectives to be reached, the actions required to achieve them and the behaviour and practices which must be changed in order to comply. Legislative ambiguity leads to prolonged arguments over meanings and scope of application, fosters delays in the development of action programmes and renders the practical implications of such measures obscure for the very same regulated entities to which they are supposed to apply. Clarity might appear to be a fundamental prerequisite for successful implementation yet it is a quality that is seldom found in highly innovative legislation, which usually requires significant compromises in the course of its approval. Thus, '[s]tatutory specificity is rare because of the chronic disinclination of legislators to confront the hard political decisions that underlie legislative precision' (p. 64). In this manner, the key task of defining terms and modes of application is delegated to the discretion of the administrative bodies charged with implementation.

The second legislative element of importance in determining the potential for successful implementation of a given regulation or law is that of *enforceability* which refers to the relationship which holds between the 'stringency of the mandate for behavioural change and the stringency of the enforcement process' (p. 64). The greater the change in behaviour on the part of regulated entities required by the law or regulation, the greater the need for well-specified enforcement procedures. The mismatch between the extent of behavioural change required by a given piece of legislation and the degree of precision with which it stipulates the necessary enforcement mechanisms represents one of the more common sources of implementation failure. Large gaps between the objectives established by new legislation and current practice among regulated entities may thus require additional efforts to ensure enforcement, from the provision of information and assistance to the imposition of sanctions.

The general concepts of specificity and enforceability may be operationalised through the development of a set of appropriate variables (each with a range of values) tailored to the specific legislation under examination. Such measures provide an indication of legislative specificity and enforceability and hence the probability of successful implementation, to the extent that it may be said to depend on these two legislative characteristics. In the case of EIA legislation, the set of variables with which to estimate legislative specificity (clarity of definitions) and enforceability (clarity of procedures) may be said to include the following:

- *specificity*: clarity of statutory objectives of EIA legislation; definition of projects subject to EIA; precision of exemptions from EIA; specification of information to be supplied in the environmental impact statement;
- *enforceability*: specification of EIA phases, timing and links to other permitting processes; provisions for access to information; provisions for public participation; centrality of the EIA procedure within the overall permitting process, i.e. whether EIA represents a veto point in permit decision making or has the status of a mere recommendation.

Of course, the problems associated with specificity and enforceability apply to both the EU's legislature and its transposition into national law. The EIA legislation of the three CECs examined here, fare less well than the EU Directive with regard to specificity, reflecting what are in each case different lacunae in the legislative texts, thus:

- for the *Czech Republic*, none of the projects included in the list of those subject to EIA are necessarily required to do so given that 'the competent authority shall decide whether the impact assess-

ment shall or shall not be carried out' (art. 5(4)) on what is effectively a case-by-case basis – i.e. there are no projects for which an
EIA is obligatory by definition;

- the legislation of *Hungary* lacks a preamble stating its overall
  objectives and defining the 'spirit of the law' – which at the level
  of a governmental decree (no. 152) is hardly surprising, but
  which is more so for the articles dealing with EIA within the 1995
  Framework Law (Act LIII, arts 67–72);
- in the case of EIA legislation in *Slovakia*, the Ministry of the
  Environment has broad powers to determine exemptions from
  the EIA provisions in 'special cases' where the information contained in the initial plan submitted is considered to be sufficient
  (art. 13(1)).

In contrast, the legislation of the same CECs does considerably
better than that of the EU template with regard to enforceability –
as is only to be expected from national level legislation which must
provide precise directions for national public administration and
regulated entities alike, thus:

- the EIA Act of *Slovakia* emerges with full points by providing for:
  set time limits for each main step in the EIA procedure; detailed
  specifications as to which public authorities are obliged to publi-
  cise, manage and provide information to the public; public participation in the initial scoping phase (with the submission of
  written comments (art. 8(5)) and in the evaluation of the Environmental Impact Statement (EIS) (in the course of a 'public
  discussion' (art. 17(2–5))); and, finally, by stipulating that without
  the final opinion of the Ministry of Environment other public
  authorities may not issue permits for projects subject to EIA
  (art. 36(1)); all of which must be subject to monitoring and evaluation (art. 23);
- the EIA Decree of *Hungary* provides generally fewer indicators of
  timing for each stage, although those pertaining to availability of
  information on the EIS and public participation (posting notice of
  the EIS and public hearing) are most clearly enunciated (art. 7;
  art. 15(1)); public participation in the preliminary EIA phase
  (scoping) is ensured (via written comments (art. 7(2c))); while
  other permitting authorities are prevented from concluding their
  procedures prior to the issue of an environmental permit for projects subject to EIA (art. 21);

- under the EIA Act of the *Czech Republic* the various stages of the EIA procedure are set out and precise indications of timing provided; it establishes that the 'documentation on environmental impact evaluation' submitted by the investor is to be made available to the public (art. 7, Appendix 3) and that a 'public discussion' of the expert opinion on the EIA documentation is to be held (art. 10) (although public participation is not foreseen at the scoping phase); finally it stipulates that without the statement issued by the competent environmental authority 'an administrative body cannot issue a permitting decision or measure following separate regulations' (art. 11(1)).

High scores for specificity and enforceability of the legislative *texts* for EIA do not necessarily translate into high levels of implementation and enforcement in practice. Needless to say, for legislative intent to be translated into practice, adequate resources for implementation of a non-legislative nature are also required.

Non-legislative: tangible and intangible resources   Clarity of legislative language and purpose is, in itself, of little use if adequate resources to fulfil the legislative mandate are not forthcoming. Formal institutional capacity for implementation thus depends heavily on non-legislative factors, including: *tangible resources* (such as budgetary, human and technological assets) and *intangible resources* (such as legitimacy and credibility) (Caddy 1996).

Although data specific to the implementation of EIA legislation in CECs is not readily available, basic comparative indicators of the level of tangible resources destined to environmental policy implementation in general may serve in their stead. These include figures for environmental expenditures and human resources employed within the public administration for the environment, as provided in tables 9.3 and 9.4.

Table 9.3   *Total expenditure on environment as % of GDP*

Country	Year	% of GDP
Czech Republic	1991	1.6[a]
Hungary	1993	0.6[b]
Slovakia	1993	1.5
OECD average[c]	1990s	1.0 – 2.0

[a] % GNP; [b] public expenditure only; [c] limited to pollution abatement and control.
Source: EIU 1995; OECD1996; REC 1994; REC 1995a, 142.

Table 9.4   *Budget share (%) and employees of national ministries of the environment*

Country	Budget share (%)	No. of employees
Czech Republic	0.39	463
Hungary	1.17	373
Slovakia	0.81	280

Source: REC 1995b.

The deep recession experienced by the CE economies during the period 1990 to 1993 had two major impacts on the environment.[4] First, it led to significant reductions in emissions into air and water (as well as of industrial waste) as large numbers of heavily polluting state owned enterprises were closed down. Second, it caused a drastic cutback in public expenditures that had disproportionately severe repercussions on environment protection budgets throughout the region (Manser 1993, 73). In contrast, if the upturn in economic growth experienced by the Czech Republic, Hungary and Slovakia from 1994 on did only result in a partial reversal of these trends, while not translating into appreciable increases in environmental expenditure levels, it did lead to a resumption of industrial emissions. Hence, we see a compounding of the accumulated effects of decades of environmental degradation under the communist command economy (Bochniarz *et al.* 1994).

It is against this background that the figures on environmental expenditures presented in table 9.2 are to be compared not only to the OECD average but also, and more importantly, with the cost of environmental damage in the region, which has been estimated to lie at between 10 and 15 per cent of GDP for the three CECs examined here (OECD 1992, 100). Such figures clearly illustrate how limited the available financial resources for environmental protection and clean-up in CECs are with respect to the true extent of the task in hand.

Tightened budgets and staff cutbacks have had a dramatic impact on all sectors of the public administration in CECs (Support for Improvement in Government and Management in Central and Eastern Europe: SIGMA 1997) and environment ministries and inspectorates are no exception in this regard. In particular, they face significant difficulties in recruiting and retaining qualified staff due to lower salaries compared to the private sector, limited career prospects and the low prestige of public service.

With regard to the implementation of EIA provisions, such general resource constraints are further aggravated by:

- the strong sectoral division of expertise within the environmental public administration which is ill prepared for the assessment of strategic documents having the multidisciplinary nature of environmental impact studies (Emmott 1996);
- the lack of qualified personnel capable of effectively managing the new relations with members of the public and environmental NGOs central to the EIA process and only limited efforts to provide re-training in this field (Vári 1995);
- the general overburdening of environmental inspectorates with new tasks and responsibilities, of which EIA procedures constitute an important element, in the face of public administration cutbacks (Radnai and Mondok 1997).

Although precise indications of the proportion of human resources dedicated to EIA procedures by the environmental administration in CECs are largely lacking, the numbers of EIA procedures handled per year are shown in table 9.5.

The presence of intangible resources for implementation and enforcement, such as *credibility* and *legitimacy*, also plays a key role in the success of actions undertaken by formal institutions for the environment. Credibility is linked most directly to the availability of tangible resources for implementation while legitimacy is generated with reference to the overarching goals pursued by the policy in question. There is no fixed relationship between the two, and indeed the implementation of a given policy goal may be considered by regulated entities and the public to be credible but not legitimate, or *vice versa*.

In the case of newly introduced EIA procedures in CECs such intangible resources for implementation are limited by, first, a lack

Table 9.5 *Number of EIA procedures (per year)*

Country	EIAs
Czech Republic	100
Hungary	130
Slovakia	129[a]

[a] in period 01.09.94 – 26.10.95
Source: Drdoš and Pavlíčková 1995, 91; Kobus *et al.* 1997, 198.

of widespread recognition of the need for and hence, legitimacy of EIA by investors and environmental enforcement officials alike:

- for investors this is due to the additional costs entailed by EIA procedures in terms of: the effort required to prepare an environmental impact study (including the cost of engaging consultants); the risk of delays in or unfavourable conclusion of permitting procedures (with consequent opportunity costs) and the need to establish contacts with affected communities (which may involve the preparation and dissemination of information on the project, the hiring of PR firms and so on);
- while for environmental enforcement officials the legitimacy of EIAs is reduced given the significant demands entailed by the organisation of these new procedures, participation in public hearings and evaluation of the comments received.

Second, the limited credibility of EIA procedures in the eyes of public officials, investors and environmental NGOs obstruct effective implementation:

- for public officials, EIA procedures and the public participation represent a superfluous complication and one less credible than expert evaluation on the basis of established internal procedures;
- for investors, EIAs widen the boundaries of participation in decision making and hence enlarge the scope for public pressure to be brought to bear on decision making, thereby reducing its credibility as a technical, impartial permitting procedure;
- for NGOs, the recurrent experience of organising public participation in EIA procedures only to see their objections and suggestions consistently fail to be incorporated into the environmental permit issued (which is a consequence of the resistance on the part of public officials and investors), contributes to a growing disenchantment with EIA as a credible and effective procedure for participatory decision making and environmental protection (Regional Environment Center: REC 1995c).

Impact of informal institutions
That the implementation of environmental policy is the responsibility of all sectors of society is recognised in the 'principle of shared responsibility' contained within the EU's Fifth Environmental

Action Programme (Commission of the European Communities 1992, 113). The role of informal institutions for the environment is greater still in the case of EIA given the explicit provisions made for public participation in the course of implementation. Among the informal institutions that may participate in EIA procedures are environmental non-governmental organisations, public advocacy groups and citizens' associations.

Some indication of the overall numbers of environmental NGOs in CECs which might potentially participate in environmental decision making under EIA may be gained with reference to the NGO Directory compiled by the Budapest-based Regional Environmental Center for Central and Eastern Europe. Note, however, that such a list is not exhaustive as it does not include short-lived, single-issue local citizens' associations which may also play an important role in EIA procedures (see table 9.6). As a conservative estimate, these figures testify to the existence of a sizeable 'green' NGO community within each of these three CECs, especially in Hungary and the Czech Republic.

Table 9.6 *Environmental NGOs in Central Europe*

Country	NGOs including EIA among their objectives	Total
Czech Republic	1	520
Hungary	2	726
Slovakia	2	141

Source: REC 1997, 11.

The presence of environmental NGOs and the existence of rights of standing enshrined in law are not sufficient to ensure their participation in the implementation of EIA legislation, however. Indeed, many obstacles to the full involvement of NGOs in EIA procedures in CE persist despite provisions for the basic preconditions of access to information, consultation and rights of standing and the growing numbers of environmental NGOs in the region. Experience with EIA procedures in CE has shown that 'many times the legal requirements are ignored ... there is a great discrepancy among projects as to the extent to which EIA is implemented' (REC 1995c, 15). This is especially true for the public participation provisions supposedly guaranteed by the EIA legislation of CECs. Problems are rife and include (REC 1994; REC 1995c):

• a lack of resources and experience of EIA procedures on the part of NGOs as well as frequent encounters with, at best, passive resistance and, at worst, a climate of hostility on the part of public authorities charged with EIA;

• a long-standing tradition of the paternalistic state which arrogates responsibility for all spheres of public life, combined with an overwhelming deference to and inordinate emphasis upon the supremacy of technical expertise in environmental decision making;

• the extreme diffidence with which investors greet the prospect of public participation in authorisation procedures they consider to be a matter for bilateral discussion with public authorities alone;

• ingrained distrust of procedures staged by public authorities on the part of the general public coupled with an equally widespread strategy of confrontation with, or distancing from, official spheres by protest-oriented environmental NGOs.

Under such conditions, in which legally sanctioned rights of access to information and public participation may not enjoy recognition in practice nor be fully utilised by representatives of the public interest, the effective impact of informal institutions for the environment may indeed prove slight.[5] Ultimately, the greatest long-term impact of EIA legislation may lie in its introduction of this new set of participants into the decision making arena under provisions for public participation, thereby opening up the resolutions of formal institutions to an unprecedented level of public scrutiny. Nevertheless, other chapters in this book hint that the provisions of the EIA Directive – or other new instruments – may not suffice to induce public mobilisation.

Evaluating success in EIA implementation

The previous sections have developed a framework with which to evaluate the capacity of CECs in implementing EU environmental legislation. Clearly, the 'tables of convergence' developed by the EU to measure the level of approximation of national legislation with that of the EU provide little indication of the potential for actual, practical implementation within the applicant countries.

While the CECs have proved quite successful in meeting the requirements of approximation, effective implementation is hampered by the severity of the policy problem, the lack of personnel and financial resources, as well as the impact of political and administrative traditions. Such factors impinge upon the credibility and legitimacy of environmental policy and hence the effectiveness of its implementation.

Furthermore, although useful as a general framework with which to review formal and informal capacities for implementation, a comparative survey such as the one outlined above tells us little about the significance of the *outcomes* of EIA implementation for the permitting of public and private projects and even less about the *processes* by which they actually unfold in contemporary CECs. Far more detailed information about actual EIA procedures in each of these countries would clearly be needed for even an initial assessment of implementation success. At the very least we would need to establish how many EIA procedures resulted in (1) the straightforward issue of development permits without additional conditions, (2) the issue of development permits subject to the inclusion of mitigation measures for expected environmental impacts or (3) the outright denial of permits. Among the key questions to be addressed by such an in-depth investigation would be the following. How much public participation was forthcoming and how effective was it? How were conflicts between the key actors (investors, public administration, NGOs) managed in the course of decision making? To what extent did EIAs prevent or mitigate the environmental impacts of proposed projects?

Yet in the context of CE transition countries, the impact of EIA as a process may be of even greater significance than the sum of its outcomes given its nature as a *deliberation forcing* provision, one whose 'ostensible purpose is not to obtain any particular result but rather to change the way decision makers think and the processes by which they reach decisions' (Landy 1993, 34). The EIA serves this cognitive function by requiring, at a minimum, the provision of information to the 'affected public' and the inclusion of opportunities for comment, review and public discussion. Viewed optimistically, the EIA may help to fulfil the requirements for effective implementation identified by Jänicke and Weidner (Jänicke and Weidner 1997; Weidner 1997):

- *capacity-building processes may be more important than their outcomes* and this is particularly true in the CEC context in which the introduction of a new policy instrument, such as EIA, generates pressure for transparency on the part of the public administration and provides the opportunity for active involvement on the part of NGOs and citizens' associations. This is not to argue that EIA serves no concrete purpose in ensuring higher levels of environmental protection in CECs – nor that environmental protection should not be the ultimate goal. Rather, it is to underline the equally significant fact that EIAs, as procedures for environmental decision making, may be more important than their specific outcomes. This is particularly the case in situations of institutional flux in which ground rules are still being laid down and whose future development may still be influenced (Kriesi 1991). Within this perspective, the processes of access to information and public participation triggered by EIA procedures may be of more far-reaching impact than the issue of whether or not an environmental permit is granted in a given instance. Indeed they may prove crucial in the implementation of environmental legislation (of EU origin and non) by raising a new set of expectations, developing capacity and awareness while mobilising a new set of actors with an interest in ensuring that policies adopted actually produce tangible results. Finally, EIA procedures may foster 'social learning' among public administration officials, investors and NGOs alike with regard to the rights and responsibilities of public participation and in so doing build up a patrimony of experience which may be applied to decision making procedures in other spheres, thus ultimately contributing to democratic consolidation in the region (Webler *et al.* 1995);
- *public pressure is a key factor in improving environmental performance* but this, in turn, depends upon the degree of public awareness of environmental problems. In the case of CECs both environmental concerns and pressure for action are limited by the overwhelming predominance of economic considerations (such as the need to create or preserve local jobs). This notwithstanding, EIA procedures may serve to air public concerns over specific projects with significant environmental impacts and ensure that environmental and economic concerns are explicitly weighed up and their relative merits openly debated in the course of environmental decision making.

Notwithstanding the specific focus on EIA, the approach to the examination of CEC implementation capacities for EU-origin environmental legislation adopted in this chapter is of more general application. One which may prove equally useful in guiding further research into the dynamics of implementation processes in CECs and in reorienting EU programmes of technical assistance to include due consideration of both formal and informal institutions when supporting future Member States'⁶ efforts to prepare for EU membership.

Notes

1 I am especially indebted to Anikó Radnai and Jiri Dusik whose suggestions and insights have proved invaluable. The opinions expressed and arguments employed in this chapter are the sole responsibility of the author and do not reflect those of the OECD or of the governments of its member countries.
2 Hungary formally applied for EU membership on 01.04.94, the Slovak Republic on 27.06.95 and the Czech Republic on 24.01.96 (Commission of the European Communities 1997a).
3 See also Knill and Lenschow in the final chapter of this book for the 'legacies' of CEE environmental policy.
4 With the worst GDP growth figures being registered in 1991: Czech Republic –14.2 per cent, Hungary –11.9 per cent; and Slovakia –14.6 per cent (EBRD 1996).
5 Compare Börzel, chapter 10, in this book for a similar finding in the case of Spain. The combination of policy misfits and lacking bottom–up capacities and mobilisation are responsible for implementation failures in the case of new as well as old instruments.
6 In the light of the decision by the Luxembourg Council of 12–13 December 1997 to open accession negotiations with five CE applicants in spring 1998, namely: Estonia, Czech Republic, Hungary, Poland, Slovenia (Commission of the European Communities 1997a).

References

Bellinger, E., Lee, N., George, C. and A. Paduret (eds) (1997) *Environmental Assessment in Countries in Transition*, Papers and Proceedings of the Central European University Summer University Workshop, July 1996, Budapest (mimeo).
Bochniarz, Z., Bolan, R., Kerekes, S., and J. Kindler (eds) (1994) *Designing Institutions for Sustainable Development in Hungary: Agenda for the*

Future, Minneapolis-Budapest.

Bozóki, A., Körösinyi, A. and G. Schöpflin (1992) *Post-Communist Transition: Emerging Pluralism in Hungary*, London: Pinter; New York: St Martin's Press.

Caddy, J. (1996) 'Building Institutions for the Environment in Central Europe', *Proceedings of the International Conference on Environmental Protection (ICEP.3)*, Budapest, Hungary, 15–19 April 1996, Volume 1, London: European Centre for Pollution Research.

Commission of the European Communities (1992) *Towards Sustainability: A European Community Programme of Policy and Action in Relation to the Environment and Sustainable Development (1993–2000)*, Brussels: European Commission.

Commission of the European Communities (1996) *Implementing Community Environmental Law*, Communication to the Council of the European Union and the European Parliament, Brussels: European Commission, 22 October.

Commission of the European Communities (1997a) *Agenda 2000: Commission Opinions on Applications for Membership of the European Union*, Brussels: European Commission, 15 July.

Commission of the European Communities (1997b) *Guide to the Approximation of EU Environmental Legislation*, Commission Staff Working Paper, SEC(97) 1608, Brussels: European Commission, 25 August.

Czech National Council (1992) Czech National Council Act on Environmental Impact Assessment, Act no. 244/1992 S.B., 15 April.

Drdoš, J. and K. Pavličková (1995) 'Slovak Republic', International Roundtable on Practical Implementation of EIA in Central and Eastern Europe, 8–10 November, Bratislava (mimeo).

EBRD (1994) *Environmental Impact Assessment Legislation: Czech Republic, Estonia, Hungary, Latvia, Lithuania, Poland, Slovak Republic, Slovenia*, London, Dordrecht and Boston: Graham & Trotman and Martinus Nijhoff.

EBRD (1996) *Transition Report 1996*, London: EBRD.

EIU (1995) *Country Report: Czech Republic and Slovakia: 4th Quarter*, London: Economist Intelligence Unit.

Emmott, N. (1996) *Requirements for the Implementation of Integrated Pollution Control in the Republic of Hungary*, LLM essay (mimeo), London: University of London, School of Oriental and African Studies.

European Council (1985) 'Council Directive 85/337/EEC of 27.06.85 on the Assessment of the Effects of Certain Public and Private Projects on the Environment', *OJ* 5 July 1985, L 175, Brussels.

European Council (1997) 'Council Directive 97/11/EC of 03.03.97 amending Directive 85/337/EEC on the Assessment of the Effects of Certain Public and Private Projects on the Environment', *OJ* 3 March 1997, L 73, Brussels.

Fülöp, S. (1995) *Analysis of Legal Institutions of Several European and EU Environmental Impact Assessment Regulation*, (mimeo), Budapest: EMLA.

George, C. (1997) 'Environmental Impact Assessment Legislation in the Slovak Republic', in Bellinger, Lee, George and Paduret (eds).

George, C., Svejdarova, H. and L. Vojtechovska (1997) 'Environmental Impact Assessment Legislation in the Czech Republic', in Bellinger, Lee, George and Paduret (eds).

Government of Hungary (1995a) 'Act LIII on General Rules of Environmental Protection', *Hungarian Rules of Law in Force*, no. VI/17, Budapest, 1 September.

Government of Hungary (1995b) 'Government Decree no. 152 of 1995 (12 December) on Activities Requiring the Completion of an Environmental Impact Assessment', (unofficial translation).

Hanf, K. (1982) 'Regulatory Structures: Enforcement as Implementation', *European Journal of Political Research*, 10: 159–72.

Jänicke, M. and H. Weidner (1997) *National Environmental Policies: A Comparative Study of Capacity-Building*, Berlin: Springer-Verlag.

Kobus, D., George, C. and N. Lee (1997) 'Comparative Analysis of EIA Practice in Transitional Economies', in Bellinger, Lee, George and Paduret (eds).

Kriesi, H. (1991) *The Political Opportunity Structure of New Social Movements: Its Impact on Their Mobilization*, FS III 91–103, Berlin: Wissenschaftszentrum Berlin für Sozialforschung.

Landy, M. (1993) 'Public Policy and Citizenship', in Ingram, H. and S.R. Smith (eds), *Public Policy for Democracy*, Washington, DC: The Brookings Institution.

Lee, N. (1995) 'Environmental Assessment in the European Union: A Tenth Anniversary', *Project Appraisal*, 10(2): 77–90.

Manser, R. (1993) *The Squandered Dividend: The Free Market and the Environment in Eastern Europe*, London: Earthscan Publications.

Mazmanian, D. and P. Sabatier (1981) 'The Implementation of Public Policy: A Framework of Analysis', in Mazmanian and Sabatier (eds), *Effective Policy Implementation*, Lexington, MA: Lexington Books.

OECD (1992) *Reforming the Economies of Central and Eastern Europe*, Paris: OECD.

OECD (1996) *Environmental Performance in OECD Countries*, Paris: OECD.

PUMA (1993) *The Design and Use of Regulatory Checklists in OECD Countries*, Regulatory Management and Reform Series, PUMA Occasional Papers, no. 4, OCDE/GD(93) 181, Paris: OECD.

Radnai, A. and Z. Mondok (1997) 'EIA Implementation in Hungary', in Bellinger, Lee, George and Paduret (eds).

REC (1994) *Use of Economic Instruments in Environmental Policy in Cen-*

tral and Eastern Europe, Budapest: Regional Environmental Center for Central and Eastern Europe, December.

REC (1995a) *Status of National Environmental Action Programmes in Central and Eastern Europe*, Budapest: Regional Environmental Center for Central and Eastern Europe, May.

REC (1995b) *Government and Environment: A Directory of Governmental Organizations with Environmental Responsibilities for Central and Eastern Europe*, Budapest: Regional Environmental Center for Central and Eastern Europe, September.

REC (1995c) *Status of Public Participation Practices in Environmental Decisionmaking in Central and Eastern Europe*, Budapest: Regional Environmental Center for Central and Eastern Europe, September.

REC (1996) *Approximation of European Union Environmental Legislation: Case Studies of Bulgaria, Czech Republic, Estonia, Hungary, Latvia, Lithuania, Poland, Romania, Slovak Republic and Slovenia*, Budapest: Regional Environmental Center for Central and Eastern Europe, January.

REC (1997) *Problems, Progress and Possibilities: A Needs Assessment of Environmental NGOs in Central and Eastern Europe*, Budapest: Regional Environmental Center for Central and Eastern Europe, April.

Rosenbaum, N. (1981) 'Statutory Structure and Policy Implementation: The Case of Wetlands Regulation' in Mazmanian and Sabatier (eds).

Sabatier, P. (1986) 'Top–Down and Bottom–Up Approaches to Implementation Research: a Critical Analysis and Suggested Synthesis', *Journal of Public Policy*, 6(1): 21–48.

Sheate, W.R. (1997) 'The Environmental Impact Assessment Amendment Directive 97/11/EC: A Small Step Forward?', *European Environmental Law Review*, 6(8–9): 235–43.

SIGMA (1997) *Promoting Performance and Professionalism in the Public Service*, SIGMA Papers, 21, Paris: OECD.

Slovak Ministry of the Environment and Comenius University (1995) International Roundtable on Practical Implementation of EIA in Central and Eastern Europe, 8–10 November, Bratislava: Ministry of Environment of the Slovak Republic and Centre for EIA, Comenius University.

Slovak National Council (1994) 'Act of the National Council of the Slovak Republic on Environmental Impact Assessment', Act no. 127/1994, 29 April.

Stec, S. (1993) 'Public Participation Laws, Regulations and Practices in Seven Countries in Central and Eastern Europe: An Analysis Emphasizing Impacts on the Development Decision Making Process', in Vári, A. and P. Tamas (eds) *Environment and Democratic Transition: Policy and Politics in Central and Eastern Europe*, Dordrecht, Boston and London: Kluwer Academic Publishers.

Vári, A. (1995) 'Environmental Policy in Hungary: History and Plans', in

Dwivedi, O.P. and J.G. Jabbra (eds), *Managing the Environment: An Eastern European Perspective*, Ontario: de Sitter Publications.

Webler, T., Kastenholz, H., and O. Renn (1995) 'Public Participation in Impact Assessment: A Social Learning Perspective', *Environmental Impact Assessment Review*, 15: 443–63.

Weidner, H. (1997) 'Implementation of EU Environmental Legislation: The Theoretical Perspective', presentation at the 1997 Spring Workshop, Implementing EU Environmental Policy, Working Group on Environmental Studies, Robert Schuman Centre, European University Institute, 10–11 April, Florence.

10 Tanja A. Börzel[1]

Improving compliance through domestic mobilisation? New instruments and effectiveness of implementation in Spain

Introduction

Overall implementation effectiveness of European environmental policy, defined as formal and practical compliance with the legislation, is rather low among the Member States. Since the mid-1980s, the Commission has hoped to increase compliance by encouraging societal participation and transparency in the implementation process. EU environmental policies, such as Environmental Impact Assessment (1985), Access to Information (1990), Eco-Audit (1993), or Integrated Pollution Prevention and Control (1996) contain policy instruments which aim at broadening the participation of societal actors in the practical application and enforcement of European environmental regulations.

This chapter tackles the question to what extent such new policy instruments (NPIs) may actually contribute to improving Member State compliance with European environmental regulations. Are European environmental policies, which aim at broadening public participation and transparency really implemented more effectively than conventional regulatory policies?

I will argue in this chapter that the effect of NPIs on Member State compliance is highly ambivalent. On the one hand, domestic mobilisation is an important factor in enhancing the effective implementation of European policies at the domestic level. Not only can domestic societal actors serve as 'watchdogs' which bring Member States' infringements of European regulations to the attention of the Commission, thus, triggering pressure from 'above'. Societal actors may also exert pressure from 'below' by pushing Member State administrations to effectively apply and enforce European policies. Hence, there are good reasons to expect NPIs, which intend to provide societal actors with additional opportunities to 'pull' European regulations down to the domestic level, to improve Member State compliance.

On the other hand, NPIs may not only help to overcome Member State resistance against effective implementation. They can also create additional implementation problems. Procedural and communicative regulations which aim at providing public access and information in the implementation of environmental policies challenge the administrative practice of many Member States, which rely heavily on interventionist command-and-control regulation, being rather hostile to broad public participation and transparency. But, the implementation of NPIs itself is likely to trigger strong resistance on behalf of the public administration, particularly if they do not 'fit' existing administrative practice (see Knill and Lenschow, chapter 2, in this book for a similarly sceptical perspective).

Spain serves as a case in point to illustrate the ambivalent effect of NPIs on Member State compliance. Spain is one of the alleged environmental 'laggards' of the EU. Its level of compliance with EU environmental policy is relatively low. Due to the strong tradition of state interventionism and more than forty years of dictatorship, the Spanish system of interest intermediation is still weak. Societal actors have little resources to pull European policies down to the domestic level against the resistance of public administration. NPIs, such as environmental impact assessment and access to information, could strengthen the power of Spanish societal actors *vis-à-vis* their administration. At the same time however, public participation and transparency strongly contradict the Spanish administrative practice of closure and secrecy and are therefore likely to meet strong opposition in the Spanish administration. A comparative study on the implementation of two 'old' and two 'new' EU environmental policies in Spain will demonstrate that NPIs do not necessarily result in a higher level of compliance. Their mobilisation effect is strongly mitigated by the additional implementation problems which NPIs create as they do not fit existing administrative practice in Spain.

The chapter proceeds in the following steps. First, I will develop a theoretical model which allows systematically accounting for the effect of new, participatory policy instruments, as compared to 'old', command and control instruments, on Member State compliance. Second, I will use this model to compare the effect of old and new policy instruments on Spain's level of compliance with EU environmental regulations. Finally, I will summarise the argument and the findings of the chapter and conclude that NPIs are facing a fundamental dilemma, which has to be overcome, if they are to promote Member State compliance with EU environmental policy: NPIs can only increase the effective implementation of a policy if they are themselves effectively implemented. Here, in turn, they face some of the same obstacles as old policy instruments.

Domestic mobilisation and compliance: conceptual considerations

Implementation failure in EU environmental policy making is discussed in the literature along two groups of factors, which Geoffrey Pridham has distinguished as *genetic* and *systemic* causes of implementation problems (Pridham 1996). *Genetic* causes arise from the specific structural character of EU environmental policy making, i.e. the nature of the policies and of the policy process (see Collins and Earnshaw 1992; Macroy 1992). *Systemic* or domestic accounts of implementation problems refer to the specific features of the political and administrative institutions of the individual Member State (see Rehbinder and Stewart 1985; Müller 1986).

As I have argued elsewhere, implementation failure is neither an exclusive feature of EU environmental policy making nor simply systemic to the political system of the Member States. Rather implementation problems are the result of an interplay between both European and domestic factors (Börzel 2000b). One way of systematically linking the European and domestic factors in explaining compliance is to conceptualise the effectiveness of implementation as a function of pressure from 'above' and from 'below'.

Pressure from above and from below: the pull-and-push model
The 'pull-and-push model' is based on two major propositions. First, implementation problems only arise if European policies impose considerable costs[2] for the public administrations of the Member States. The less a European policy fits the legal and administrative structure of a Member State, the higher the adaptational costs in implementation and the lower the willingness of the public administration to ensure effective implementation. Second, the willingness and/or ability of the public administration to bear the costs of implementing poorly fitting EU policies is influenced by additional pressure for adaptation from 'below' by societal actors

mobilising against ineffective implementation at the domestic level (pull), and from 'above' by the European Commission introducing infringement proceedings (push).

External pressure for adaptation: policy misfit as the necessary cause of implementation failure   EU environmental policy making is strongly influenced by the regulatory competition among highly regulated countries such as Germany, the Netherlands, Denmark, or the UK. These Member States seek to bring EU policies into line with their own administrative traditions and regulatory standards in order to minimise the costs of institutional adjustment and to avoid disadvantages for their economies (Héritier 1996). This regulatory competition has given rise to a 'patchwork' of EU environmental policies (Héritier1996), where different regulatory approaches are often linked even within one single policy. As there is no consistent regulatory framework in EU environmental policy, the individual Member States face different levels of pressure for adaptation, depending on the extent to which an EU policy 'fits' the national approach and standards. The more an EU policy challenges or contradicts the corresponding policy at the national level, the higher the adaptational pressure a Member State faces in the implementation process (Knill 1997, 19).

It is assumed that implementation problems only occur if there is pressure for adaptation. If an EU policy fits the problem solving approach, policy instruments and policy standards adopted at the national level, there is no reason why the public administration should resist implementation. The EU legislation can be easily absorbed into the existing legal and administrative system. Only if the implementation of an EU policy requires considerable legal and administrative changes imposing economic and political costs on the public administration, implementation failure should be expected. Thus, there is hardly any incentive for a local administration to practically apply environmental standards if monitoring requires considerable financial and human resources or if enforcement challenges powerful economic interests.

External pressure for adaptation arises from a 'misfit' or incompatibility of the problem solving approach, policy instruments and/or policy standards of an EU policy and the corresponding policy at the national level. Only if an EU environmental policy challenges one (two, or all) of these three elements, i.e. imposes significant costs of adaptation, its implementation gives rise to problems for the national administrations.

1   The problem solving approach refers to the general understanding of an administration about how to tackle problems of environmental pollution. Two ideal types of problem solving approaches can be conceptualised:[3]

    • *a precautionary, technology and emission based approach*, which is based on imposing legally binding standards to be uniformly applied by all polluters irrespective of the differing local quality of the environment and the application of the available technology irrespective of the cost involved compared to the potential benefit for the environment;

    • *a reactive, cost–benefit and quality based approach*, which builds on the setting of quality standards for a certain area and on balancing the costs of a technology against potential environmental improvements;

2   Policy instruments refer to the 'techniques' applied to reach a policy goal by inducing certain behaviour in actors. They can be classified according to the following dimensions:[4]

    • *regulatory, command and control instruments*, which regulate behaviour through prescriptions and prohibitions threatening negative sanctions in case of non-compliance vs. *market-oriented*, offering financial incentives, and *participatory, communicative*, providing information, encouraging public participation and deliberation;

    • *substantial*: regulation by legally binding standards vs. *procedural*: regulation through procedures, such as the balancing of costs and benefits or the public participation in authorisation procedures.

3   Policy standards, which can be quantitative or qualitative in nature (see above), refer to the guiding values set by a policy, e.g. for air or water quality.

Yet, policy misfit causing external pressure for adaptation does not necessarily lead to implementation failure. The mobilisation of domestic actors who pull the policy down to the domestic level pressuring the public administration to properly apply it, may persuade national public actors 'to give priority to environmental policy and to embrace new directions' (Pridham 1994, 84). Legal action or public campaigns of environmentalist groups against the

Member State administration denouncing it for not applying EU legislation, often provide an additional 'incentive' for implementation. Such domestic mobilisation very often triggers additional external pressure for adaptation from 'above' by the European Commission, which opens infringement proceedings against recalcitrant Member States.

Domestic pressure for adaptation from 'below': the pull factor Internal pressure for adaptation arises from domestic mobilisation. EU policies usually have direct effects on domestic actors, imposing constraints for some and offering opportunities to others. It is typical for (EU) regulatory policies (like environmental policy) that their costs are allocated to those actors who are in charge of implementation and to those who are the target group of the policy. The domestic actors (public and private) who have to bear the costs of EU environmental policies (very often subnational authorities and economic actors), tend to resist the practical application and enforcement of a policy. This resistance, however, can be counterbalanced by other domestic actors who strive to 'pull down' an EU policy to the domestic level pressuring the public administration to practically apply and/or enforce it. This domestic pressure can be exercised through various channels (Pridham 1994, 94–9). First, political parties can raise concerns about the proper implementation of policies *vis-à-vis* the government, like the Catalan socialists did in 1989, when they questioned the non-application of the Environmental Impact Assessment Directive in the authorisation of a motorway cutting through a nature reserve.[5] Second, environmental organisations can act as a 'watchdog' drawing the attention of both public authorities (national and European) and public opinion on incidents of non- or improper application of EU environmental legislation. Third, the media can play a crucial role for domestic mobilisation. Media coverage often decides whether an environmental issue gains public attention and support. And fourth, business and industry can mobilise in favour of the implementation of a policy. The Eco-Audit Regulation is an example of economic interests having a promoting rather than obstructing impact on the implementation of an EU environmental policy. Domestic mobilisation is most effective if it is able to link up with European institutions, reinforcing external pressure for adaptation by initiating infringement proceedings.

In sum, if the public authorities get 'sandwiched' between

adaptational pressure from above (EU) and below (domestic actors), EU environmental policies have a good chance of being more effectively implemented, even if implementation involves high costs due to policy misfit.

According to the pull-and-push model, NPIs, which aim at enhancing public participation and transparency in the implementation process, may improve the level of Member State compliance as they provide societal actors with additional resources, strengthening their position *vis-à-vis* public administration and, thus, enabling them to pull down a European policy to the domestic level (see figure 10.1.

Figure 10.1 *The pull-and-push model of implementation*

```
┌─────────────────────────────────────────────────────────────────┐
│   External pressure for adaptation                                │
│  Misfit between EU and national policy                            │
│     EU infringement proceedings                                   │
│                                                                   │
│                  ⇩                                                │
│                                                                   │
│     Public administration      ⇨      Effective implementation    │
│                                                                   │
│                  ⇧                                                │
│                                                                   │
│   Internal presure for adaptation                                 │
│     Domestic mobilisation                                         │
└─────────────────────────────────────────────────────────────────┘
```

Yet, the pull-and-push model also points at a fundamental constraint that may severely limit the capacity of NPIs to promote Member State compliance. To some Member States, NPIs like environmental impact assessments or access to information are in fact not 'new' but already constitute administrative practice (Denmark, the Netherlands, Great Britain). But Member States, such as Germany or Spain, which rely heavily on interventionist, command-and-control regulatory instruments imposing material standards, face significant problems in incorporating new, procedural and communicative instruments into their legal and administrative structures. This misfit between European and domestic policy instruments is likely to provoke the resistance of public administration in implementation. Rather than facilitating implementation, NPIs become an implementation problem themselves. The comparative study on the implementation of two old and two new EU environmental policies in Spain will elucidate this dilemma.

The implementation of European environmental policy in Spain

The empirical study will look at the implementation of the following EU environmental policies:

- the Directive on the Combating of Air Pollution of Industrial Plants;[6]
- the Large Combustion Plant Directive;[7]
- the Access to Information Directive;[8]
- the Environmental Impact Assessment Directive.[9]

All four policies exert significant pressure for adaptation on the Spanish legal and administrative system due to policy misfit. The two air pollution control Directives are examples of old policies which do not include any special provisions for public participation and transparency while environmental impact assessment and access to information represent the new type of policy instruments.

In order to assess the effectiveness of implementation of these four policies, I will analyse both transposition and practical application in each case. A policy will be considered effectively implemented if (1) it is completely and correctly transposed into national law, (2) conflicting national provisions were amended or repealed, (3) the administrative infrastructure and resources were provided to put the objective of the policy into practice, and (4) the competent authorities encourage or compel others to comply with the legislation by monitoring, positive and negative sanctions, and compulsory corrective measures.[10]

Before analysing the implementation of the four policies, the major features of Spanish environmental policy making are briefly outlined.

Environmental policy making in Spain

Before accession to the EC, Spain had already enacted some substantial environmental legislation (such as the Law of Air Protection of 1972). But environmental policy has not been a priority on the political agenda. When Spain joined the EC in 1986, it committed itself to incorporate the total of European environmental legislation enacted before 1986 without asking for any transitional period or special conditions of application. The process of incorporation took more than two years and caused a severe policy overload for the Spanish administration. Nevertheless, most implementation problems arose at the level of practical application rather than transposition.

In Spain, the responsibility for environmental policy is strongly decentralised. In the implementation of EU environmental policy, the central state is concerned with the transposition of EU directives into national law, whereas practical application and enforcement lie with the responsibility of the Comunidades Autónomas (CCAA) and the municipalities. Despite gradual improvements, mechanisms of vertical coordination between the central state and the regions are still weak (Börzel 2000a). This has given rise to a number of implementation problems, not only in terms of compliance but also with regard to the uniform application of EU policies throughout Spain. Vertical fragmentation used to be complemented by 'intersectorial discoordination' of environmental responsibilities at the central state level. Horizontal coordination, however, has been improved by an upgrading of the administrative unit responsible for the environment, culminating in the creation of the Ministerio de Medio Ambiente in May 1996. At the regional level, all CCAA established an administrative body responsible for the environment, which, however, does not always enjoy the status of an independent ministry (Departamento, Consejería).

The Spanish state has historically been a 'strong', interventionist one, heavily regulating and interfering in most sectors of social life (Aguilar Fernandez 1992, 149–52). Together with the particular evolution of capitalism in Spain (strong preference for state protectionism) and almost forty years of authoritarian rule under Franco (1939–1975), state interventionism has led to a very weak system of interest intermediation. The degree of self-organisation is low, and policies have been made without any substantive participation of societal actors. Whereas economic interests have been enjoying some informal but discontinuous relations with the public administration, other societal actors used to be excluded from the policy making process (see Aguilar Fernandez 1994). Consequently, environmental policy making in Spain has been characterised by a non-cooperative, interventionist and reactive policy style (Font Borras 1996). It evolved through laws and regulations addressing specific and urgent environmental problems. Environmental policies are not based on some clear principles derived from a certain philosophy of environmental protection.

The Industrial Plant Directive: ineffective implementation due to policy misfit and the lack of domestic mobilisation

The Industrial Plant Directive, adopted by the Council on 28 June 1984, provides a framework legislation for preventing and reducing air pollution caused by industrial plants. The Directive does not set any substantive emission standards but establishes an administrative framework containing procedural requirements for the authorisation of the operation of any new industrial plant and the substantial modification of existing plants. It thereby follows the principle of procedural regulation embracing a precautionary and technology-based problem solving approach. From 1 July 1987, the authorisation of a new plant, or of the substantial modification of an already existing plant, especially if they fall under one of the 19 categories specified in Annex I of the Directive, is only to be granted if (1) all appropriate preventive measures against air pollution were taken, including the application of the best available technology not entailing excessive costs (BATNEEC), (2) the emission of the plant will not cause any significant air pollution, especially with regard to those polluting substances listed in Annex II of the Directive, and (3) none of the emission or air quality limit values applicable will be exceeded. The Member States are to ensure that applications for authorisation and the respective decision of the competent authority are made available to the public concerned. The Directive establishes the categories of industrial plants which require prior authorisation. It also makes specific provisions for existing industrial plants predating 1 July 1997. The Member States must implement measures in order to gradually adapt existing plants falling into the categories specified in the Directive to the best available technology. This adaptation of existing plants is to be carried out in taking into account the technical characteristics of the plant, the nature and volume of its polluting emissions, and the costs of adaptation. The Directive finally stipulates the possibility for the Council to fix 'emission limit values', based on BATNEEC, but only if it appears to be strictly necessary and by the unanimous vote of the Member States.

Triggered by the developments in international environmental policy and a concern about an increasing level of CO_2 emissions, Spain initiated a series of legislative measures to combat air pollution in the early 1970s. The Air Protection Act[11] of 1972, which provides a first legal framework for combating air pollution, lays out some general regulations for the authorisation of new industrial installations and the modification of existing plants.

A Decree of 1975[12] regulates in more detail the authorisation of new industrial installations and the modification of existing plants. As in the procedure prescribed by the Industrial Plant Directive of 1984, all new industrial installations and the modification of existing industrial plants which are likely to increase their emission level, are subject to prior authorisation by the municipalities.[13] Authorisation is only granted if the installation does not exceed the emission standards applicable and has adopted certain measures allowing for a dispersion of polluting substances to prevent the exceeding of air quality standards. Besides, the environmental impact of an industrial plant has to be assessed by the national or regional Ministry of Industry, in cooperation with the environmental authorities (*evaluación del impacto ambiental*).

At first sight, Spanish legislation appears to fulfil the major requirements of the Industrial Plant Directive. A closer look at the regulations, however, reveals important deficiencies. First, the formal requirements of the impact assessment as well as the consideration of corrective measures are certainly not sufficient to meet the respective regulations of the Directive. Second, dispersion measures do not really qualify as appropriate preventive measures against air pollution. Third, the importance of technological progress in combating air pollution is acknowledged in the legal texts. But any reference to available technology is linked to considerations about how environmental legislation must always be a compromise between public health considerations on the one hand, and economic imperatives and the available technology on the other hand. Moreover, the criterion of 'best available technology' (BAT) is nowhere defined nor is its application explicitly required.

Due to these considerable misfits between the problem solving approaches implicit in the EU legislation and Spanish regulatory practice, the Industrial Plant Directive has never been transposed into Spanish law. In 1987, the Directorate-General for Environment had announced the intention to amend existing legislation in order to comply with the Directive acknowledging the misfit between Spanish and European regulations (Bennett 1991, 184). The Ministry of Industry, however, which is in charge of compliance with the

Directive, claimed that Spanish legislation already fulfilled the requirements of the Directive.

As the Industrial Plant Directive has never been formally transposed, it does not come as a surprise that those parts which do not correspond to Spanish legislation, are not practically applied either because of the high costs involved. In order to avoid any additional workload and to avoid the opposition of industry, public administration has refrained from systematically considering preventive measures in the authorisation of industrial plants. Nor is BAT enforced on Spanish industrial plants. Some environmental administrators even consider BAT as a 'Northern European invention', which does not fit into Spanish environmental policy (interviews, March 1997). Moreover, due to the large number of small and middle-sized enterprises in Spain, the enforcement of BAT would only be feasible if the state provided some subsidies.

Environmental groups have been aware of the ineffective implementation of the Industrial Plant Directive. But they refrained from mobilising against public administration because they strive to concentrate their resources on more 'important issues' (interviews, March 1997). Air pollution is not a high ranking issue either in public opinion or on the political agenda of the environmentalists.

In sum, there is a considerable misfit between the Industrial Plant Directive and Spanish air pollution control legislation. Public administration refrained from effective implementation due to the adaptational costs. In the absence of pressure from above by the Commission in response to incomplete transposition, and pressure from below by societal actors because of non-application and non-enforcement, Spain's compliance with the Industrial Plant Directive remains low.

The Large Combustion Plant Directive: overcoming ineffective implementation through domestic mobilisation
The first time the Council set emission limit values previewed by the Industrial Plant Directive was in 1988 when it adopted the Directive on Large Combustion Plants (LCP). Being based on the 1984 Industrial Plant Directive, the Large Combustion Plant Directive shares the same precautionary, technology- and emission-based problem solving approach. Although the Directive contains procedural requirements for the authorisation and monitoring of plants, it predominantly relies on substantial command and control regulation in

order to prevent and reduce air pollution. For large combustion plants with a thermal output greater than 50 MW that enter operation after 1 July 1987, the Directive defines binding emission values for three pollutants: sulphur dioxide (SO_2), dust, and nitrogen oxides (NO_x). New plants to be authorised or licensed have to comply with these emission limit values and use BATNEEC to reduce air pollution. Old plants are not subject to emission standards as such, but their aggregated annual emissions have to be progressively reduced. For this purpose, the Member States have to draw up national programmes setting out the timetable and the implementing procedures. By applying the best available technology, the emission for SO_2 and NO_x have to be reduced by an increasing percentage over 1980 levels in three phases – 1993, 1998, and 2003. The emission ceilings to be achieved (national bubbles), however, vary among the Member States according to their economic, energy and environmental situation. Finally, BATNEEC has to be applied to the measuring methods used by the Member States to monitor compliance with the Directive.

Spanish legislation provides both quality and emission standards in order to control air pollution. The already mentioned decree of 1975 lays down a number of air quality standards, including sulphur dioxide, nitrogen oxide, suspended particulates, and lead and emission limit values for SO_2, and solid particles, such as smoke, soot and dust, which may be different for new and existing plants. And it also sets requirements for progressively reducing the level of total emissions. Yet, the SO_2 emission limit values for old as well as for new combustion plants were nowhere near the limit of the LCP Directive. In other words, there was a clear misfit between European and Spanish substantial air pollution standards. Moreover, as Spain did not implement the Industrial Plant Directive, Spanish air pollution control legislation was still lacking the precautionary and technology-based problem solving approach adopted by the LCP Directive.

In order to bring Spanish emission limit values for combustion plants up to European standards, and to incorporate the total emission reduction levels for existing plants, Spain transposed the LCP Directive into Spanish law by a Royal Decree in 1991.[14] The text of the Royal Decree is almost a literal copy of the Directive. It is to simply replace the Decreto 833/1975 in all the parts in which the Decree does not conform with the Directive. The 'automatic' suspension of conflicting national provisions brought Spain into formal compliance with the LCP Directive. But it resulted in a lack of domestic regulations, which would operationalise certain regulations of the Directive, such as the application of BATNEEC in reducing emissions and monitoring compliance.

Due to a considerable misfit with respect to policy standards and BATNEEC requirements, the practical application and enforcement of the LCP Directive imposes considerable costs. First, Spain will have to cut its total SO_2 and NO_x emission by half till 2003. And second, Spain has to upgrade its measurement technology in order to meet the BATNEEC requirements.

Spain is the third largest SO_2 emitter in OECD Europe (after Germany and the UK). Compliance problems with (SO_2) emission standards of the LCP Directive for existing plants have been basically limited to Spain's two largest central power stations, As Pontes (Galicia) and Andorra (Aragón), which account for more than half of the total SO_2 emissions in Spain. Andorra is considered the second most contaminating central power station in Europe. Following the requirements of the LCP Directive, the Ministry of Industry and Energy developed a National Plan, which requires a 42 per cent reduction of SO_2 emissions and a 28 per cent reduction of NO_x emission between 1990 and 2000. These reductions go well beyond those required by the LCP Directive and can only be achieved by systematically applying BAT, or, by importing better quality coal (interview, June 1998). Both central power stations burn up to 80 per cent indigenous high sulphur coal, and coal mining is the major source of socio-economic development in the areas where the central stations are located. This was the reason why the Spanish administration initially did not take any measures to practically apply and enforce the ambitious emission reductions of the National Plan.

Yet, at the beginning of the 1990s, massive *Waldsterben* (forest dying) was observed in the neighbouring provinces of the Andorra plant. Local municipalities, environmental groups (Greenpeace among others), trade unions, and political parties started to mobilise against the pollution caused by the central power station. After a fierce public campaign, which included an environmental liability law suit (see Font Borras 1996, 250–71), the management of the Andorra power station agreed to implement an environmental plan, which anticipates an SO_2 emission reduction of 90 per cent till the end of 1998, thereby superseding the reduction required by the LCP Directive by 40 per cent. Over-compliance with the Directive can only be explained by the continued domestic mobilisation due to massive environmental deterioration, which is linked to the pollution caused by the power station. According to a recent OECD report, Spain succeeded in significantly reducing its SO_2 emission over the last years. The reduction, however, has been mainly achieved by substituting indigenous low quality coal through higher quality imports, not by introducing BAT (OECD 1997). The Spanish administration and industry alike justify the *non*-introduction of BAT on the grounds of too extensive costs, as most of the existing combustion plants date back to the 1960s and 1970s (interviews, March 1997).

The BAT(NEEC) requirement also causes implementation problems with respect to monitoring air pollution. Due to the uneven geographical distribution of measurement stations and a measurement technology which is not always up to standard, the Spanish monitoring system is not able to provide reliable data on air pollution for all areas. Monitoring air pollution falls under the responsibility of the Spanish regions of which many lack the financial resources to invest in better monitoring technology, additional manpower and expertise (interviews, March 1998). While air pollution monitoring has improved over recent years, the Spanish system – depending on the region – is often still not up to BAT (OECD 1997; Instituto para la Política Ambiental Europea 1997) .

To conclude, due to the considerable policy misfit between the LCP Directive and Spanish air pollution control legislation, Spanish administration and industry alike resisted effective implementation due to the high costs which the systematic introduction of BAT in reducing and monitoring emissions would have involved. Only after societal actors and municipalities started to form a powerful coalition pressuring both central state administration and industry to enforce existing air pollution standards, were steps taken to comply with the LCP Directive, even though the technological emphasis of the legislation continued to be ignored. While compliance has thus improved, the BAT requirement is still not systematically imposed on existing combustion plants and monitoring networks. An operationalisation of the concept is still missing.

The Environmental Impact Assessment Directive: policy misfit
partly compensated through domestic mobilisation
The EU's 5th Environmental Action Programme indicated a change in European environmental policy making. The traditional

command and control approach will be complemented by the principle of shared responsibility between state authorities, industry, consumers, and the general public. The Directive on Environmental Impact Assessment is one of the first policies to implement this new approach. Environmental impact assessment (EIA) is based on a precautionary problem solving approach. It constitutes an instrument of procedural regulation, which assesses in a systematic and cross-sectoral way the potential impact of certain public and private projects on the environment. The policy also contains a strong element of public participation. The basic principle of the EIA Directive is that any project that is likely to have significant effects on the environment is subject to an environmental impact assessment prior to authorisation by the competent authority. The developer of a project has to provide information on the characteristics of the project, the measures envisaged in order to avoid, reduce and remedy significant adverse effects, and the data required to identify and assess the main potential effects of the project. The Member States can establish a procedure, in which the competent authority and the developer informally agree upon the precise scope of the required information ('scoping procedure'). This information (in the form of environmental impact statements, EIS) shall be forwarded to public authorities likely to be concerned by the project. The information is also to be made available to the public with the possibility that those concerned by the project can make complaints. The details of the information and consultation procedure are to be arranged by the Member States. Finally, the information, together with the public complaints, is to be considered by the competent authorities in the development of the consent procedure. The public must be informed about the final decision and the reasons and considerations that form the basis of the decision.

The Member States have a lot of discretion in the implementation of the EIA. The environmental impact assessment may be integrated into the existing authorisation procedures or established as a separate procedure. While any project listed in Annex I of the Directive has to be subject of an EIA, the projects of Annex II shall only be made subject to an EIA where the Member States consider that their characteristics so require.

Before the EIA Directive, there was no comprehensive environmental impact assessment procedure in Spain. Yet, environmental impact assessment was not entirely new to Spain either. As in other

Member States, different sectoral environmental regulations require the assessment of certain environmental impacts of a planned project. The most important predecessor of EIA is the Regulation on Irritating, Unhealthy, Harmful, and Dangerous Activities (RAMINP).[15] This administrative decree of 1961, partly modified in 1965, requires a sort of EIA for so called 'classified activities'. Before local authorities grant the licence required for a new classified activity, or the modification of an already existing one, the impact of such an activity on environmental conditions relevant to public health has to be assessed. Similar to the EIA Directive, the promoter has to provide information on the characteristics of the activity, its potential repercussions on the environment, and corrective measures to remedy such adverse effects. And the procedure also includes a period of public information of 10 days, in which the public concerned can make their complaints. The environmental impact of a classified activity is assessed by the regional environmental authority. In case of a negative assessment, the local licence must be denied.

Although not entirely new to Spanish environmental policy, the European EIA procedure does not fully fit the corresponding domestic procedures. The Spanish EIA lacks the explicit precautionary approach of the Directive. And the concept of public participation and transparency in administrative procedures contrasts with the Spanish administrative practice of closure and secrecy. More specifically, the requirements for information to be provided by the developer are much less demanding. The period of public information and consultation is shorter. Requirements for corrective measures are lax to non-existent. Cross-media effects are not systematically considered. And a project has only to be assessed with respect to its negative effects on public health, not on the environment as such (Font Borras 1996, 119–20).

Due to the 'misfit' between European and Spanish EIA regulations, Spain opted for a proper law to implement the EIA Directive, rather than integrating it into the different pieces of sectoral legislation.[16] Yet, the new EIA law does not correctly implement the EIA Directive.

Spanish national transposition norms only include six projects of Annex II: large dams, initial afforestation, airports for private use, marinas, and extraction of coal and lignite as well as minerals by open-cast mining. After the Commission had sent a reasoned opinion in 1992 threatening legal proceedings, the Spanish government finally agreed to remedy the matter in 1994. Yet, the Spanish EIA legislation has not been modified so far. To date, the Spanish Ministry of the Environment announced that it would correct its legislation when the revision of the EIA Directive decided by the Council of Ministers in 1997 (97/11/EEC) will be transposed.

While transposition is already incomplete, the practical application of the EIA Directive has also been of little effect. Administrative changes have been small. The EIA procedure was incorporated into the existing administrative procedures for the implementation of RAMINP. These procedures were merely formally adjusted to the requirements of the European EIA procedure. Consequently, there is a lack of sufficient human resources and expertise, especially if the relatively short time period for the assessment and the cross-media approach of the Directive is taken into account. The EIA are often still carried out 'in the old spirit', i.e. in the way former national EIA under RAMINP used to be conducted. As a result, the quality of the EIS produced is often low (Commission 1993). Alternatives are not really discussed; the 'zero alternative' is not considered at all (Escobar-Gómez 1994). The elaboration of adequate EIS requires expertise in which many enterprises are not willing or able to invest.[17] Environmental authorities seem to be equally unwilling to invest additional resources to ensure the good quality of EIS, its appropriate assessment, and the enforcement of corrective measures. Hardly any public and industrial projects are turned down (Escobar-Gómez 1994). Many projects still proceed without any authorisation at all, or only ask for it when they are already implemented. Local authorities, in charge of monitoring, often cover up for this 'circumvention' of authorisation procedures in order not to suffer socio-economic disadvantages.

In general, the effectiveness of EIA implementation is rather low in Spain. In a number of cases, however, EIA has turned out to be more than merely 'rubber stamping' the authorisation of a project. Societal actors have been mobilising against ineffective application of the EIA Directive, trying to pull the policy down to the domestic level. Societal actors emphasise that, if correctly applied, the new EIA procedure strengthens their position in the authorisation process of public and private projects in three respects (interviews, March 1997). First, the period of public information is longer (30 instead of 10 days) giving societal actors more time to prepare their complaints. Second, the information on the environmental impact of a project is more detailed and has to take into account the cross-media effects – not only on public health but on the environment as a whole. This procedure gives the public concerned a broader basis on which to make their complaints. And third, the European Commission is a powerful ally to whom societal actors may turn with their complaints about ineffective implementation. Appeals to the Spanish courts are time consuming, costly, and very often unsuccessful.

And indeed, environmentalists and citizen groups, often in coalition with the local administration, have increasingly made use of the participatory opportunities provided by the EIA to oppose the authorisation of public and private projects. There is a series of authorisation procedures where due to domestic mobilisation a project was stopped or, far more likely, substantive corrective measures were imposed. A case study on the authorisation of nine different projects subject to EIA – eight public, one private – indicates that domestic mobilisation can indeed make a difference. In all cases but one, environmental groups, often together with the local governments concerned, strongly opposed the project. In three cases, they even made a formal complaint to the Commission. Three of the public projects were not authorised due to a negative EIA, and the authorisation of another three projects was made conditional on substantial corrective measures. Hence, in two-thirds of cases, the EIA had a significant impact on the outcome of the project (Font Borras 1996).

Even broader empirical data show that the EIA Directive had a positive impact on domestic mobilisation in Spain. Denouncements and petitions made to the Spanish parliament with respect to infringements of the EIA regulations account for about 40 per cent of the total number in the environmental sector. Together with the Habitat and Wild Bird Directive, EIA also represents the highest number of Spanish complaints to the Commission (about 30 per cent) (see table 10.1).

Yet, the Spanish case points to an important caveat with respect to the effect of this new policy instrument. The empirical study shows that *if* societal actors mobilise against the authorisation of a project, EIA strengthens their position *vis-à-vis* public authorities, enabling them to prevent a project altogether or, at least, to impose corrective measures. Yet, societal actors, particularly at the local level, have only limited resources to mobilise in the first place. They often lack

Table 10.1 *Sectoral distribution of petitions and denouncements made to the Spanish parliament in 1994 and of complaints made to the European Commission in 1996*

Sector	Number of petitions and denouncements made to the Spanish Parliament in 1994	Number of complaints to the European Commission in 1996
Air	23	2
Water	20	6
Waste	91	9
Nature conservation	50	21
Environmental impact assessment	66	18
Total	250	56

Source: *Medio Ambiente en España 1996 and 1994* (annual reports of the Spanish Environmental Ministry).

the necessary human resources, expertise, and money to oppose the non-application of EIA regulations such as a cross-media assessment of the potential environmental impact or the elaboration of corrective measures. In other words, societal actors often do not have the necessary resources to exploit the opportunities for mobilisation offered by EIA. The EIA Directive represents a useful tool in public campaigns but has only limited mobilising effects per se (see also Knill and Lenschow in chapter 2 of this book). As a result, societal mobilisation to pull EIA down to the domestic level is concentrated on issues which seriously affect the 'backyard' of a larger group of people who then decide to join forces in mobilising against public authorities (Not In My Back Yard: NIMBY effect).

The Access to Information Directive: policy misfit and limited domestic mobilisation

One of the most important efforts of the European Commission to improve Member State compliance through public participation is Directive 90/313 on Freedom of Access to Information on the Environment (the AI Directive). The goal of the Directive is to broaden public access to environmental information to increase transparency and openness, thereby encouraging citizens to participate more actively in the protection of the environment. Entailing elements of procedural and communicative regulation, the Directive aims to ensure freedom of access to information on the environment held by public authorities as well as the distribution of information. It defines the basic conditions under which environmental information should be made accessible. Public authorities holding information on the environment, or bodies with public responsibility for the environment have to make such information available to any natural or legal person at his or her request without his or her having to prove 'direct effect'. The Directive allows for refusal if a request concerns information which affects public security, the confidentiality of the proceedings of public authorities, international relations, national defence, matters which are under legal inquiry, commercial and industrial confidentiality, the confidentiality of personal data, material voluntarily supplied by third parties, unfinished documents and internal communications, and where disclosure of the information may damage the environment. A request can also be refused when it is manifestly unreasonable or formulated in too general a manner. It must be possible to seek judicial and administrative review against the refusal of or failure to provide a requested item of information. Besides the obligation to make environmental information available upon request, Member States are called upon – however not obliged – to actively provide general information to the public.

In Spain, access to information held by public authorities has traditionally been highly restricted and not freely available either to ordinary citizens or to NGOs. During the Franco dictatorship, the Law of Administrative Procedure of 1958[18] allowed for restricted access to certain documents or records, provided the person could claim a personal, direct and legitimate interest. Public authorities were obliged to reply to all requests within six months. If a request was not answered within this time, the 'administrative silence' had to be understood as a refusal, against which an administrative appeal was to be lodged before the case could be taken to the administrative courts. In the democratic constitution of 1978, Spain recognised the general right of citizens to access files and public registers, except where such access could affect national security and defence, criminal investigations or personal privacy (art. 105b). Art. 105b, however, has a declaratory character, i.e. it does not constitute a subjective right to which citizens can refer in claiming access to a specific piece of information.

Moreover, Spanish legal provisions and administrative practices of granting access to information only in justified cases is in sharp contrast with the AI Directive which demands general access to information for anybody, only to be refused in justified cases. This 'misfit' produces intense pressure for adaptation in the implementation of the AI Directive. The costs of such adaptation do not lie so much with an additional working load for the administration. Broader access to information provides the public with an effective means of controlling administrative behaviour such as monitoring compliance with environmental legislation. It also allows for more transparency in administrative decision making. Not surprisingly, Spanish administration, not being used to public scrutiny, has shown little enthusiasm in an effective implementation of the AI Directive (see Kimber, chapter 8, in this book for a similar assessment).

When the AI Directive had come into force in December 1992, the European Commission started receiving complaints from Spanish environmental NGOs about the non-implementation of the Directive. In March 1993, the Spanish government notified the Commission that the AI Directive had been implemented by the new Law on the Legal Regime of Public Administrations and Common Administrative Procedures passed in 1992.[19] Yet, this law did not properly implement the AI Directive. The regulations of the new law concerning access to information contradict the AI Directive on several points. First, the right of access to information is only granted to Spanish citizens and NGOs and not to any natural and legal person irrespective of nationality, as stipulated by the Directive. Second, access is limited to files and documents, which are held in administrative registers, are part of a record and belong to completed administrative proceedings. In order to get information relating to proceedings which are unfinished and incomplete, the requester needs to prove an interest which is in contrast to the Directive.[20] Third, the law of 1992 fixes a time period of three months for the public administration to respond to requests, whereas the Directive requires Member States to respond as soon as possible and at the latest within two months. Fourth, the Spanish law includes exceptions, which go beyond those permitted by the Directive. These exceptions refer to files and documents, which form part of registered and closed files and dossiers. Fifth, the convention of 'administrative silence' is confirmed. If a request is not answered within three months, this is to be considered as a refusal. The Directive, however, states that a refusal has to be justified by the public authority.

Due to the incomplete transposition of the AI Directive, complaints to the Commission continued.[21] In March 1994, the Commission started an infringement proceeding against Spain sending an article 169 letter. Spanish NGOs strove to invoke the 'direct effect' of the AI Directive (Sanchis Moreno 1996: 234–5), and the Commission also intervened in some cases of refusal of information. In view of this pressure from above and from below, the Spanish government prepared a new Draft Law on the Right of Access to Information on the Environment, which was sufficient for the Commission to stop the infringement proceeding.[22] In 1995, the AI Directive was finally transposed into national law.[23]

The law transposing the Directive closely follows the structure and content of the Directive. It even includes one positive improvement on the Directive. If the information is available in different formats, the requester can choose the format in which he or she likes the information to be provided. Nevertheless, the new law does not fully implement the European norm. First, the right of access to information is still not granted to everybody but restricted to nationals or residents of states forming part of the European Economic Area (EEA). Second, the principle of administrative silence still holds. A request not answered within two months is to be considered a refusal, even if no justification is provided. Finally, authorities can make charges for supplying requested information. There is no mentioning that such charges should not exceed a reasonable cost. Each authority is free to make its own charges[24] and there is no obligation to inform the requester in advance of the charges that will be made.

In light of the still incorrect transposition of the AI Directive, complaints by societal actors to the Commission have continued. In February 1996, Greenpeace presented a third complaint to the Commission arguing that Spanish legislation did still not effectively implement the AI Directive. Spain is currently facing another infringement proceeding for not properly transposing the Directive.

As with formal transposition, practical application has not been very effective in Spain. Most of the Spanish regions have not enacted any legislation developing the national law on access to information on the environment. Hence, there are no practical arrangements for regulating access to information.

A study of 105 cases of requests for environmental information, collected by AEDENAT, Greenpeace, and the Fons de Documentació i Medi Ambient, illustrates the difficulties in gaining access to information. Eighty per cent of these requests, all however prior to the formal transposition of the Directive in 1995, are cases of non-reply. Only in 5 per cent, was access to information provided. Against five cases, an administrative appeal was lodged. Two appeals were decided by the administration, both positively, i.e. the information was granted. In five cases, a complaint was submitted to the Commission. The case study also reveals some clearly unintended change of behaviour on behalf of several authorities. Whereas previously no charges had been made for providing information, some authorities have started to take advantage of the possibility of charging. The charges are sometimes so high that they can only be meant as a means of dissuading requests (Sanchis Moreno 1996).

The implementation of the AI Directive reveals the same dilemma as we found in the case of the EIA Directive. AI has triggered some domestic mobilisation but this mobilisation is concentrated at the level of already mobilised and, in terms of resources, capable actors, in this case (trans)national environmental organisations. The Spanish branch of Greenpeace has filed three complaints to the Commission for incorrect transposition which resulted in the opening of two infringement procedures. National environmental groups, such as AEDENAT and CODA, have organised nationwide campaigns against the ineffective practical application of the AI Directive. At the local level, however, public demand for environmental information is still low. As in the case of the EIA Directive, local environmentalists and citizen groups have only limited resources to push their rights to information against the resistance of the public administration. On this broader societal level the 'misfit' between EU policy instruments and national practices effectively constrains the mobilising effect of the Directive. Suing public authorities takes about three years and involves high costs. Hence, there is little systematic pressure 'from below' on public authorities to correctly apply the Directive.

Conclusion: new policy instrument and domestic mobilisation – strengthening the already strong?

This chapter explored whether new policy instruments (NPIs), which aim at broadening public participation and transparency in the implementation process, can contribute to a higher level of Member State compliance with European environmental policy. A theoretical model was developed which conceives of implementation problems as a function of policy misfit and lacking domestic mobilisation. According to this pull-and-push model, the positive impact of NPIs in promoting effective implementation is not as clear cut as often suggested. While NPIs can help overcome implementation problems by providing societal actors with tools to mobilise against 'recalcitrant' public authorities, they may also face significant implementation problems themselves. In Member States like Germany or Spain, the underlying problem solving approach as well as the procedural and communicative character of the NPIs do not easily fit the traditional administrative practice of closure and secrecy in (environmental) policy making. As a result, public authorities in these countries can be expected to oppose the effective implementation of NPIs, hence blocking the anticipated mobilising effects of these policy instruments (see Knill and Lenschow, chapter 2, in this book).

The comparative study on the implementation of two old and two new EU environmental policies confirms the propositions of the pull-and-push model. First, the case of the LCP Directive demonstrates that domestic mobilisation can help overcome the resistance of public authorities against the effective implementation of a costly (because poorly fitting) policy. Second, the case of the EIA Directive shows that NPIs can strengthen the position of domestic actors *vis-à-vis* public authorities in the implementation of a policy. Moreover, the relatively high number of petitions and complaints against the ineffective implementation of the EIA Directive, as well as the complaints and public campaigns against both the incorrect transposition and non-application of the AI Directive, indicates the potential of NPIs to promote domestic mobilisation.[25] Yet, when it comes to practical application and enforcement, domestic mobilisation has proved (so far) insufficient to systematically bring about better compliance. This failure relates to the third major finding of this study: the implementation of EIA and AI in Spain demonstrates that societal actors with little resources are not able to use NPIs in their mobilisation effort, particularly if NPIs do not fit the administrative practice of the Member State and therefore create additional resistance. In other words, NPIs are less likely to initiate domestic mobilisation by providing additional resources. Rather, NPIs tend to strengthen those societal actors who already have a minimum of resources, which are necessary to exploit the new avenues created by the NPIs.

The three major findings of this chapter are confirmed in the comparative case study presented by Knill and Lenschow in chapter 11. They point at a serious limitation, if not a dilemma, of NPIs in promoting Member State compliance with European environmental policy. The effect of NPIs on Member State compliance is likely to vary across the Member States depending on the fit between NPIs and existing administrative practice on the one hand, and on the relative strength (resources) of societal actors *vis-à-vis* public administration, on the other hand. In 'fit' countries, such as Great Britain or Denmark, NPIs do not cause additional implementation problems. But as public participation and access to information already constitute administrative practice, the added value of NPIs for societal actors may be limited. In 'misfit' countries, such as Spain and Germany, NPIs face their own implementation problems. As a result, societal actors can only use NPIs to pressure the public administration if they have a minimum of resources like German environmental organisations and citizen groups, which are even at the local level far more powerful than their Spanish counterparts (see Börzel 2000b).

To conclude, NPIs appear to predominantly strengthen the already stronger (more resourceful) societal actors while those who would really need to be strengthened are not able to systematically use NPIs because they lack the necessary resources to invoke their rights provided by NPIs. As the Member States with the lowest compliance record are often those with the weakest societal actors, the potential of NPIs to improve Member State compliance is indeed questionable.

Notes

1 I would like thank Andrea Lenschow, Christoph Knill and Geoffrey Pridham for their comments on earlier versions of this chapter. The empirical results are part of my dissertation project (Börzel 2000a). They are partly drawn from a research project which was conducted at the European University Institute in 1997 and which was funded by the legal unit of DG XI of the European Commission.

2 Costs are not understood in merely economic terms. They can be also political, e.g. with respect to public support (endangering jobs) or political credibility or reputation (being a 'good European' or an 'ecological leader').

3 The classification draws on the categories developed in a research project on the impact of national administrative traditions on the imple-

mentation of EU environmental policy guided at European University Institute, Florence in April 1997 (Knill 1997; see Héritier *et al.* 1996).

4 It will be apparent from the following criteria that 'new' and 'old' instr-ments may cause adaptation costs. For a discussion of how this is often overlooked in the literature on new instruments see Knill and Lenschow in the introductory chapters to this book.

5 First, the socialists raised the issue in the Catalan Parliament and then made a complaint to the Commission and the European Parliament. The Commission decided to freeze the loan granted to the promoter of the project by the European Bank for Reconstruction and Development and asked for the elaboration of an environmental impact assessment including corrective measures (Font Borras 1996, 137).

6 84/360/EEC.

7 88/609/EEC.

8 90/313/EEC.

9 85/337/EEC.

10 Hence, the concern of the case study lies with the output rather than the outcome of the different EU environmental policies (see chapter 2 of this book).

11 Ley 38/72, 22.12.1972 de Protección del Ambiente Atmosférico, BOE 309, 16.12.1972.

12 Decreto 833/1975, BOE 96, 22.4.1975 which is further specified in a ministerial circular of October 1976 (Orden de 18 de octubre 1976, BOE 290, 3.12.1976).

13 Reglamento de Actividades Molestas, Insalubres, Nocivas y Peligrosas, Decreto 2414/1961, 30.11.1961, BOE 292, 7.12.1961.

14 Real Decreto 646/1991, 22.4.1991, BOE 99, 2.4.1991, modified by the Real Decreto 18000/95, 3.11.1995 (BOE 293, 8.12.1995).

15 Reglamento de Actividades Molestas, Insalubres, Nocivas y Peligrosas (RAMINP) de 30 de noviembre 1961 (Decreto 2414/1961; BOE 292, 7.12.1961).

16 Real Decreto Legislativo 1302/1986; BOE 155, 30.6.1986, executed by Real Decreto 1131/1988; BOE 239, 5.10.1988.

17 The EIA increases both the costs and the time scale of a project, the former by an estimated 5–10 per cent, and the latter by a couple of months delay (Commission 1993: 241).

18 Ley de Procedimiento Administrativo de 17 de julio 1958.

19 Ley 30/1992 de 26 de noviembre, de Régimen Jurídico de las Admin-istraciones Públicas y del Procedimiento Administrativo Común, BOE 285, 27.11.1992.

20 Kimber points to the legal ambiguity with respect to cases involving unfinished administrative proceedings. Nevertheless, the Spanish practice indicates resistance to the general idea of administrative transparency.

21 Two complaints were made by Greenpeace, one in February 1993, and the other in January 1994 (De la Torre and Kimber 1997).

22 A non-legislative proposal of the Izquierda Unida (a left party coalition) submitted before the National Congress further increased the pressure on the Spanish government to finally transpose the Directive (Sanchis Moreno 1996: 233).

23 Ley 38/1995 de 12 deciembre sobre el Derecho de Acceso a la Información en Materia de Medio Ambiente, BOE 297, 13.12.1995.

24 However, the 1989 Public Charges and Prices Act (Ley 8/1989, de 13 de abril, reguladora de las Tasas y Precios Públicos) is applicable, of which art. 7 establishes a principle of equivalent charges.

25 So far, domestic mobilisation focuses on the correct implementation of the NPIs themselves; environmental mobilisation beyond this narrow perspective, effecting bottom–up forms of control of environmental policy performance in general still needs to develop. Given the 'youth' of NPIs, this is hardly surprising, however.

References

Aguilar Fernandez, Susana. 1992. 'Políticas Ambientales y Disenos Institucionales en Espana y Alemania: La Comunidad Europea como Escenario de Negociación de una Nueva Area Política'. Doctoral Thesis, Departemento de Sciencies Políticas, Universidad Complutense de Madrid, Madrid.

Aguilar Fernandez, Susana. 1994. 'Spanish Pollution Control Policy and the Challenge of the European Union'. *Regional Politics and Policy* 4 (1, special issue): 102–17.

Bennett, Graham, ed. 1991. *Air Pollution Control in the European Community. Implementation of the EC Directives on the Twelve Member States*. London: Graham & Trotman.

Börzel, Tanja A. 2000a. 'Europeanization and Territorial Institutional Change. Towards Cooperative Regionalism in Europe'. In *Europeanization and Domestic Political Change*, edited by J. A. Caporaso, M. G. Cowles and T. Risse. Ithaca, NJ: Cornell University Press.

Börzel, Tanja A. 2000b. 'Why There Is No Southern Problem. The Implementation of EU Environmental Policy in Germany and Spain'. *Journal of European Public Policy* 7 (1): 141–62.

Collins, Ken, and David Earnshaw. 1992. 'The Implementation and Enforcement of European Community Legislation'. *Environmental Politics* 1 (4): 213–49.

Commission, of the European Communities. 1993. *Report from the Commission of the Implementation of Directive 85/337/EEC on the Assessment of the Effects of Certain Public and Private Projects on the*

Environment. Brussels: Commission of the European Communities.

De la Torre, Maria, and Cliona Kimber. 1997. 'Access to Information on the Environment in Spain'. *European Environmental Law Review*, February: 53–62.

Escobar Gómez, Gabriel. 1994. Evaluación de Impacto Ambiental en Espana: resultados prácticos. *Ciudad y Territorio* 2 (102): 585–95.

Font Borras, Nuria. 1996. La Europeizacion de la politica ambiental en Espana. Un estudio de implementacion de la directiva de evaluacion de impacto ambiental. Ph.D. thesis, Departamento de Ciencia Politica y Derecho Publico, Universitat Autonoma de Barcelona, Barcelona.

Héritier, Adrienne. 1996. 'The Accommodation of Diversity in European Policy Making and Its Outcomes: Regulatory Policy as a Patchwork'. *Journal of European Public Policy* 3 (2): 149–76.

Héritier, Adrienne, Christoph Knill and Susanne Mingers. 1996. *Ringing the Changes in Europe: Regulatory Competition and the Redefinition of the State: Britain, France, Germany.* Berlin and New York: De Gruyter.

Instituto para la Política Ambiental Europea, Madrid. 1997. *Manual de Política Ambiental Europea: la UE y Espana.* Madrid: Fundación MAPFRE.

Knill, Christoph. 1997. 'The Impact of National Administrative Traditions on the Implementation of EU Environmental Policy'. In *The Impact of National Administrative Traditions on the Implementation of EU Environmental Policy. Preliminary Research Report for the Commission of the European Union, DG XI*, edited by C. Knill. Florence: European University Institute, Robert Schuman Centre, 1–45.

Macrory, Richard. 1992. The Enforcement of Community Environmental Laws: Some Critical Issues. *Common Market Law Review* 29: 347–69.

Müller, Edda. 1986. *Die Innenwelt der Umweltpolitik: sozial-liberale Umweltpolitik: (Ohn)macht durch Organisation?* Opladen: Westdeutscher Verlag.

OECD. 1997. *Environmental Performance Reviews: Spain.* Paris: OECD.

Pridham, Geoffrey. 1994. 'National Environmental Policy making in the European Framework: Spain, Greece and Italy in Comparison'. *Regional Politics and Policy* 4 (1, special issue): 80–101.

Pridham, Geoffrey. 1996. 'Environmental Policies and Problems of European Legislation in Southern Europe'. *South European Society and Politics* 1 (1): 47–73.

Rehbinder, Eckard, and Richard Stewart. 1985. *Environmental Protection Policy.* Vol. 2. Berlin: de Gruyter.

Sanchis Moreno, Fe. 1996. 'Spain'. In *Access to Environmental Information in Europe. The Implementation and Implications of Directive 90/313/EEC*, edited by R. E. Hallo. London, The Hague and Boston: Kluwer Law, 225-48.

11 Christoph Knill and Andrea Lenschow

Do new brooms really sweep cleaner? Implementation of new instruments in EU environmental policy

Introduction

In view of an ever widening implementation gap (CEC 1996), we observe in recent years a significant shift in the Community's policy making and implementation approach. This shift is characterised by the emergence of so-called new instruments, such as procedural regulation, self-regulation, public participation and voluntary agreements. In the hope of improving implementation effectiveness, new instruments are increasingly replacing or supplementing 'command-and-control' regulations which prescribe uniform and substantive objectives (such as emission standards, best available control technologies) in a detailed way.

New instruments are expected to improve the effectiveness of EU environmental policy in basically two ways. First, they leave Member States more leeway to comply with EU requirements by taking account of domestic context conditions. In fact, the new flexibility may ease the decision making process as well as the subsequent implementation. Second, in promoting the role of the general public in the implementation process (by strengthening public access and self-regulation), the Commission aims at increasing the societal support and awareness with respect to its policies. Strong societal support and awareness, in turn, increases the pressure on domestic administrators to properly comply with EU legislation. This strategy shift is supported by implementation scholarship which suggests that successful implementation depends on the preferences, capabilities and resources of subordinate administrative actors dealing with practical enforcement as well as societal actors addressed by the policy in question (Hanf and Downing 1982; Mayntz 1983; Peters 1993). The so-called bottom–up approaches are perceived most promising in cases with complex policy problems, controversial objectives and solutions (Ingram and Schneider 1990). These are typical aspects of the environmental field, which is characterised by high scientific uncertainty, and of European policy making in general, with its difficult task of accommodating diverse regulatory approaches and preferences in a centralised mode of policy formulation.

Considering these general features characterising both the environmental field and European policy implementation, the Commission's move towards new instruments may represent an appropriate step to promote effective implementation. In this context, new instruments may be viewed as particularly promising in order to address the far-reaching environmental problems of future Member States from Central and Eastern Europe (CEE), given the particular risk of resistance towards environmental regulations on the ground. However, a look at the implementation record of 'new' EU policies hardly confirms such positive implementation expectations. Comparative research reveals that implementation effectiveness for European policies varies from country to country and policy to policy; new instruments do not perform significantly better than policies in line with the traditional top–down approach (Knill 1998; Knill and Lenschow 1998a, 1998b).

This chapter advances two arguments. First, to understand the implementation effectiveness of European policies, the choice of policy instruments has to be considered in a broader institutional context. The institutional fit or misfit of national administrative traditions and European requirements is the decisive factor explaining implementation effectiveness, not the type of the policy instrument *per se*. Second, at least in the shorter term most new instruments have only limited capacities to mobilise support for environmental measures. Experience in CEE, especially, indicates that more direct capacity-raising instruments are required here. Nevertheless, considering the insufficient financial means targeted at making top–down regulatory instruments effective in CEE, even the limited effects of new communicative and economic instruments may make some difference.

To elaborate on these arguments, the chapter proceeds in three steps. In section two, we compare the implementation of old and new instruments in Germany, Britain and France. Whereas the Directives on Large Combustion Plants (LCP) and Drinking Water reflect the top–down regulatory approach, the Directive on the

Freedom of Access to Environmental Information (Information Directive) and the Environmental Management and Audit Scheme (EMAS) Regulation represent the new approach. In section three we elaborate on our institutional explanation for the observed patterns of implementation effectiveness. Section four considers the implications of our research in Western Europe for the future Member States in CEE.

We define effective implementation as the degree to which the formal transposition and the practical application of European policies at the national level correspond to the objectives defined in European legislation. Rather than analysing the accomplishment of policy objectives in terms of normative outcomes, we restrict our investigation to the compliance with the legal-administrative tasks specified in the legislation. As further elaborated in chapter 2 of this book, the application of this relatively narrow definition allows us to establish a clear link between EU policy making and implementation effectiveness; furthermore we are able to compare implementation processes across individual policies and policy instruments.

New instruments but old problems

To investigate the impact of the EU's new strategy for ensuring policy implementation, we selected four pieces of EU legislation with two each representing the contrasting regulatory approaches. Evidence drawn from Britain, France and Germany indicates that the choice of regulatory strategy makes no systematic difference with respect to the effectiveness of formal and practical compliance at the national level. Let us begin by briefly characterising the four pieces of legislation under investigation before turning to the country experiences.

The old approach: top–down implementation
With the emergence of environmental policy as an EU policy area in its own right, the 1980s saw a significant growth in European legislation. For the most part, these policies were characterised by hierarchical patterns of regulation. Detailed substantive requirements, such as emission, product or quality standards were prescribed at the European level in order to protect air, water, and soil. Following this top–down approach, uniform and detailed requirements applied to all national administrations involved in

practical implementation and enforcement, as well as to private actors, such as industrial operators, who were addressed by the European policy in question.

Two classical examples of this top–down approach are the Directives on LCP and Drinking Water. The 1988 LCP Directive attempts to tackle one of the principal causes of acid rain by limiting emissions of sulphur dioxide and nitrogen oxides from fossil-fuelled power stations and other large combustion plants, such as oil refineries. Different requirements are set for new and existing plants. With respect to already existing plants Member States were required to draw up programmes for the progressive reduction of total annual emissions. For new plants uniform emission limits applicable to individual authorisations were defined (Haigh 1996, 6.10). Although at least the application of a so-called 'bubble-concept' concerning old plants left it to the Member States to select appropriate means for achieving the limit values, leeway for national decision making was generally quite restricted. Given the dependence of domestic energy generation on high sulphur coal in most Member States (except the nuclear dominated industries in France and Belgium) as well as the considerable reduction rates required by the Directive, the 'bubble concept' in many instances required the installation of flue gas desulphurisation technology. Implicitly, European legislation not only prescribed national emission limits, but also the technological means towards fulfilling European standards.

The implications of the 1980 Drinking Water Directive are similarly demanding. The Directive defines standards concerning the quality of water intended for drinking or for use in food and drink manufacture. The Directive covers all water for human consumption including public and private water supplies. It lays down over sixty water quality standards and guidelines for water quality monitoring. Member States must set national values in order to comply with the standards defined in the Directive. In addition, Annex II of the Directive defines the analytical measurement methods as well as minimum monitoring frequencies (Haigh 1996, 4.4–2). Hence, similar to the LCP Directive, the detailed specification of mandatory standards and appropriate technologies leaves little scope for choosing an adaptation strategy to meet these requirements while remaining in line with domestic conditions and capacities.

The new approach: bottom–up implementation

Room for flexible adaptation and the mobilisation of domestic support for environmental improvements became more central to EU policy after the mid-1980s. The Information Directive and the EMAS Regulation represent European measures of this new regulatory orientation, intended to change the level of environmental awareness, environmental attitudes and behaviour in society, industry and the public sector. The 1990 Information Directive is part of the Commission's attempt to make environmental information more easily available to the public and – through increasing public control – reduce the enforcement and monitoring difficulties experienced with EU environmental policies. To make both public authorities and the regulated industries accountable to the public, the Directive requires that relevant authorities holding information on the environment make this information available to persons requesting it. Procedural requirements aim at open and transparent patterns of administrative interest intermediation strengthening the opportunities for access by third parties.

The emphasis on procedural rules also characterises the 1993 EMAS Regulation. The Regulation intends to change the behaviour of economic actors *vis-à-vis* the environment by targeting the polluters' perception of the economic incentives to use environment friendly production methods. Industry's implementation of environmental management systems occurs on a voluntary basis. The EMAS Regulation defines procedural requirements for the establishment of internal management systems, which have to be approved by external verifiers. Member States must create competent bodies for the accreditation of the verifiers and the certification of participating companies in the EMAS.

The Information Directive and the EMAS Regulation are characterised by regulatory patterns, which are diametrically opposed to the regulatory approach underlying the Directives on LCP and Drinking Water. Instead of hierarchy, they emphasise participation, self-regulation and voluntarism. Rather than prescribing detailed and substantive objectives, they contain procedural requirements in the hope that procedural compliance will lead to the achievement of substantive environmental objectives.

Implementation effectiveness in comparison

A comparison of the implementation effectiveness of the four pieces of European legislation in the three largest Member States of the EU, Britain, France and Germany, gives results that question the special promise of new policy instruments. There is no evidence that they are generally implemented more effectively than top–down regulation. Although the Information Directive and the EMAS Regulation are explicitly oriented towards creating and motivating broad support at the national level, their overall implementation record in these three countries does not differ significantly from corresponding results in the cases of LCP and Drinking Water (table 11.1).

Table 11.1 *Implementation effectiveness of EU environmental policy in three Member States*

| | Top–down approach | | Bottom–up approach | |
	LCP	Drinking water	Information	EMAS
Germany	Effective	Delayed, but effective	Ineffective	Effective
Britain	Effective	Delayed, but effective	Effective	Effective
France	Effective	Ineffective	Effective	Ineffective

To summarise the results briefly,[1] neither country had much trouble in implementing the LCP Directive. Germany's existing legislation already corresponded generally to the EU legislation and went beyond it in some substantive standards. France had to adapt its legislation slightly but benefited from the structure of its energy market with about 70 per cent of its energy nuclear generated. In Britain the implementation of the Directive followed the privatisation of the energy sector and general public sector reforms which facilitated a smoother adaptation process than the previous EU negotiations would have suggested. Implementation of the Drinking Water Directive proved generally more difficult. Germany long resisted implementing the Directive due to some inconsistencies in the legislation; it implemented once technological innovations and the adoption of new economic instruments allowed it to overcome these inconsistencies. France, by contrast, continued to implement deficiently, resisting the high quality standards and the inflexible form of legal implementation implied in the Directive. Similar to the LCP case, privatisation and public sector reforms allowed the British government to impose the new regime on the sector without incurring additional costs for the state budget; hence, implementation of the Drinking Water Directive was delayed but in the end successful.

Turning to the new instruments, the Information Directive was implemented quite effectively in France and Britain. In France, the Directive corresponded with already existing practices and in Britain it fitted well into the general development towards building a more consumer-oriented and transparent public sector. In Germany, the formal transposition of the Directive was minimalist, and ongoing proceedings of the ECJ indicated further deficiencies in practical implementation (see Kimber, chapter 8, in this book). In the EMAS case, in turn, Germany performs as the declared 'front-runner' in implementing the Regulation (see Bouma, chapter 6, in this book). In Britain industry is slightly less responsive with regard to this new EU instrument (in part due to its international outlook and use of equivalent international norms), however, the Regulation has been implemented without problem. Only in France, does scepticism with regard to the new instrument prevail among the targeted industrial actors, resulting in rather poor practical implementation of the Regulation.

From the perspective of implementation theory, this empirical evidence confronts us with a puzzle: why are the new instruments not implemented more effectively than the old ones although they fulfil a central condition for successful implementation, namely, the mobilisation of support from below? We are going to argue that the implementation results of (West) European policies can only fully be explained when this 'support argument' is placed into a broader institutional context.

The explanation: effective implementation from an institutional perspective

Here we argue that it is not the choice of the policy instrument *per se*, but the degree of institutional fit between national administrative arrangements and corresponding European requirements that affects implementation effectiveness. Our case is based on three considerations.

First, we assume that depending on the compatibility of European policies with domestic administrative arrangements, administrative practices and structures at the domestic level may be faced with institutional pressures for adaptation. Adaptation pressure on domestic arrangements may equally emerge from old and new instruments, given the fact that the latter are in many instances procedurally demanding.

Second, following propositions of the institutionalist literature, we hypothesise that domestic adjustment and hence implementation effectiveness depends on the institutional scope of the required adaptation. It is widely acknowledged that institutions do not smoothly adapt to external pressures. The 'normal life' of institutions is characterised by continuity and persistence. It is only in exceptional cases of fundamental performance crises or external shocks, that the discrepancy between exogenous pressure and adaptive capacity becomes too big and that old continuities are given up in order to create new ones (Krasner 1988; March and Olsen 1989). The emphasis on institutional persistence does not preclude that institutions routinely modify their processes and structures in the light of exogenous pressures, however, they do so without changing their institutional core. Institutional change is incremental rather than revolutionary.

Based on these considerations, we expect effective implementation to be more likely if the adaptation required by European policies can be achieved by changes *within* rather than a change *of* the core of national administrative traditions. In other words, general characteristics shaping administrative practices and structures within a country, which follow from the specific constellation of the macro-institutional context, including the state tradition, the legal system, as well as the political-administrative system. If European adaptation requirements remain within the range of options defined by national administrative traditions, this does not automatically imply that these adaptations will actually take place. We suggest that it is in these institutionally less demanding constellations; that is, when European adaptation requirements can be achieved by changes *within* the core of national administrative traditions, that we need to observe a second condition for effective implementation, namely the level of domestic support for administrative adaptations.

It follows from this that the effectiveness of new instruments may be hampered in two cases. First, their implementation will be seriously constrained if they are in contradiction to core features in the respective Member States. Second, in cases of a less determinant or a fluctuating core, new instruments depend on a favourable domestic support structure. Here, the very nature of new instruments may constitute great potential as they help to mobilise such support on the lowest level. This mobilisation capacity is generally lacking in top–down instruments; in institutionally open situations these depend on coincidentally favourable societal conditions.

Finally, even though the core features of state, legal or administrative structures are by definition rather stable, in response to extraordinary internal or external pressures some core dynamic could be possible. We will observe below that 'movement of the core' played a role in the UK's shift from a resistant to a positive attitude towards the implementation of certain European Directives. Even more central will be the role of macro-institutional dynamics in the discussion of CEE environmental policy implementation.

Based on this analytical framework, we now interpret the empirical findings drawn from the implementation of EU environmental policy in Germany, Britain and France, before turning to the implications for CEE countries. On the basis of the West European cases, we elaborate first on instances of institutional fit and hence expected effective implementation, then on cases of institutional contradiction and therefore ineffective implementation. Finally, we discuss the institutionally open situations. In these now more narrowly defined cases, we investigate whether new instruments have lived up so far to their declared special potential for mobilising additional support for effective implementation.

Cases of confirmation
The LCP Directive in Germany and France, the Information Directive in France, as well as the EMAS Regulation in Britain represent cases of confirmation. Here, effective implementation is explained by the fact that domestic arrangements basically corresponded to European requirements; i.e., European legislation implied no or only negligible adaptation pressures. Given that few domestic changes were necessary for full compliance, the degree of domestic support and hence the approach to implementation made no difference in terms of effective compliance.

Since the LCP Directive was modelled after a corresponding German regulation, it is not surprising that European legislation could be implemented easily, without any changes in administrative practice and structures (Héritier *et al.* 1996; Lenschow 1997). In the French case, some adaptations would have been necessary as the

Directive required the introduction of uniform emission standards, which reduced the previous leeway of the regulatory authorities to interpret regulatory requirements in light of the local situation. However, given the low number of fossil-fuelled combustion plants in France, the Directive was of little practical relevance. Hence, adaptations could be restricted to the formal level and had no impact on well-established administrative practices (Bailey 1997). Consequently, also in France implementation was effective as core principles remained unaffected in the practical implementation of the Directive.

Similarly, the Information Directive confirmed existing arrangements in France. The relevant national legislation, the 1978 Act on Access to Administrative Documents, went even beyond EU requirements and was part of a group of laws enacted in the late 1970s designed to promote public trust in administrative decision making through greater transparency. At first sight, the French tradition of an 'enlightened bureaucracy', which is superior to society, seems challenged by this approach. However, greater transparency actually served to strengthen the position of the bureaucracy, increasing its legitimacy and authority at a time of intensified technocratic intervention (Winter 1996). Even though formal and practicable implementation in France were effective given the absence of institutional contradiction, there is some doubt as to whether the Information Directive succeeded in mobilising public support, i.e. whether it achieved its political objective (Bailey 1997). This is a point to which we return in our discussion of CEE.

Turning to the implementation of the EMAS Regulation in Britain, pressure for administrative change was very low, since the adoption of the EU Regulation took place at about the same time as the British environmental management system was put into place. In fact, the British example had even been used as a reference point (Héritier *et al.* 1996). Hence, the adaptations required by EU legislation were minimal. Rather than implying changes to existing practices, the Directive merely demanded the introduction of additional elements to the national system based on British Standard 7750. Moreover, with respect to structural requirements, the UK could rely on administrative structures already in place to implement the national system as well as the ISO 9000 quality management (Knill 1998). Given the general compatibility of EU legislation and national administrative traditions, EMAS is implemented effectively in the UK. Looking beyond our narrow definition of effective (formal) implementation, the EMAS Regulation seems to perform positively also in terms of mobilising companies to use this voluntary tool: forty-eight companies are currently registered under the scheme (see Bouma, chapter 6, in this book, table 6.1 quoting 1998 date); many more operate under international EMS standards that are considered equivalent by the EU.

Cases of contradiction
In two cases, namely access to information in Germany and drinking water in France, we can explain ineffective implementation because European requirements contradicted the core of national administrative traditions. These situations of institutional contradiction suggest that the choice of either top–down or bottom–up approaches makes no systemic difference for implementation effectiveness.

Although the Information Directive is explicitly directed at the mobilisation of domestic support and Germany is generally known as a country with a strong environmental movement and considerable political influence of environmental associations, the German implementation record is characterised by ineffectiveness and administrative resistance to change (see Kimber, chapter 8, in this book). Considering the seemingly favourable support conditions, this outcome can only be explained by the high level of institutional adaptation pressures created by the Directive. Thus, the requirements of the Information Directive stand in sharp contrast to the German tradition of restricting access to administrative data to parties directly affected by recorded activities. In the German tradition, the civil service is accountable to the state and to the law rather than to society; hence there is no particular necessity for administrative transparency (König 1996). Moreover, the *Rechtsstaat* principle places its emphasis on the protection of subjective individual rights rather than the transparency of administrative decision making to the general public. Access to administrative decision making therefore, is limited to cases that are exactly specified by administrative law (Winter 1996). Considering these core principles of administrative behaviour, the German resistance to the European legislation makes sense. Besides the fact that implementation was delayed and formal transposition occurred in a very restrictive way, practical application indicates far-reaching deficits (Scherzberg 1994; Lenschow 1997).

The degree of German resistance becomes evident in view of legal proceedings already brought before the European Court of Justice (Kimber, chapter 8, in this book).

Turning to the implementation of the Drinking Water Directive in France, the domestic patterns of sectoral regulation seemed to be well in line with the regulatory style implied by the Directive. The French regulation of drinking water relies on uniform and substantive standards, which basically correspond with the European values (Bailey 1997). Despite this compatibility, however, European requirements were in contradiction with a deeply rooted core element of French administrative practice, namely the considerable autonomy of the local level to negotiate regulatory arrangements with its clientele. Although administrative activities are legally specified in a detailed way, the local services have acquired a *de facto* power of decision, allowing for the interpretation of legal rules in light of the particular local situation. These 'normes secondaires d'application', which are often defined in informal and consensual negotiations between the regulators and the regulated, 'se révèlent plus déterminantes que la législation de référence' (Lascoumes 1994, 169). In view of this contradiction, we understand how many standards laid down by the Directive could be considered too strict by French authorities and therefore were intentionally ignored (Knill 1998).

Required adaptations within the core: the impact of domestic support

The remaining six cases refer to constellations where European legislation required substantive adaptations at the domestic level, however, without challenging fundamental core patterns of national administrative traditions. In these institutionally undetermined constellations the extent to which European legislation is supported by domestic actors crucially influences the extent to which adaptation takes place or not. The question arises whether the support-generating new instruments do better in these cases. Considering our limited empirical base, we cannot achieve conclusive evidence. However, since we chose 'easy' cases, in the sense that in France, Germany and the UK the level of environmental mobilisation and awareness is already relatively high and hence, societal actors are well prepared to react to the signals sent via new instruments, a negative performance of new instruments would quite seriously question their effectiveness in general.

As suggested above we shall distinguish two situations: First we have constellations where EU requirements amount to adaptations *within a 'static' core* of national administrative traditions. Second, initial European core challenges may be reduced as a result of national administrative reforms which alter the initial core and hence the scope for adaptation. Such core shift may result in a situation that permits compliance *within the (new) core*.

'Static' core   Cases where European legislation required domestic adaptation within a static core of administrative traditions refer to the implementation of the EMAS Regulation in Germany and France, as well as to the implementation of the Drinking Water Directive in Germany.

The moderate institutional scope of the EMAS Regulation can be attributed to the fact that it constitutes a regulatory instrument supplementing the tools already in place rather than replacing existing core arrangements. Moreover, in the case of Germany the industrial self-regulation as advanced by the Regulation corresponds with an important element of the German state–industry relations, namely, the tradition of corporatist arrangements, which are reflected in a whole range of intermediary organisations that partly assume public functions and partly represent private interests (Lehmbruch 1997). In France, in turn, the spirit of the Regulation is well in line with the French practice of voluntary agreements on industrial emission reductions (*contrats de branche*) and the use of economic incentives (Héritier *et al.* 1996). In neither country, does EMAS closely correspond with already existing practices, however, and hence some institution building is required. Therefore, we consider these as institutionally ambiguous cases.

As outlined in our explanatory framework, moderate adaptation requirements do not automatically imply effective implementation. This now depends on the degree of support by national actors which is no longer pre-determined by institutional conditions. In the EMAS case domestic support was mobilised in Germany but it remained low in France. EMAS did not fulfil its bottom–up mobilisation potential in France.

In Germany, the political arena was characterised by broad support for the Regulation from both industrial and environmental organisations, which could be traced partly to the fact that implementation happened to resonate with concurrent national debates on 'slimming the state' and deregulation (Lenschow 1997). A policy coalition favouring the intentions of the Regulation and, specifically, supporting patterns of corporatist self-regulation, formed with administrative, industrial, and environmental actors represented (Héritier *et al.* 1996). In France, by contrast, industrial support was not sufficient to trigger domestic adaptations, which would have allowed for the effective compliance with the Regulation. A major problem in this context consists in the homogeneous character of the French bureaucracy, which facilitates exchange of information between different authorities dominated by the same *grands corps.* Industry is concerned that information voluntarily provided within the context of EMAS might be used against it during authorisation and inspection procedures. As this problem was not explicitly addressed in the context of the formal transposition, the Regulation so far failed to achieve its objectives (Bailey 1997).

Turning to the case of the Drinking Water Directive in Germany, it took considerable time to find a domestic solution to comply with the Directive's requirements within the core of national administrative traditions. Initially, the implementation of the Directive was characterised by strong administrative resistance to adapt to European requirements. The Directive demanded stricter standards with regard to nitrate and pesticide pollution, requiring high investments in new abatement technologies. Most Member States avoided these investments by taking advantage of an inconsistency in the Directive, namely the fact that the measurement procedures prescribed by the Directive were insufficient for detecting breaches of these quality values. In contrast, Germany did not make use of this 'pragmatic' approach to reduce adaptation pressure since this would have been in contradiction to its strongly embedded legalistic and interventionist tradition and the principle of the *Rechtsstaat.* The latter implies that, as a general rule, the scope and mode of administrative activity is specified by law, leaving public administration little flexibility and discretion when implementing legal provisions (Ellwein and Hesse 1989, 392). The pragmatic solution to escape adaptation pressure would have delegitimised the German regulatory logic of interventionist arrangements by questioning the credibility of the law as the basis for administrative action. Instead of taking an easy route towards compliance, Germany resisted the implementation of the Directive until it had found the required technical and economic solutions to comply with the Directive and remain within the core of national administrative traditions. In short, the available measurement technologies were upgraded and complementary economic instruments were adopted, as so-called water taxes were introduced in certain regions in order to finance the installation of new cleaning technologies.

'Dynamic' core The traditional regulatory style characterising British environmental policy was based on procedural principles, which were never legally defined by numerical standards. These principles reflected a flexible approach allowing for high administrative discretion in adapting control requirements in light of the particular local situation (Vogel 1986). These sectoral patterns corresponded with the general British policy style (Jordan and Richardson 1982), rooted in the state tradition of the 'society-led state' (Badie and Birnbaum 1983, 83). Also the British tradition of secrecy, which almost entirely excluded access and participation opportunities for third parties with respect to environmental regulation (Vogel 1986), can be understood against the background of the British state tradition, namely the supremacy of parliament. Administrative accountability towards society is perceived as sufficiently guaranteed due to the parliamentary control over the executive (Steel 1979). These core features are in contradiction to the requirements implied in the LCP, Drinking Water and Information Directives. However, a range of national reforms led to modifications of the old core that not only reduced the institutional scope of European requirements but also strengthened the position of those national actors supporting effective implementation.

This change in the core of national administrative traditions emerged as a result of the far-reaching public sector reforms initiated by Conservative governments from 1979 onwards. At the centre of the domestic reform programme was the improvement of efficiency and effectiveness of the public sector. Policies were directed at administrative reorganisation, management reforms and privatisation. Important structural changes implied the creation of independent agencies responsible for operational management, separating these management functions from policy making functions which remained the responsibility of the relevant departments. Private sector management and performance regimes introduced noteworthy operational reforms. The performance drive, but also the need to compensate for lacking democratic control of the independent agencies, produced a tendency to make the agencies' activities more transparent and accountable to the public. A further feature of national reforms was the privatisation of public utilities, including the nationalised energy and water supply industries. Regulatory regimes were created to control the market activities of these privatised utilities (Hood 1991; Knill 1995; Rhodes 1996). As a consequence of the reforms, the regulatory approach became more formal, legalistic and open (Rhodes 1996). The shift towards the legal definition of substantive, performance-related criteria was particularly facilitated by the fact that privatisation shifted the economic costs of compliance with European standards to the private sector and no longer interfered with the Conservative government's objective of reducing public spending. These developments permitted implementation of the LCP, Drinking Water and Information Directives to be approached within a modified core of British standard administrative procedures which happened to fit better with the regulatory principles embodied in EU legislation (Knill 1998).

The fact that Britain actually adjusted to EU requirements cannot be sufficiently explained by domestic core changes, which reduced the institutional scope of European adaptation pressure. In the end, it was a consequence of a now more supportive actor constellation, also as a result of the institutional changes introduced by national reforms. The establishment of independent regulatory agencies for the control of the economic and environmental activities of the privatised industries strengthened the voice and influence of environmental and consumer groups, and hence provided a new institutional context favouring compliance with European objectives also from an actor-centred perspective (Knill 1995; Maloney and Richardson 1995). Moreover, in the context of general public sector reforms, windows of opportunity opened for reform-oriented actors to provide some input in particular (policy-specific) processes of change. In this context, the Royal Commission on Environmental Pollution, environmental organisations and the Campaign for the Freedom of Information, who had all called for the adoption of more transparent environmental information and reporting practices in Britain since the mid-1970s, were finally heard in their demands (Knill 1998).

In view of these developments, we observe substantial administrative reforms facilitating effective compliance with the Directives.

In the cases of LCP and Drinking Water, these adaptations include a more substantive orientation in state intervention by relying on legally binding standards, a shift toward more formal and legalistic patterns of administrative interest intermediation and significant investment programmes in order to meet EU requirements (Maloney and Richardson 1995, 145; Knill 1998). The Information Directive was implemented in a way that in part even went beyond European provisions. The Environmental Protection Act of 1990 requires regulatory authorities to establish so-called public registers which contain all relevant permitting and operational data as well as the results of emission monitoring for all processes falling under the Act. In contrast to the EU Directive, which provides only an obligation of public authorities to present environmental information on request, the British rule establishes a positive duty to inform the general public. The Directive applies to all environmental data, however, while the public registers cover only certain data pertinent to authorisation procedures. Certain legal adaptations were therefore still necessary in the UK; these were implemented rather effectively in this context of more favourable framework conditions (Knill 1998).

Summary
Table 11.2 summarises the implementation performances in the respective institutional contexts: effective implementation in the cases of core confirmation; ineffective implementation in cases of

Table 11.2 *Implementation effectiveness in the national institutional context*

| | Top–down approach | | Bottom–up approach | |
	LCP	Drinking water	Information	EMAS
Germany	Confirmation of the core	Sufficient support for change within the core	Contradiction of the core	Sufficient support for change within the core
Britain	Sufficient support for change within the core	Sufficient support for change within the core	Sufficient support for change within the core	Confirmation of the core
France	Confirmation of the core	Contradiction of the core	Confirmation of the core	Insufficient support for change within the core

core contradiction; effective or ineffective implementation (depending on specific actor constellations) if pressure occurred within the core of administrative structures.

Our analysis of the implementation of four pieces of European legislation in three Member States points to three general conclusions.

1 The choice of either a top–down or bottom–up approach to the implementation of EU environmental policy makes no difference in principle for implementation effectiveness. Rather, the response to old and new policy instruments is pre-structured by national institutional characteristics. Thus, due to core contradictions, the Information Directive had little chance of effective implementation in Germany.

2 Even in institutionally more open situations, where domestic support is expected to play a decisive role on implementation effectiveness, the 'success rate' of bottom–up policies, which are explicitly directed towards the motivation and creation of support, is not different from results achieved by top–down measures. Hence, in Britain after the national reforms we observe favourable reactions to top–down as well as bottom–up directives. No such support developed in the French EMAS case although the adaptation pressure seemed equally moderate.

3 As illustrated by the case of Britain, the domestic institutional context is nothing static, but may be subject to changes that alter the institutional scope of European adaptation pressure. Although changes coincide with the persistence of other elements (otherwise it would make no sense to speak of a core), dynamic developments at the national level may create new opportunities for effective administrative adaptation to European requirements.[2]

Based on our theoretical and empirical evidence, we will now consider the opportunities for effective implementation of EU environmental policy in future Member States from Central and Eastern Europe. It is of particular interest to what extent the combination of 'political revolutions' and persisting traditions, i.e. the combination of change and persistence, will create opportunities for effective adaptation to European requirements. In the following section we will also raise a second issue relevant to the discussion of new and old instruments, namely the impact of economic and administrative capacity. With respect to top–down instruments, constraints linked to insufficient economic resources are recognised; with regard to new instruments, however, we argue that their support and capacity generating potential is often exaggerated (see Börzel, chapter 10, in this book for similar conclusions with regard to Southern Europe).

Implications for Central and Eastern European EU applicant states: legacies, imperatives and a 'very dirty floor' to be swept

Turning to CEE applicant states to the EU, only few conclusive statements can be made about the chance of and conditions for eventual compliance – formally and practically – with EU environmental directives. The process towards compliance with the EU *acquis* is a structured one and assisted by bi- and multilateral as well as EU-led programmes (see Caddy 1997; and Klarer and Francis 1997 for good overviews). In this section we use the framework developed above and some empirical material already available to hypothesise about this process. Due to our limited empirical basis, we treat CEE as one case, using country examples for illustrative purposes. To arrive at the general trends and problems in implementing EU environmental legislation this treatment seems defensible; nevertheless we realise that in concrete cases the context and institutional path-dependencies vary from country to country (Baker and Jehlička 1998). First, we consider the role of an institutional core in these 'transition countries'. We elaborate on what appears to be a dynamic situation between continuity and change – the continuing effects of political, administrative and societal legacies as well as dramatic reforms following new 'imperatives'. There does not yet seem to exist a new and stable core in CEE states. Hence, still torn between old structures and new imperatives, what are the consequences for the implementation of the four pieces of legislation investigated in this chapter? In the absence of clear institutional signals, will command-and-control or new, communicative instruments lead to a higher level of success?

Legacies and imperatives
Beverly Crawford and Arend Lijphart (1995) reviewed the literature on the general political and economic transition process in CEE. They found two contrasting positions. One argues that legacies from the socialist era will hamper political, administrative, economic and

societal reforms. The 'core features' of the pre-1989 era will continue to shape political and economic performance in these countries. Others argue that the 'imperative' of political and economic liberalisation is too strong to allow the continuation of contradictory old traditions. The collapse of the Soviet system has been too dramatic to keep even an invisible hold on the reform process in CEE.

Both positions can be transferred to the specific case of CEE countries adapting environmental legislation and implementation structures to the EU model. On the one hand, the desire to join the EU and hence the need to implement the *acquis communautaire* may work as the imperative to reform poorly fitting national structures quickly; this assumes that the 1989 revolution managed to wipe out or uproot old structures. On the other hand, it seems conceivable that socialist administrative and legal structures, state–industry relations, and the role of civil society will shape politics for some time to come and work to resist such easy adaptation. Before evaluating these two competing claims empirically, let us elaborate briefly on the nature of the legacies and imperatives in the environmental case.

Turning to the legacies first: what was the nature of (environmental) law in the socialist states of CEE; how did (polluting) industry operate in these regimes; and what about an (environmentally active) civil society? It seems that three points – unfavourable for implementing *any* environmental instrument – can be made: First, CEE during the socialist era was not rooted in the principle of a *Rechtsstaat*, with a body of law regulating processes in politics and society. Laws and regulations certainly existed, but the ideologically legitimised political leadership exceeded them in authority. Environmental legislation in particular, even though strict by international standards, was habitually ignored by those addressed; its function was to symbolise to the outside world that the 'products' of the Eastern bloc were superior to those in the West (Klarer and Moldan 1997, 21). On the other hand, the effectiveness of the hierarchical leadership in terms of securing implementation on the ground was weak: The 'rules' of state and ideology were undermined by the ineffectiveness of the central planning and control system, leaving the implementation level without resources and incentives to comply with environmental law. Such traditions question the effectiveness of the authoritative, legalistic, top–down measures in the EU environmental *acquis*, among those the LCP and Drinking Water Directives.

Second, the centralised structure of economic planning and the absence of market forces discouraged the development of industrial management. There existed no regulatory regime that imposed a rational use of resources or restricted polluting practices, nor did the market push toward efficient and effective production methods – not to mention the internalisation of external (environmental) costs. The proverbial wastefulness of production, in particular in terms of the utilisation of non-renewable natural resources such as coal, was the result. Equally, the poisoning of water streams through industrial (but also household) effluents was normal business.[3] Considering these past practices, both effective top–down regulation and control of industrial locations as well as the rationalisation of production and the introduction of environmental management tools seem a world apart and confronting a legacy hard to break.

Finally, the authoritative socialist regimes in CEE generally oppressed an active civil society that could have potentially mobilised for higher environmental standards. The limits of the oppression strategy became apparent in 1989; nevertheless, there was no participatory, democratic political culture. The old administration had never been exposed to public participation and operated in secret. Societal actors were equally neither used to, nor could they expect much from, a flow of communication and information from public authorities.[4]

Considering these 'legacies' the implementation of all four pieces of legislation is in conflict with core principles of the old regime. Will this be the end of the story? What are the 'imperatives for change' allowing for a possibly less pessimistic perspective?

The general impetuses for change, mentioned already by Crawford and Lijphart, are democratisation and market liberalisation. In brief, democratisation points also in the environmental context to more transparency in the political process and the acceptance if not encouragement of public participation. Market liberalisation introduces new pressure towards rationalising production processes and improving managerial practices; further, we may assume – or at least hope – that the liberal market regime will eventually be embedded in stable framework conditions in the social and environmental field in order to restrict competitive abuses. These pressures coming out of the 1989 'revolution' itself are presently strengthened by the CEE countries' applications to join the EU in due time. The so-called Copenhagen principles, drawn up as a baseline for the applicant countries to meet in order to be considered as future Member States, underline the significance of political and economic liberalisation. More specifically in the environmental context, the EU application process implies clear environmental targets for CEE as all future members must be in conformance with the entire *acquis communautaire*. Are these sufficient 'imperatives' to overcome the legacies of the past? To begin an answer to this question, we will take a look at concrete experiences in the respective countries.

Approaches and limits to adaptation in practice
Information directive   Merely looking at the legal level of implementing the Access to Environmental Information Directive suggests that the legacies of an authoritative state and oppressed civil society have been left behind in large parts of CEE. Interestingly, all five CEE countries considered for a first round of enlargement were initially paying great attention to the role of the public in environmental policy. Most new constitutions establish an explicit right to a favourable environment and to information on the state of the environment (see Whitehead and Woodford 1996); many of these provisions go beyond Western European constitutions and legal frameworks.[5] The explicit mention of public access to information can be traced to the strong post-1989 desire to firmly establish democratic principles in the legal foundations of the new regimes. The particular attention that was paid to the environment in this context probably resulted from the special role played by environmentalist groups during the turnaround; many more (mostly local) came to life shortly afterwards (Klarer and Moldan 1997, 23). An opinion poll conducted in 1990 in Czechoslovakia confirmed this high level of public support; 80 per cent of the Czech citizens considered the environmental clean-up the very first priority of the new government, even before economic problems (Moldan 1997, 118). This attitude was also reflected in political terms. For instance, in Poland the opposition insisted on the environment as one of the main topics to be discussed in the so-called 'round tables' with the old government (Nowicki 1997, 222). Throughout the region many environmentalists were elected to the first newly established parliamentary assemblies.

However, while public interest and pressure was certainly instrumental in making the environment a priority in constituting the new regime, this interest and its representation was rather quickly ebbing away. Earlier patterns of a relatively subdued civil society are re-emerging. In part responsible for this downturn in public mobilisation is the economic situation. Economic concerns are now dominating the political agendas and environmental protection is often perceived as too costly and hampering economic 'catching up'. Such linkage between economic well-being and environmental awareness is not exclusive to CEE; but its structural impact on the evolution of the civil society may be greater, given the legacy of the past forty years. The question arises whether the progressive legal framework in terms of access to information is capable of securing a fertile ground for environmental awareness raising and mobilisation? The EU Information Directive, for instance, seems inherently weak in this respect due to its exclusive focus on administrative duties to respond to public requests. Few inquiries will emerge from an increasingly unmotivated public. The Regional Environmental Center for CEE (REC) observes:

> Participation is in a way like spinach. In theory, no one questions that it is good for you – participation is after all, the keystone to and a precondition for an effective, dynamic democratic system. In practice, though, participation is something hard to swallow and even more difficult to digest. In addition to legal and constitutional provisions for rights for participation, true participation requires an informed, active public with knowledge of their rights and the motivation to exercise it. (REC, Spring 1996, 19)

The REC lists several initiatives under way to (re)mobilise the population with an active information policy. National and regional inspectorates are being installed all over CEE. Also some governments are setting examples with a proactive information policy. For instance, Hungary adopted a regulation for public participation in legislative drafting in August 1996. It invites environmental groups to participate in legislative preparation; furthermore, it established an information office to facilitate the environment ministry's communication and information dissemination efforts (REC, Winter 1997, 11). Such active policy depends on political commitment and resources, as well as on good cooperation between central and local levels. Here the encouraging examples of the REC must be countered by some less hopeful instances. For example, the initial opening on the political elite level had ceased in the Czech Republic, where in 1995 several green NGOs were temporarily listed as 'extremist organisations' and general access to the policy process was limited (Fagin and Jehlička 1998, 121–4). This reflects an authoritarian understanding of the state, not conducive to the implementation of new instruments. Also, the attitude of the implementing public administration, being still unaware, unwilling or helpless in dealing with public information requests or with public involvement in impact assessment procedures remains frequently resistant (see REC, Summer 1995, 12–13). This may be part of the undemocratic legacy as much as the consequence of a still ineffective information infrastructure, i.e. means to collect and disseminate data.

In short, the departure from authoritarian and secretive legacies is partial. Progressive legal structures were established immediately following the revolution. But both on the state and the society level we observe relapses to old attitudes and practices. Furthermore, as in all European countries, the actual effectiveness of the legal provisions for public access to environmental information is influenced by the general socio-economic situation leading to fluctuation in public interest and in the quality of information available. The nature of EU information policies seems insufficient to tap societal interests and resources for their effective implementation as well as the generation of bottom–up support for environmental law in general.

EMAS   EMAS is a scheme exclusive to EU Member States; hence presently CEE countries cannot be officially registered under it. Nevertheless, CEE businesses have the option of using international environmental management systems (EMS), such as ISO 14001, or they may adopt EMAS without yet becoming officially certified. Given the non-applicability of the EMAS scheme to CEE, we cannot empirically evaluate its implementation. Assuming that the political and economic transition has created a principally adaptable core also with respect to management practices, we will observe in this section to what extent there has emerged a favourable support structure for the actual implementation of the Regulation in the future.

Despite almost non-existent management practices that would pay attention to either rational use of resources in the production process or to the production of high-quality goods, the window of opportunity for change stands wide open. In many cases new management is not the same as old management; pressures to become competitive nationally as well as internationally make the modernisation of production processes imperative (through investments in new, and cleaner, technologies); the demands of consumers shift toward higher quality items; industry will be forced to comply with increasingly rigid environmental standards; new investments will be subject to environmental impact assessments. The installation of an environmental management system will help businesses to identify the most cost-effective means to meet these challenges; hence incentives to apply an EMS are numerous.

Recent data show that CEE businesses are mainly interested in ISO 14001 since the institutional framework required for EMAS is not yet in place. The actual number of CEE companies certified under ISO 14001 remains small however – seven in the Czech Republic, five in Hungary and five in Poland. Interestingly, some CEE businesses or firms are starting to show an interest in EMAS as well. Two companies in the Czech Republic and one in Hungary have implemented EMAS; they were certified by organisations officially recognised by the competent bodies of other countries. The government-led institution building, i.e. the establishment of the 'competent body', has hardly begun, though (REC, Autumn 1997/Winter 1998, 10).

Considering that EMAS is not yet applicable in CEE and that the scheme is voluntary, the limited level of institution building as well as the few responses on the part of the policy's addressees are not surprising. The window of opportunity to use EMAS not only for environmental purposes but also to increase the competitiveness of industry is large, however. The emerging interest on the part of industry for the scheme may serve as an indicator for rising bottom-up support for the implementation of EMAS eventually. For large parts of the industrial sector as well as in the administration we must assume great unfamiliarity with and possibly resistance to self-regulatory policies, however. In this respect, the EMAS scheme standing alone is poorly suited to build greater familiarity and to reduce resistance. Such capacity and support generation may depend on more direct initiatives. For instance, EMSs may be used more effectively if the management training programmes that are emerging all over CEE also take account of the role of environmental management – a task to consider by international assistance projects. In other words, similar to the information legislation the voluntary EMAS scheme assumes the automatic response on the part of its addressees (the general public in the former case, business and firms in the latter). In reality such responsiveness may require some additional push and active capacity creation to make these new instruments truly effective.

LCP and Drinking Water   The problem of complying with the Drinking Water and the Large Combustion Plant Directives is twofold. On the one hand, the EU legislation needs to fit into the legislative and administrative framework: most CEE applicant states had some legislation dealing with air and water pollution in place; this was embedded in a top–down regulatory structure and a fragmented and ineffective implementation and control 'infrastructure'. Despite the traditionally more endemic implementation deficit in CEE, the problem of adaptation regarding the LCP and Drinking Water Directives may be comparable to that in Western Europe – i.e., what is the nature as well as stability of the sectoral core features framing the old practices. To what extent did the transformation in CEE undermine also the basis of these existing structures? First evidence seems to suggest that the open and dynamic situation had a more positive effect in the case of air than in the case of water pollution. In short, the ongoing liberalisation of the energy sector in CEE and the related restructuring on the plant level has reduced the adjustment pressures with respect to the LCP case to – however significant – changes within the (new) core. The level of support for such adaptation varies depending on the available capacities and resources to actually comply with the requirements. Ongoing economic and administrative reforms in CEE did not have the same impact on the water sector. Here old structures prevail and pose a greater challenge for the implementation of EU drinking water legislation.

Besides the difficulty of administrative adjustments, we need to consider the technical and economic challenges implied in meeting the substantive environmental parameters as main obstacles to compliance. In this respect, we face a sizeable difference between East and West; the distance between present pollution and the EU standards is enormous and not easy to reach even by following the regulatory philosophy behind the legislation. The specified timeframe may be entirely inappropriate; probably even more importantly, full compliance with top–down instruments may require investment in new installations and technologies that by far exceed the available resources of CEE countries. These context conditions are the primary determinants for the level of support during the practical implementation of the relevant legislation.

Regarding the formal approximation of EU legislation commentators seem to agree that much progress has been made. Whitehead and Woodford surveying ten CEE countries with respect to their environmental 'road to EU membership' (1996) observe a rather high level of approximation with EU law. Especially in terms of air pollution, the problem is identified not as the acceptance of new standards but as finding the technical capacity to implement and enforce them. In administrative terms a comprehensive framework for inspection and monitoring is being developed quickly. For instance, a network of national and regional inspectorates is being built.

Progress in the case of air pollution in all CEE states is due to a radical restructuring of the industry, i.e. the shutdown of many plants and forced restructuring of others. In Poland, formerly 100 per cent dependent on coal-based energy generation, several plants were forced to close due to environmental dangers, others are presently installing desulphurisation technology, furthermore there is a shift from coal to gas (Nowicki 1997). The shift to gas energy is visible throughout the region; in addition, nuclear energy is gaining in attractiveness (considering the technical standards of these plants and the unresolved nuclear waste problem a less than ideal substitute) (REC, Winter 1996, 12–16). Somewhat comparable to the British case, even though exceeding it in magnitude, the complete restructuring of the sector had significant environmental consequences.

Despite these efforts and the apparent high level of adaptability, the problem remains immense and it is hard to see how EU standards could be reached any time soon.[6] For their practical implementation, most substantive EU environmental regulation depends on large scale investment efforts and capacity building programmes. Considering the scale of the investment requirements and the limited resources available, there is a need for an optimisation of spending as well as a successful economic and fiscal policy. This raises additional constraints for the emergence of a supportive implementation context due to the fluctuations and continuing uncertainties in the economic development of these countries. In this context, the utilisation of economic instruments, for instance, is difficult to do – besides the fact that the necessary reforms in the fiscal and economic sectors have not yet resulted in the required institutional foundation for their application. Due to these obstacles, economic instruments are primarily used so far for fund raising rather than effective incentive building or sanctioning (Lehoczki and Balogh 1997, 153–8), hence they have only limited utility in complementing other policy instruments. More central to the analytical questions posed in this chapter, the unfavourable economic context has helped to select the wheat from the chaff as the least economic and most polluting plants were closed. On the other hand, the economic capabilities of the existing plants pre-structure their support for practical compliance with environmental legislation.

Economic and political restructuring did not have the same positive effect in the water sector as they had overall for the reduction of air pollution. Implementation requirements still constitute to a large degree challenges to the core of administrative structures and traditions. Most notably, turf battles related to the establishment of environment ministries as well as coordination problems deriving from the decentralisation of responsibilities constrain the adaptation process. Local administrations are typically responsible for implementing the drinking water legislation; naturally they have little influence on controlling polluting agents 'upstream'; not even regional governments may be able to coordinate in this respect. Nevertheless, decentralisation has had the positive effect that local authorities are gaining control over more financial resources, though still over an insufficient amount. On the national level there tends to be the additional problem of an unclear organisation of competencies between the environment ministries and ministries (or national institutes) of health, or physical planning (Lehoczki and Balogh 1997; Nowicki 1997). The unclear attribution of responsibilities often goes hand in hand with different interpretations of the nature of the problem (and hence appropriate solutions). In Estonia, for instance, we find a great degree of legal approximation but a continuing disparity in the conception of the problem compared to the EU. In other words, 'the rationale behind [Estonia's] 1994 law [applying to the water sector] is that water is primarily a natural resource for industrial and domestic consumption rather than an environmental resource' (Whitehead and Woodford 1996, 7).

Administrative coordination is not the only difficulty for effective water regulation. There is also the nature of the pollution problem. In contrast to controlling individual polluting plants as in the LCP case, the control of adequate drinking water quality occurs at the end of a long chain of pollution and outdated systems. Hence, while the initial focus in CEE environmental policy on cleaning up efforts and end-of-pipe measures led to short term improvements on the level of individual plants (significant for the implementation of the LCP Directive), the effect of such approach is more limited in the more complex structure of water provision with numerous and sometimes hard-to-identify sources of pollution. Analytically, this problem has an institutional and a support-building dimension: First, old legal and administrative structures in CEE were rarely appropriate to deal with the complexities of the problem. For instance, the regulation of industrial and municipal wastewater – i.e. one of the main causes for poor water quality – has been negligible in the past and is only slowly developing. Considering this, the fact that even in Poland, where the development of a more responsible environmental policy had begun even prior to the regime change, the 'Water Management and Protection Act of 1974 has survived with little changes so far' (Whitehead and Woodford 1996, 4) is not particularly encouraging. Looking from the perspective of generating support for effective implementation, in the water case such support would need to come from a multitude of actors, many of whom will be hardly aware of their role in the chain of clean water provision. This structure of the sector poses a challenge to effective implementation in the East and the West.

In sum, in the case of industrial air pollution the overall restructuring of the economy has created a favourable base condition to begin complying with EU law. The issue here seems less one of regulatory style and formal implementation than one of financial resources and the magnitude of the problem for practical implementation. Here the mere imposition of strict standards will not suffice; active support for the necessary investments is closely linked to the development of the economic and financial framework conditions. By contrast, compliance with the Drinking Water Directive does not benefit much from the general restructuring efforts, and institutional limits to adaptation are greater. Aside from still unresolved problems related to administrative structure, implementation success will also depend on significant institutional as well as attitudinal changes in industry, agriculture, housing and waste management.

Summary
What are the conclusions of the experience so far in CEE in the context of the general questions asked in this chapter?

1   Analogous to our results in the West European cases, there is
    little evidence that bottom–up instruments can be implemented
    easier and more effectively. Even in the case of access to infor-
    mation, where the willingness to adapt seems relatively high, the
    effectiveness is constrained by frequently resistant local admin-
    istrations and, more importantly, by a rapidly decreasing
    interest on the part of the population. But neither are top–down
    measures easy to implement as they stand. In addition to insti-
    tutional traditions we need to consider here the economic and
    financial dimension of the environmental problem as a con-
    straining factor. Compliance with the LCP and the Drinking
    Water Directives will depend on the commitment of important
    financial resources, besides the systematising of the overall
    legislative framework and administrative coordination.

2   Second, legacies of the past – i.e., the equivalent to institutional
    core features in Western Europe – do play a role in the adapta-
    tion process, but a more limited one. We observe remnants of
    past structures and practices, for instance the return to a situa-
    tion with a low mobilisation of the population, backward
    management practices and administrative structures resistant to
    work in an integrated way. Nevertheless, compared to Western
    Europe we seem to be dealing with a generally more open and
    adaptable situation. Hence, there is movement especially in
    areas were the restructuring of the economy and the political
    system is leaving strong imprints, i.e. in terms of encouraging
    public participation and in the revolutions taking place in the
    industrial sector.

3   Our empirical evidence from France, Germany and Britain indi-
    cated that – contrary to the expectations drawn from imple-
    mentation theory – bottom–up concepts are not principally
    superior (depending on whether support is already present or
    easily mobilised) to top–down approaches even in the context
    of institutionally more open cases (changes *within* the core).
    Considering the open-ended situation in CEE, it is hard to judge
    the special potential of new instruments. Baumgartl in his study
    of environmental policy evolution in Bulgaria, points to the
    legitimacy-building potential on the one hand, but the absence
    of clear guidelines and targets on the other (1997, 250–1). We
    can critically observe that the support building capabilities of
    both investigated new instruments appears limited; they need to

be complemented by more active measures (see Börzel, chapter 10, in this book for a similar conclusion with respect to Spain).

Conclusion

In recent years, EU environmental policy has been characterised by a regulatory shift towards so-called new instruments associated with a bottom–up approach to implementation. New instruments are expected to improve the implementation effectiveness of environmental policy by mobilising domestic support for proper compliance at the domestic level. In comparing the 'success rates' of top–down and bottom–up approaches, however, we found no evidence confirming this expectation. We suggest that this can be explained by the fact that implementation effectiveness is primarily dependent on the degree of institutional compatibility of national administrative traditions and European requirements, rather than on the choice of implementation approaches. Given that both top–down and bottom–up concepts imply institutional requirements for domestic adaptation, no approach can *per se* be judged as being superior to the other. The choice of approach should therefore be taken in the light of national institutional constraints, rather than of its theoretical support-building potential.

This general statement holds true also for the case of future Member States from Eastern Europe. The 'moving institutional core' in these countries generally reduces the institutional scope of European adaptation requirements, regardless of the policy approach. However, it seems unlikely that the newly emerging core, shaped by democratisation and market liberalisation, is by itself producing advances in environmental policy making. Equally, external pressure would not have sufficed without internal striving for environmental improvement (for instance, the Conference on Security and Cooperation in Europe, CSCE, negotiations have long pressured the countries of the socialist bloc to improve environmental performance, only to be ignored in practice). The bringing together of dramatic domestic restructuring, the political will to improve the state of the environment and the concrete policy formulations offered from the EU are presently guiding the creation of an environmental policy regime in CEE, without indicating a clear superiority of either new or old approaches. Rather, it seems that both instruments need to be embedded in a coherent larger system.

The process of adopting the EU environmental *acquis* that is ongoing in CEE has many parallels with earlier Southern European experiences. Greece, Portugal and Spain needed to integrate the (at that point still smaller) body of EU environmental legislation into national structures. The chapter (10) by Börzel shows that, besides the institutional constraints or misfits, the capacity issue forms the main obstacle to successful implementation. Similar to the evidence that is emerging from CEE, Southern Europe faced substantial financial constraints in implementing top–down standards and mobilisation problems to make new instrument effective. These two challenges apply to the 'non-pioneers'[7] of EU environmental policy in general and indicate that new instruments are not spared from encountering capacity gaps.

Notes

1 For a more detailed summary, see Knill (1998) and Knill and Lenschow (1998a, 1998b).
2 Conversely, a core shift could create new constraints to effective administrative adaptation. Such a case, which is not considered empirically in this chapter, would inhibit the implementation process.
3 Mismanagement of natural resources has also been a feature of capitalist development. The emphasis on economic growth, industrialisation and technical progress at the expense of the protection of natural resources is common to the thinking of the Enlightenment (see Baumgartl 1997, 48–9; Baker and Jehlička 1998, 6–7). The centralised planned economy, however, further enforces the tendency toward resource exploitation.
4 This legacy may be weakest in Poland where environmental groups could operate relatively freely and a green party was established prior to 1989 (Millard 1998).
5 CEE countries also participated actively in the United Nations Economic Commission for Europe's convention on access to environmental information. Countries blocking a progressive draft were from Western Europe (most notably Germany) and Russia (EWWE, 19 September 1997, 14; EWWE, 20 March 1998, 11; REC, Spring 1997, 4–5).
6 On the optimistic end, Nowicki expects that Poland will reach EU standards within 15–20 years; others assume that expenditures of about 5 per cent of the national GDP (i.e. 3 to 4 times the present level) would be necessary to reach that goal (W. Lauber at a presentation for the Austrian Wirtschaftskammer, 7.5.1998).

7 See Mikael Skou Andersen and Duncan Liefferink (1997) on 'the pioneers'.

References

Badie, Bertrand and Pierre Birnbaum (1983). *The Sociology of the State.* Chicago: Chicago University Press.

Bailey, Patricia (1997). 'The Implementation of EU Environmental Policy in France'. In Christoph Knill (ed.), *The Impact of National Administrative Traditions on the Implementation of EU Environmental Policy*. Interim Research Report. Annex 3. Florence: European University Institute.

Baker, Susan and Petr Jehlička (1998). 'Dilemmas of Transition: The Environment, Democracy and Economic Reforms in East Central Europe: An Introduction. *Environmental Politics*, 7(1), 1–25.

Baumgartl, Bernd (1997). *Transition and Sustainability: Actors and Interests in Eastern European Environmental Policies.* London, The Hague and Boston: Kluwer Law International.

Caddy, Joanne (1997). 'Harmonisation and Asymmetry: Environmental Policy Coordination between the European Union and Central Europe'. *Journal of European Public Policy*, 4(3), 318–36.

CEC (1993). *Towards Sustainability: A European Community Programme of Policy and Action in Relation to the Environment and Sustainable Development*. Luxembourg: Office for Official Publications of the European Communities.

CEC (1996). *Implementing Community Environmental Law*. Communication to the Council of the European Union and the European Parliament. Brussels: Commission of the European Union.

Crawford, Beverly and Arend Lijphart (1995). 'Explaining Political and Economic Change in Post-Communist Europe: Old Legacies, New Institutions, Hegemonic Norms, and International Pressures'. *Comparative Political Studies,* 28(2), 171–99.

Environment Watch: Western Europe (EWWE), Cutter Information Corp., 19. Sept. 1997 and 20 March 1998.

Ellwein, Thomas and Joachim Jens Hesse (1989). *Das Regierungssystem der Bundesrepublik Deutschland*. Opladen: Westdeutscher Verlag.

Fagin, Adam and Petr Jehlička (1998). 'Sustainable Development in the Czech Republic: A Doomed Process?' *Environmental Politics*, 7(1), 111–28.

Haigh, Nigel (1996). *The Manual of Environmental Policy: The EC and Britain*. London: Catermill Publishing.

Hanf, Kenneth and Paul B. Downing (1982). 'Introduction: A Perspective for the Study of Regulatory Enforcement'. In Paul Downing and Kenneth Hanf (eds), *International Comparisons in Implementing Pollution Law*.

Dordrecht: Kluwer-Nijhoff, 1–25.

Héritier, Adrienne, Christoph Knill and Susanne Mingers (1996). *Ringing the Changes in Europe: Regulatory Competition and the Transformation of the State*. Berlin: de Gruyter.

Hood, Christopher (1991). 'A Public Management for all Seasons?'. *Public Administration*, 69, 3–19.

Ingram, Helen and Anne Schneider (1990). 'Improving Implementation Through Framing Smarter Statutes'. *Journal of Public Policy*, 10(1), 67–88.

Jordan, Grant and Jeremy Richardson (1982). 'The British Policy Style or The Logic of Negotiation'. In Jeremy Richardson (ed.), *Policy Styles in Western Europe*. London: Allen and Unwin, 80–109.

Klarer, Jürg and Francis Patrick (1997). 'Regional Overview'. In Jürg Klarer and Bedrich Moldan (eds), *The Environmental Challenge for Central European Economies in Transition*. Chichester: John Wiley & Sons, 1–66.

Knill, Christoph (1995). *Staatlichkeit im Wandel: Großbritannien im Spannungsfeld innenpolitischer Reformen und europäischer Integration*. Opladen: Deutscher Universitätsverlag.

Knill, Christoph (1998). 'European Policies: The Impact of National Administrative Traditions'. *Journal of Public Policy*, 18(1), 1–28.

Knill, Christoph and Andrea Lenschow (1998a). 'Coping with Europe: The Implementation of EU Environmental Policy and Administrative Traditions in Britain and Germany'. *Journal of European Public Policy*, 5(4), 595–614.

Knill, Christoph and Andrea Lenschow (1998b). 'Change as "Appropriate Adaptation": Administrative Adjustment to European Environmental Policy in Britain and Germany'. *European Integration online Papers* (EIoP), 2(1), (http: //eiop.or.at/eiop/texte/1998–001a.htm).

König, Klaus (1996). 'Unternehmerisches oder exekutives Management: die Perspektive der klassischen öffentlichen Verwaltung'. *Verwaltungs-Archiv*, 87(1), 19–37.

Lascoumes, Pierre (1994). *L'Éco-Pouvoir*. Paris: Éditions La Découverte.

Lehmbruch, Gerhard (1997). 'From State of Authority to Network State: The German State in a Comparative Perspective'. In Michio Muramatsu and Frieder Naschold (eds), *State and Administration in Japan and Germany: A Comparative Perspective on Continuity and Change*. Berlin: de Gruyter, 39–62.

Lehoczki, Zsuzsa and Zsuzsanna Balogh (1997). 'Hungary'. In Jürg Klarer and Bedrich Moldan (eds), *The Environmental Challenge for Central European Economies in Transition*. Chichester: John Wiley & Sons, 131–68.

Lenschow, Andrea (1997). 'The Implementation of EU Environmental

Policy in Germany'. In Christoph Knill (ed.), *The Impact of National Administrative Traditions on the Implementation of EU Environmental Policy*. Interim Research Report. Annex 1. Florence: European University Institute.

Maloney, William A. and Jeremy Richardson (1995). *Managing Policy Change in Britain: The Politics of Water*. Edinburgh: Edinburgh University Press.

March, James G. and Johan P. Olsen (1989). *Rediscovering Institutions*. New York: Free Press.

Mayntz, Renate (1983). 'Implementation von regulativer Politik'. In Renate Mayntz (ed.), *Implementation politischer Programme II*, Opladen: Westdeutscher Verlag, 50–74.

Mayntz, Renate and Fritz W. Scharpf (1995). 'Der Ansatz des akteurzentrierten Institutionalismus'. In Renate Mayntz and Fritz W. Scharpf (eds), *Gesellschaftliche Selbstregelung und politische Steuerung*. Frankfurt/Main: Campus, 39–72.

Millard, Frances (1998). 'Environmental Policy in Poland'. *Environmental Politics*, 7(1), 145–61.

Moldan, Bedrich (1997). 'Czech Republic'. In Jürg Klarer and Bedrich Moldan (eds), *The Environmental Challenge for Central European Economies in Transition*. Chichester: John Wiley & Sons, 107–29.

Nowicki, Maciej (1997). 'Poland'. In Jürg Klarer and Bedrich Moldan (eds), *The Environmental Challenge for Central European Economies in Transition*. Chichester: John Wiley & Sons, 193–227.

Peters, B. Guy (1993). 'Alternative Modelle des Policy-Prozesses: Die Sicht "von unten" und die Sicht "von oben"'. In Adrienne Héritier (ed.), *Policy-Analyse. Kritik und Neurorientierung*, PVS Sonderheft 24, 289–306.

Regional Environmental Center for Central and Eastern Europe [REC], *The Bulletin*, quarterly newsletter (several issues since 1995).

Rhodes, Rod A.W. (1996). *The New European Agencies: Agencies in British Government: Revolution or Evolution?*, EUI Working Papers, RSC No. 96/51, Florence: European University Institute.

Scherzberg, Arno (1994). 'Freedom of Information: deutsch gewendet. Das neue Umweltinformationsgesetz'. *Deutsches Verwaltungsblatt*, July, 733–45.

Skou Andersen, Mikael and Duncan Liefferink (eds) (1997). *Issues in Environmental Policy. European Environmental Policy: The Pioneers*. Manchester: Manchester University Press.

Steel, D.R. (1979). 'Britain'. In F.F. Ridley (ed.), *Government and Administration in Western Europe*. Oxford: Oxford University Press, 71–99.

Vogel, David (1986). *National Styles of Regulation: Environmental Policy in Great Britain and the United States*. Ithaca, NJ: Cornell University Press.

Whitehead, Cynthia and Jerôme Woodford (1996). 'On the Road to EU Membership: an Environmental Overview of Central and Eastern Europe'. *Environment Watch: Western Europe*, 5(16), special issue.

Winter, Gerd (1996). 'Freedom of Environmental Information'. In Gerd Winter (ed.), *European Environmental Law: A Comparative Perspective*. Aldershot: Dartmouth, 81–94.

Index